RANDOM TREASURE

RANDOM TREASURE

ANTIQUES, AUCTIONS AND ALCHEMY

ROGER STEWART

The Book Guild Ltd

First published in Great Britain in 2017 by
The Book Guild Ltd
9 Priory Business Park
Wistow Road, Kibworth
Leicestershire, LE8 0RX
Freephone: 0800 999 2982
www.bookguild.co.uk
Email: info@bookguild.co.uk
Twitter: @bookguild

Typeset in Adobe Garamond Pro

Printed and bound in Great Britain by CPI Group (UK) Ltd, Croydon, CR0 4YY

ISBN 978 1912083 558

British Library Cataloguing in Publication Data.
A catalogue record for this book is available from the British Library.

To Frances

CONTENTS

INTRODUCTION

To transmute base metal into gold, you need four ingredients. First, the raw material, a quantity of lead or mercury or unpurified ore. Second, the catalyst: the Philosopher's Stone, a mythical substance taking more or less any physical or elemental form. Third, a magic spell, a word or incantation to spark the process, which you'll find in a cobwebby vellum-covered tome lying open upon a curiously-carved lectern. Fourth, a suitably atmospheric location: a low vault or a high tower, sparks from a glowing crucible, pungent smoke, deep shadows. Bring them all together and *abracadabra!* There's gold!

And you need an alchemist. Imagine the archetype: an elderly man, learned and obsessive, complete with grey beard, black cloak, magic wand, pointed hat.

There's no magic in this book, but there is a kind of alchemy, in the transformation of worthless junk into precious treasure. Here, the raw material is a jumble of unwanted and unrecognised objects made from clay or metal, wood or rags. The catalyst is the antiques auction. The book of spells and incantations is replaced by the internet. The location is a semi-detached house in a northern suburb of Edinburgh. How prosaic. How mundane.

And the alchemist? That would be me. True to type, I'm elderly, grey-bearded, studious and borderline obsessive. But sadly no pointy hat. No magic powers.

But I'm not being fanciful. I've done it many times, and I can prove it. A brown pottery Jug, bought in a local back-street saleroom and sold at Bonham's in London for a record-breaking sum. A miner's safety lamp, auctioned on the internet to a French collector for an unbelievable profit. A vase found in a charity shop and sold for almost two thousand times its purchase price. A little porcelain bowl bought for a trivial amount, kept and used roughly in the kitchen until discovered to be 900 years old, and then packed off to Sotheby's for sale. A carved wood statue of a Saint, bought on a whim and sold in Paris as one of the highlights of the French auction year. Five items, total outlay less than £1,500, total proceeds more than £250,000. And there are many more.

Of course, it's not real alchemy, but a second-hand variety, somehow appropriate for second-hand goods, because these objects have all been through a transmutation once before. When fashioned by their original artists or craftsmen they were important, top-of-the-range, desirable items. But over time they degraded to dross, bottoming out as pieces of bric-a-brac in seedy, unfashionable Leith. That's where I spotted them and subjected them to a secondary alchemical process, regenerating them and sending them on to their next owners as important and valuable antiques with documentation and provenance.

What were the chances? Were these five items and all the others merely random treasure randomly unearthed, or are their identical trajectories capable of more complex and thoughtful interpretation? What brought them to the saleroom or charity shop in the first place? What took me there to spot them? What were the unique qualities in these particular objects that demanded and caught my attention? What gave them their desirability and their cash value?

I'm setting out in this book to answer these questions. To do so I'll be telling the stories of many remarkable antiques collected over more than sixty years, with a particular focus on two very special items: the brown pottery Jug and the wooden Saint.

I'll also be seeking an understanding of exactly *what* it is that I do when I buy and sell antiques, and *how* I do it, and *why* I do it. I think of myself as a very ordinary and run-of-the-mill sort of amateur enthusiast and collector, with occasional forays into part-time dealing, operating on a modest budget, mostly within one mile from home. Nothing noteworthy about me. Why, then, was it me and no-one else out of a whole roomful of collectors and dealers who competed for and won these items? Was it down to good luck and nothing else? Do I know more than other people? Do I work harder? Do I have better taste or a better eye? Am I cleverer? Do I take more risks? Or is there indeed a magic spell, a Philosopher's Stone, or a goose which regularly lays a golden egg for me?

Almost certainly, none of the above. To find an answer, I'll need to investigate my own motivations, responses and behaviours, and I won't be able to do so without including some elements of autobiography. But I'll write about myself and my life not because (or not merely because) I like to talk about myself, but because I suspect that what drives me might also drive others who share the same interests. My hope is that my story might help to explain more generally why so many of us love to spend so much time at auctions, or in charity shops or at car boot fairs, up to our elbows in other people's cast-off stuff.

Proposing a general explanation of a facet of human behaviour feels like an ambitious task. To succeed, I'll need to show that I am indeed representative of my species, and a suitable subject for a case study. I'll have zero credibility as an exemplar of the breed of amateur antique collectors and dealers if self-examination reveals that I am atypical, that readers will share no common ground with me, that I am, after all, a one-off eccentric alchemist.

Attentive readers might already be flummoxed. This book purports to be about matters which are truly exceptional and entirely non-typical, and yet here's the author claiming that his personal story provides a valid general account of the behaviour of an entire population. Really?

It's a fair point, but what I'm hoping to show is that it is possible to be both typical and exceptional at the same time. My story is a unique one, but so is every other individual's story unique. Perhaps once or twice or more in a lifetime *every* antiques enthusiast has a coup which gives similar cause for self-congratulation. Perhaps *everyone* has a touch of the alchemist. It doesn't have to be about money. It might be about finding the final missing piece of a set, or discovering something unknown about a maker or artist, or proving that an item dismissed as a fake is in fact the real thing. Maybe it's typical for *everyone* to be exceptional now and again. In the context of antique collecting and dealing, I must try to define what it means to be *average* or *normal.*

The stories to be told in this book are true, and the facts about the objects described will be as accurate as my historical research can make them. But when writing about recent people and events, I'll withhold or alter a few names and places, firstly to protect the confidentiality and spare the blushes of some of those involved, and secondly (if possible – but I don't really think it will be possible) to preserve my anonymity in my local auction room.

And why do I seek anonymity? Simple – if I get to be known as the chap who makes all that money from his winning bids, then the other auction regulars might take notice of what I'm competing for, and force up prices by bidding against me. I'll do much better if I continue to be thought of as that stand-offish old bloke who buys up the ugly junk that nobody else wants.

1

THE SAINT, 1426–2012

The Setting

Here is a small log of walnut wood from a tree felled in a forest in eastern France during the lifetime of Joan of Arc. Now it's a sculpture, a masterpiece from a royal workshop. And now it's an unrecognised and unwanted piece of junk in a back-street auction room. The Saint has hit rock bottom after a bumpy 600-year slide. There is a story to be uncovered.

First, a short historical snapshot (true) and a conversation (made up). We are in Dijon, the capital city of the Duchy of Burgundy. The year is between 1406 and 1439. We'll choose 1426 because it's as likely as any other year, and because choosing 1426 provides a neat half-millennium gap between the tale of The Saint and the tale of The Jug.

France is fighting sporadic battles with England in Year Ninety of the Hundred Years' War, with Burgundy on the sidelines. In her home village of Domremy about 160 miles north of Dijon, Joan of Arc is fourteen years old and has recently had her first vision, a visit from the Archangel Michael, Saint Margaret, and Saint Catherine who instructed her to help King Charles VII to recover France from English domination. In four years' time Joan will lead the French army to victory at Orleans, but there won't be a happy ending for her because she will be captured and then handed over by Philip the Good, Duke of Burgundy, to the English army for trial and execution by burning at the stake.

Across the channel in England, the infant King Henry VI is just five years old. His regent, John, Duke of Bedford, is the husband of Duke Philip's sister Anne.

In Italy, the early artists of the renaissance are at work, notably Donatello. Leonardo da Vinci won't be born until 1452, Michelangelo until 1475.

It will be sixty-six years until Christopher Columbus sets out from Spain to sail across the Atlantic Ocean.

The Valois Duchy of Burgundy has a short and glorious history, covering the reign of just four Dukes over 113 years from 1364 to 1477. Through a series of canny marriages between Dukes and assorted heiresses, the Burgundian lands have expanded hugely, and include much of northern France and the Low Countries – now the Netherlands and Belgium.

Despite economically bad times after the devastating reduction of population from the Black Death, despite almost constant bickering and fighting between various royal families over succession and territory, and despite vast differences in living standards between rich and poor, the Dukes are doing very nicely.

Duke Philip's court is a model of extravagance, regarded as the most splendid in Europe. The Duke is the acknowledged leader of taste and fashion. This fact has helped the Burgundian economy considerably: the productions of Burgundian artists and craftspeople are sought by the élite of Europe.

Obsessed with mediaeval ideas of knightly chivalry, Philip holds grand feasts and tournaments. He is the greatest patron of the arts of his day, commissioning illuminated manuscripts, tapestries, paintings, works from goldsmiths and silversmiths, jewellery, and other works of art.

And sculpture. Philip the Good's grandfather, Philip the Bold, set up a ducal sculpture workshop in Dijon, and in 1385 Claus Sluter came from his native Holland to act as assistant to the chief sculptor Jean de Marville. Four years later, Marville died and Sluter took over. Today (in the twenty-first century) Sluter is regarded as the most important northern European sculptor of his age, introducing a new realism and individual characterisation into his statues, and bridging a gap between the late Gothic and early Renaissance styles.

In 1406, Sluter died and was succeeded as the Duke's chief sculptor by his nephew Claus de Werve. From then until his death in 1439, Claus de Werve was hard at work running the most important and successful sculpture workshop in Burgundy.

A Conversation

Anyone who has read the *Canterbury Tales* by Geoffrey Chaucer (died 1400) will know that despite the period costume and the absence of computers and smartphones, people in the late middle ages (and for that matter in any other era of human existence) generally thought, acted and spoke very much as they do in our own century.

The scene that follows is entirely imagined. But there's no reason to suppose that a conversation between a customer and a tradesperson in the early fifteenth century would have been much different from what you might expect today.

The year: 1426

The place: Dijon, the Duke of Burgundy's sculpture workshop.

The scene: Claus de Werve in his parlour, a door open to the rear from which workshop noises (mallets, chisels, planes, etc) are heard distantly.

Enter a richly dressed Donor. Donating works of art to the church is a good way to ensure that prayers will be said for you after your death, easing your passage from Purgatory into Paradise on Judgment Day. It's also a good way to show off your wealth and good taste to other members of the Duke's court. Our Donor might be a landowning aristocrat, or perhaps a bishop or a rich abbot, or a member of the Duke's family, or maybe even the Duke himself.

WERVE: *Good day to you, my lord / your grace / your highness (as it might be). How may I be of assistance?*

DONOR: *Good day, Master Sculptor. I want to commission you to carve a Calvary Group for me to donate to the Abbey / Church / Basilica / Cathedral of (unknown location in Burgundy) in memory of / in honour of / for the greater glory of / in the hope that (Donor to complete).*

WERVE: *Certainly, my lord. We've done a few of those and I'm sure we can fix you up with something suitable. Have you thought about the material?*

DONOR: *No, not really – what've you got?*

WERVE: Well, we do them in three ranges. The most expensive is alabaster like the mourning statues that we carved for the tomb of Duke Philip the Bold a few years ago, but they only come in white. Then there's limestone, like the big ones my Uncle Claus made for the Well of Moses at the Charterhouse of Champmol. They take colouring beautifully and they'll last a lifetime. And the Duke got us to do some smaller ones for the new convent at Poligny. If you'd like to pop over there, I'm sure the Abbess will be happy for you to take a look at them.

DONOR: I think you said there are three ranges…?

WERVE: Ah yes, so I did. The third range is the wooden ones. They're much easier and quicker to carve, so they're a bit cheaper, and once they've got a few coats of polychrome paint and some gold on them you wouldn't know they aren't made of stone. I just happen to have some lovely seasoned walnut in the store room. What sort of size were you thinking about?

DONOR: Oh, you know, the figures maybe so high (indicates about two feet high) and the cross about as tall as me or a bit taller. And lots of bright colour and gold leaf.

WERVE: Where in the abbey will you be putting the group? It's cheaper to have them standing on an altar against a wall, so that we can just give the figures flat backs. But if they'll be somewhere where people can walk all round them, then we'll need to carve the backs too.

DONOR: Hmmm… They are thinking of putting the group on a high beam near the abbey entrance, so people will be able to see it from both sides, so it would be better for the figures to be carved all round. I'll need to see your estimate to decide if it's affordable.

WERVE: And who do you want to be in the group?

DONOR: I think just the usual characters in a Calvary – Jesus on the Cross in the centre, the Virgin to the left, and St John the Evangelist to the right. Maybe Mary Magdalene kneeling at the foot of the Cross?

WERVE: Ah… there might be a bit of a problem if you want Mary Magdalene.

If she's kneeling she will have a wider outline than the standing figures, and it might not be possible to get that width out of my piece of timber.

DONOR: *Yes I see what you mean – right, let's forget about Mary Magdalene and that will free up some of the budget to pay the extra costs of carving the backs.*

WERVE: *OK my lord. Think I get what you want. Shall I do you some sketches? I'm beginning to get a few ideas in my head already. I could carve the Virgin with some of that drapery over her face that everyone thought looked so effective on the alabaster mourners. And for the St John I'd like to try making him look up quite sharply over his right shoulder at Jesus. I can get the boys in the workshop started on it as soon as you approve the drawings and the price.*

DONOR: *Yes that sounds fine Master Werve. I'm sure you'll do a splendid job. If you can just send me the sketches with your estimate… Now I'll need to get along – I've an appointment with the Duke's armourer for a fitting for my new helmet. Thank you and good day.*

WERVE: *Thank you, my lord. I'll be in touch soon.*

Exeunt

The Calvary Group

In due time, the Calvary group is delivered and installed. It's everything that the Donor requires, and more – realistic, poignant, expressive of the deepest emotions, superbly carved, richly decorated, up-to-the-minute and exquisitely fashionable.

We can't describe Jesus or the Cross – they are lost and gone, but there are a few surviving crucifixion sculptures from the period, and we can get a general idea of how they may have looked. We do however know what the Virgin looked like. As we will see, she is still very much with us. According to the experts:

"One can note the influence of the mourners from the tomb of Philip the Bold… As with those figures, the emotion-filled sorrow – all the greater here since it seems modest – is revealed in details that are subtler than incipient tears or painfully furrowed brows. Here, there is

5

the apparent withdrawal of the body, the tilt of the head, the drooping shoulders, and the force with which hands press down [to] express the figure's grief"[1].

Her "head and body are shrouded in the manner of a pleurant by de Werve on the tomb of Philip the Bold; the drapery, in its long, soft folds with horizontal indentations, recalls that on the Metropolitan Museum [New York]'s Virgin [from Poligny]"[2].

As for the figure of St John the Evangelist – there is more, much more, to be said.

The Donor is delighted. There's a big dedication ceremony. Maybe a procession. Perhaps even the Duke and Duchess attend. The statues are of exceptional quality, not merely deeply worthy of reverence and conducive to worship, but outstanding examples of the wholly innovative Sluter/Werve style. To eyes familiar with the stiff, lifeless and formulaic statuary of the middle ages, this Calvary group might appear uncannily realistic and almost magically lifelike.

Intermission

We must suppose that this group of statues, along with many other productions of the Dukes' sculpture workshop, were highly popular religious artefacts throughout Burgundy for many years after Claus de Werve's death. He was succeeded by two further notable sculptors, Antoine le Moiturier and Jean de la Huerta, who completed the tomb of Duke John the Fearless in the same style as Sluter and de Werve's tomb for Philip the Bold.

But in 1477 the Duchy of Burgundy fizzled out and the title and lands reverted to the King of France. Burgundy soon became a cultural backwater and the centres of artistic taste and innovation moved south to Italy and north to the Netherlands.

For the next three centuries, as far as our particular Calvary group was concerned, nothing much happened.

Revolutionary Times

It is not known which abbey (or church, etc) the statues were originally made for. But – now well over 300 years old, and venerable as well as venerated – they were still in a religious establishment in Burgundy in 1794 when everything changed. In a series of decrees, the atheist French Revolutionary government had introduced a vigorous policy of "dechristianisation". Public worship was forbidden. Priests were turned out of their churches and many were put on trial for crimes against the Revolution. Religious buildings were nationalised and then demolished, or sold off to Revolutionary supporters, or turned into "Temples of Reason".

One of the policies most enthusiastically pursued was the removal of all visible signs of Christianity. The Revolutionary armies were eager to seek revenge on the institution that had harboured so many counter-revolutionaries. Church bells were pulled down and melted, crosses were taken from churches and cemeteries, and statues, relics and works of art were seized. Most objects were destroyed, some were sold by auction, others simply disappeared.

This policy was not supported by all members of the Revolution. For example Henri Grégoire, Bishop of Blois, who managed to remain a devout Catholic despite being an ardent supporter of the Revolution, was appalled. In 1794 he even coined a new word to describe what was happening – *"vandalisme"*.

Within a very few years, the Catholic religion began to make a comeback, but by then a huge proportion of France's cultural heritage had been destroyed or dispersed.

Despite its age and its beauty, the Calvary group commissioned around 1426 from Claus de Werve was not immune from the general upheaval. The statue of the Virgin Mary survived unscathed. We can't be certain where she was between 1426 and 1794, but we do know that after the Revolution she re-emerged in the parish church of Saint Genest in Flavigny-sur-Ozerain, Burgundy, about 80 miles from Dijon where she was carved. She's still there today.

The statue of Jesus on His Cross disappeared and nothing further is known of it.

The third statue in the group – Saint John the Evangelist – also disappeared without trace. But not forever.

Survival Story

As an aside from the main thread of this narrative, it is interesting to speculate on whether it was pure random chance that the dispersal of the Calvary group happened in the way that it did: Virgin (survived); Christ (lost presumably destroyed); Saint John (lost but re-discovered). I think perhaps not. Here's a conjecture:

Suppose that you are a village priest, or monk, or nun, or parishioner, and it's 1794. A messenger has arrived to say that the Revolutionaries are in the next village hard at work on destroying the local place of worship, and are heading your way. One of the most prized artefacts of your church or your Order, along with silver and gold communion plate, jewelled crucifixes and reliquaries, is the ancient and venerated Calvary group comprising Jesus on the Cross, the Virgin and Saint John. You know that the vandals will be looking for everything they can take. Desperate, you think you might be able to save one piece by hiding it under your bed. Which one do you choose?

The statue of Jesus is fixed to a two-metre high Cross. Even if you could detach Him easily, you still have problems. He has His feet nailed together so He won't stand upright by Himself, and He has His arms outstretched, so He'll be difficult to wrap up and hide. In any case, you think (probably rightly) that the Revolutionaries will be most interested in finding and destroying Jesuses. So saving Jesus is the awkward and high-risk choice.

As for Saint John the Evangelist, yes, he does get top billing over the other Apostles in the conventional iconography of Calvary groups, but you don't have nearly the same level of attachment to him as you have to the other two statues in this particular group, which lacks the customary Mary Magdalene. If the Revolutionaries want him, they can destroy him or sell him off as they like.

That leaves Mary. Traditionally, in the Catholic Church in France, she has the highest status, sometimes depicted at one level below the Almighty, and above, or in pole position between, Christ and the Holy Ghost. The Mary statue from our Calvary group is about 67 centimetres tall and weighs just 7 kilograms. It will be no trouble at all to take her from the church and wrap her in a blanket. Which you do. And you keep her hidden for a few years until all the fuss dies down. Which, sure enough, it does.

Now suppose that you're a member of the Revolutionary army, roaming from village to village around Burgundy under orders to enforce the new government's decrees on dechristianisation.

You arrive at an abbey. You find rich pickings in terms of crosses, assorted statues, metal plate, vestments. There isn't a written inventory, and you might not notice that a small statue of the Virgin is missing. Or perhaps you do notice but in relation to images of the Virgin, your upbringing as a good Catholic trumps your Revolutionary fervour. So you don't make a special effort to search under the abbot's bed to seek her out.

But you do find the statue of Jesus on the Cross, and you dutifully destroy it. You might – consciously or unconsciously – have no problem at all with holding diametrically opposite views at the same time, so perhaps you're comfortable venting your anger against religion by focussing your destructive urges on Jesus, while at the same time being unable to overcome your emotional attachment to His Mother.

And then there is St John, the remaining statue in this particular tableau. With regard to him, you might think on the one hand that he isn't the main object of your anger and doesn't need to be incinerated or chopped up. But on the other hand you have no especial sentimental or spiritual attachment to him or incentive to save him. At the same time, you are bearing in mind that this type of object has a market value, and that of course the Revolution needs funds. It's OK here in 1794 to sell religious statues off to the highest bidder. In fact it's the law. So that's what you do.

There's no positive evidence to support this fanciful explanation. Alternative interpretations are available. "Vandalism" at this time didn't have the connotations of random mindless violence against objects that it does today. In some parts of France, vandals were inspired by the Enlightened ideals of the Revolution, and their version of dechristianisation meant iconoclasm in its most cerebral form – an intellectual exercise, accompanied by careful selection, description and cataloguing of items to be destroyed or sold. In other areas, the process was quick and violent. For two centuries French historians have been energetically debating the methods and motivations of the vandals. But whether they acted mindlessly or deliberately, it is indisputable that the type of behaviour conjectured above in relation to one small walnut wood Calvary group was being replicated all over France at this time, with similar fates befalling myriad other religious artefacts.

Historians agree that the overall result was destruction and dispersal of art and heritage on an epic scale, comparable to what happened in countries invaded by the Nazis or in the Cultural Revolution in China.

Switching to an almost microscopic scale, it would be interesting to look at the outcome in the context of the number of mediaeval French statues from Calvary groups still existing today. If, for example as a subject for a PhD thesis, a bright young art history graduate were to carry out a census, my hypothesis would be that the survivors among the Virgins would get the highest headcount, Saint Johns would come next some distance below, but that only a few complete or fragmentary Jesuses remain with us.

Flavigny-sur-Ozerain

If you have seen the film *Chocolat,* released in the year 2000 and starring Juliet Binoche, Johnny Depp and Judi Dench, you have an idea of what Flavigny-sur-Ozerain looks like, because many of the exterior shots were filmed in the village's narrow, steep lanes and streets.

Flavigny was prosperous during the Middle Ages, but now has fewer than 400 year-round residents, although this number increases in the summer with the arrival of tourists and holiday home owners. The Romanesque ruins of the abbey of St Peter house a factory and shop making and selling Les Anis de Flavigny, delicious aniseed flavoured pastilles with a world-wide reputation. There are a couple of decent restaurants, a textile studio and museum run by a rather fierce lady who wouldn't let us in, and a Catholic seminary. And lots of beautiful mediaeval houses, some restored and some derelict, and some at every stage in between.

In late June 2013 on the day of our visit, my wife Frances and I found the weather unseasonably damp and chilly. The village was oddly deserted – in fact it felt rather more like a run-down film set than a real village which had recently come in at Number 15 in the annual vote for the one hundred most beautiful villages in France.

The parish church stands in the square in the middle of the village. It is dedicated to St Genest, and was built and rebuilt and adapted between the thirteenth and seventeenth centuries. The outside is unspectacular, but internally the layout is interesting and unusual, with the nave overlooked on all four sides by a wide gallery.

Sadly, whereas many Burgundian churches have been beautifully repaired and restored by their local communities, the Flavigny church is unrestored and appears to be in urgent need of serious attention. The main problem seems to be from damp, which has caused a tsunami of mould and mildew to spread unchecked over much of the lower walls of the church. It's very sad to see such a marvellous building in such a dilapidated state, all the more so because the encrustations of thick black fungus are in some places threatening to engulf the remarkable mediaeval statues displayed on pedestals and on brackets and in niches.

The objects in the church, mostly from the fifteenth century, are indeed very remarkable. The walnut wood choir stalls have extraordinary carvings on the stall ends and misericords; there's a lovely polychromed limestone *Vierge Allaitant*, a Virgin and St John from another Calvary group, charming but much inferior in quality to the work of Claus de Werve's workshop; and a tall, slim, smiling but incomplete Angel of the Annunciation which has been authoritatively attributed to Claus.

The Mourning Virgin, attributed to Claus de Werve, in the parish church of Saint Genest, Flavigny-sur-Ozerain, Cote d'Or, France

And there, to the right of the high altar, in a niche, alone and decidedly forlorn, stands our Virgin, *la Vierge de douleur de l'Eglise de Saint-Genest de Flavigny-sur-Ozerain*, one of the masterpieces of Burgundian sculpture.

Alone, forlorn, but not ignored. In fact she's quite famous. She has been the subject of a number of scholarly articles and in 1907 she was designated

11

by the French Government as a Historic Monument. She hasn't always been confined to her niche in Flavigny either: she travelled to Dijon for exhibitions in 1949, 1976 and 2004, and to Rotterdam in 1950. Also in 2004, she crossed the Atlantic and was exhibited in Cleveland, Ohio.

But at no time has it been suggested that any other components from her Calvary group survived the depredations of the Revolution. At least not until 2013, when the Virgin was re-united, albeit only for an hour, with her pendant Saint John.

The Lost Years of Saint John the Evangelist

In October 2012, a statue appeared in my local auction house here in Scotland. It was described in the catalogue as "a carved wooden figure of a monk", and after some not-very-competitive bidding, was knocked down to me for a hammer price of £340. As will be related in much more detail in a later chapter, the statue turned out to be the lost Saint John of Flavigny.

So where was it during the missing 218 years between its disappearance in 1794 from a church or abbey in Burgundy at the hands of Revolutionary vandals, and its re-emergence in 2012 in a small saleroom on the northern edge of Edinburgh, Scotland? Or, in antique-dealer-speak, what was its provenance?

We'll discuss the whole question of provenance a little later, but for now, I'll attempt to bring the story from 1794 up to date. It has been possible to piece together some genuine information about Saint John's whereabouts, and to fill in some of the rest using a bit of research, some more or less informed guesswork, and a generous dollop of imagination. But – except in very rare cases where an object is in a collection or a particular location and always has been, and where there is detailed documentation covering the entire period – there will always be gaps.

A very well-known family-run firm of Scottish furniture and antique dealers, interior designers and church furnishers operated in Edinburgh from the early nineteenth century until the early twenty-first century. Let's call them MacGregor's of Edinburgh.

They bought in and sold new furniture and carpets of the highest quality; they manufactured furniture in the latest fashionable styles in their workshops, both in standard ranges and one-off designs made to order; they bought, sold and restored high-end antique furniture and works of art from Britain and continental Europe. They employed their own taste-leading in-house team of furniture designers, and partnered with the best of Scottish interior designers and architects for fit-outs of stately homes, town and country mansions and churches. They were patronised in the richest and most aristocratic echelons of Scottish society; they held a Royal Warrant as furnishers to successive sovereigns in Scotland for more than 150 years. Antique dealers today in Scotland and further afield will instantly recognise the MacGregor's style and quality in a piece of furniture, and will give it a premium price to reflect its premium status.

I recall making occasional visits to the firm's august and intimidating premises during the 1970s and 1980s, always to look and never to buy. I did, however, back in 1983, sell them something. It was a gigantic faded orange-ground antique Turkey carpet which had been left in our run-down Georgian Edinburgh New Town flat by the previous owner. We were about to move house and the carpet was miles too big to fit into any room – in fact into any two rooms – in our next property, a slightly less decrepit Victorian terraced house in the suburbs.

So I do have some dim personal recollections of the MacGregor's antique showrooms. At that time they were in a converted nineteenth-century mill building, and I can visualise a vast space full of good quality stuff, much of it oversized furniture suited to the needs of the oversized properties of their clientele. In particular I remember (because – for some reason which I have now outgrown – I desperately wanted one) noting a number of huge French provincial walnut armoires ranged around the walls.

This memory has some significance because it indicates that MacGregor's were engaged in importing French furniture to Scotland for sale. Perhaps one of the firm's directors travelled regularly to France to select suitable stock from dealers there. Or perhaps there were arrangements with French agents or dealers to send over consignments of saleable furniture and other antique items in bulk.

But one way or another, presumably through the French antique trade (because a private sale direct to MacGregor's seems unlikely, and there are no records of a sale at a public auction), a small wooden religious statue ended up in Scotland in the possession of MacGregor's. We don't know when it arrived, but we can hazard a guess that it was between, say, 1880 and 1930.

Then something unusual happened. By whatever means it reached Scotland, the statue wasn't simply taken into MacGregor's showroom and sold. It wasn't included in an interior design scheme for a makeover of a Scottish baronial castle or a Georgian villa. It didn't feature in a fashionable arts and crafts interior for a Scottish church. Instead it was taken into the family home of whichever Mr MacGregor was the patriarch of the firm at that time.

What makes an antique dealer take an object off the market and take it home? It could be that the item has been on display in the showroom for x months and isn't selling so it might as well be taken out of stock and brought home; or on the other hand it could be that the dealer thinks the statue so superbly beautiful that it's too good for non-discerning customers and deserves a prominent place in his or her private collection.

We don't know the motivation. But we can guess at the following course of events after Mr MacGregor's decision to take the statue home.

1. Mr MacGregor looks it over and decides that its faded polychrome and gold leaf decoration is
    a. Too badly damaged and flaking to restore or be acceptable in his tasteful Edinburgh home; and/or
    b. Too unfashionable at a time when bare polished wood surfaces in the arts and crafts taste are the thing; and/or
    c. Too inauthentic, in the belief (widely held but in most cases incorrect) that statues such as this started out as bare wood and were decorated later on by inferior hands; and/or
    d. Too Popish.

2. Mr MacGregor puts the statue into his firm's restoration workshop (the best one in Scotland) to have it stripped and polished and restored. It might be at this time that some sympathetic work is done to give Saint John a replacement nose and to treat a little woodworm. As you would expect, they do a lovely job. Sadly, in the process St John loses what little remains of his original glowing enamel and gold appearance, but he does look gorgeous in his new and fashionable coat of beeswax polish.

3. Mr MacGregor instructs his firm's cabinet-making workshop (the best one in Scotland) to make a suitable wall-mounted corner bracket for the statue to stand upon in his home. The bracket is duly made, incorporating part of a reclaimed English oak mediaeval church misericord or corbel. The corbel has on it a high-relief carved face of a cheery-looking jester, clown or rustic

with a large collar ruff (**See Illustrations,** *Picture 1*). I know this part of the story to be true because I bought the bracket in the same auction as the statue, and the MacGregor's workmanship is unmistakeable. It's a nice piece by itself, but of no special value, and I decided to keep it. It's now fixed high on the wall in the corner of my kitchen, supporting an as-yet unidentified eighteenth century French faience charger.

4. Mr MacGregor fixes the bracket with the statue standing atop in a corner of a room in his house. The dining room? The hall? A staircase landing? Perhaps a surviving family member recalls the statue *in situ*, but I simply don't know. There it stays for an indeterminate number of years, admired, ignored or derided, but not abused.

5. Decades pass. Early in the twenty-frist century the firm finally closes down after some years of poor trading. There's a spectacular auction of the residual contents of the showrooms before they are sold for redevelopment, but the statue isn't included because it belongs to the family and not to the firm.

6. It's 2012. The current Mr MacGregor (two, three generations in descent) has an old statue and an old bracket that he doesn't want in his home any more. He takes them into an Edinburgh auction room owned by his friend Malcolm Andrews, and asks the auctioneer to sell the items on his behalf.

2

THE MYTH OF PROVENANCE

Who Cares?

People who watch antiques programmes on the television are accustomed to hearing the word "provenance". The experts insist that it's the magic key to establishing (or boosting) the authenticity and value of an object. Where does this item come from? How did it come to be in your possession? What is its history?

At the top end of the art and antiques market, auctioneers do indeed place enormous emphasis on provenance. Naturally, a jewel worn by Elizabeth Taylor or a dress worn by Princess Diana will be worth hugely more than the identical jewel or dress bought in a charity shop. A Rembrandt etching with a documented history from a known (preferably aristocratic) private collection will command a higher price than an identical one from an unknown source which has been doing the rounds in the trade for a few years.

But in the hundreds of small "provincial" auction salerooms all over Britain, and to the tens of thousands of buyers who frequent those rather faded locations – and also to the huge majority of buyers and sellers at antiques fairs and car boot sales and using online auction sites – the question of provenance in the buying and selling of antiques is simply not an issue.

I can think of three reasons for this.

The first reason: the seller often just doesn't know the object's history. It might simply have been acquired from a dealer, a charity shop, a car boot sale or another auction house, with no documentation and no back-story.

Or, with a family heirloom the seller might be telling a handed-down tale which doesn't bear close scrutiny. Stories have an infallible way of changing and degrading over time. You're selling Great-Granny's uncharacteristically sumptuous diamond brooch and you say "she was in service as lady's maid to the Countess of Borsetshire and was given the brooch as a memento when she left to marry the footman". But the truth might be "she was dismissed for stealing the brooch and then had to marry the footman".

Or you're selling the animalier bronze that Granddad found in the bombed-out ruins of a house in Berlin at the end of the last War and brought back as a souvenir – but how do you know that it isn't looted property from a lost Jewish family?

The second reason: the buyer would rarely get the opportunity to question the seller and find out the story, reliable or otherwise. The auctioneer is acting as agent for the seller, and the default position would be that the auctioneer is prevented by data protection laws from giving out personal information and contact details to buyers.

Here is what Sotheby's say in their Conditions of Sale:

"In certain circumstances, Sotheby's may print in the catalogue the history of ownership of a work of art if such information contributes to scholarship or is otherwise well known and assists in distinguishing the work of art. However, the identity of the seller or previous owners may not be disclosed for a variety of reasons. For example, such information may be excluded to accommodate a seller's request for confidentiality or because the identity of prior owners is unknown given the age of the work of art."[3]

In practice, at the lower end of the market where most people do their buying and selling, you won't get much of a story from the catalogue. It might be nothing more than: "Lot 32: Carved wood figure of a monk" (as the statue of Saint John was described) or it might be "Lot 52: Continental pottery jug decorated with incised fish and motto decoration" (as my very special Jug was described).

The third reason and the main one: who cares? Provenance isn't actually of any interest or significance to the multitude of small-time dealers and hobby collectors who frequent local auction houses:

- If you're a dealer at this modest level, for most objects which you buy or sell, knowledge of provenance won't add to the value of the object when you sell it on. A Clarice Cliff plate obtained in a small terraced house clearance in one street won't get any extra glamour or cachet from its provenance when it's sold on to a collector living in a small terraced house in the next street.

- If you're a collector, it might not be of any interest to you to know the history of the particular object which you have just acquired. Many collectors simply want an object for its own sake, and my perception is that in the very large majority of cases it wouldn't matter to you one jot where the item came from. In fact you might decide positively not to make enquiries, just in case you find out that its provenance is dodgy and you end up losing a precious addition to your collection. Let's say that you're a Clarice Cliff collector and have bought a plate. The things that matter to you are the pattern, the shape, the colourway, the condition, the markings on the back, the scarcity, and for some of the rarer hand-painted patterns, the quality of the composition and brushwork. You probably couldn't care less about who owned it before you. I'm not a Clarice collector, but I do happen to own one of her plates. I'll write more about it in Chapter 6.

When Provenance Matters

But sometimes provenance does matter. The reason that I made efforts to gain the small knowledge that I have about the provenance of my statue of Saint John the Evangelist is that when it was properly identified and authenticated, it turned out that it wasn't an ordinary sort of object at all. Before putting The Saint up for re-sale at auction in Paris I needed to know something about where he had been since his disappearance around 1794. This was in part for my own interest because a major element of the enjoyment of many of the works of art and antique items that I collect comes from researching their background. Then, I needed to be comfortable that I had full and incontestable ownership. And finally I had a clear incentive to investigate: in preparing the description for the auction catalogue, the Paris expert wanted to include something credible about provenance.

From her own knowledge and from extensive published scholarship and research, my expert Laurence knew or could readily conjecture the history of the statue from 1426 to 1794. Her version of the story would be something fairly similar to but distinctly more scholarly than my account given in Chapter 1. But she could know nothing of how The Saint crossed the Channel, the loss of the polychrome decoration, and the long sojourn in the late Mr MacGregor's private collection. I made it my business to try to piece this part of the statue's history together.

The most important and urgent question to be answered: was the statue indisputably mine to sell? The law says you don't own an object that you buy if the person who sells it to you doesn't own it him- or herself. So if you buy a piece of stolen property, it doesn't belong to you and it doesn't belong to the person who sold it to you. It still belongs to the person from whom it was stolen, and you may be required to return it to that person regardless of whether or not you get your money back. If you have bought stolen property in an auction and then have to give it up, you might have a negligence claim against the auctioneers for failing in their duty to take reasonable care that the seller has the right to sell. But establishing such a claim would be an expensive and tedious task.

So before sending The Saint off for re-sale, I needed to be satisfied on three key ownership points.

First of all, I wanted to be certain that the statue hadn't been stolen in the recent past from a local house or church or museum. One way to check this would have been to have a search done by the Art Loss Register, who say on their website:

> "To the purchaser, a search minimises the chance of acquiring a work of art which has been stolen. Alternatively there may be some question concerning its past ownership, which could have a substantial impact on its future value and marketability.
>
> "To the vendor, a search not only minimises the chance of acquiring or dealing in stolen items, but also acts as an encouragement to buyers to know that they are acquiring the work with good title"[4].

So it seemed as if using the Art Loss Register would be a good idea. But in the event, for reasons which will become clear, I decided it was unnecessary to commission a search.

Loot

The second ownership issue to be settled was to be comfortable that The Saint wasn't on any list of looted art which, if discovered, must be restituted to the original owner or his/her surviving family or heirs. This can be a major issue, particularly where there is a possibility that the object might be one of the countless works of art stolen in Europe by the Nazis from the private collections of Jews or many other categories of victim.

Clearly The Saint was a major work of art. He could have been in occupied territory (in Burgundy, in North-East France not far from the German border) during the years of Nazi looting. The fact that he was a Christian religious artefact would not disqualify him from having been in the collection of a Jewish connoisseur. The fact that he had turned up in Scotland would not necessarily indicate that he hadn't been looted.

So the statue was certainly a candidate for being a piece of looted art. And here I have to make my first digression into autobiography. As a fourth-generation British Jew I need to declare a special interest.

My forebears, maternal and paternal, were all Dutch and for the most part middle-class, middle-income, middle-brow Jewish merchants, craftspeople and small-time professionals. My great-great-grandparents arrived in London, apparently en masse, from Amsterdam in the mid-nineteenth century, leaving behind them a very large extended family. Over the next eighty years or so, there was close contact and much coming and going between Amsterdam and the East End of London, involving trade in diamonds, cigars, textiles and clothing, foodstuffs (one great-grandfather is listed in the 1881 census as a "dealer in lemons") and, as might be expected, the giving and taking of wives and husbands between the various branches of the families.

My multitude of Amsterdam relatives weren't the kind of people who would have accumulated grand private collections of works of art, but between the German invasion of the Netherlands in 1940 and the end of the war in 1945, every item of petit bourgeois property that they did possess was taken from them, including, in all cases except one, their lives.

By contrast, my own parents and their London families, while suffering the same dangers and privations in wartime as non-Jewish Londoners, were never under direct threat of mass extermination.

My personal memories begin in the austere post-war years of the early nineteen-fifties. By then we and most of our aunts, uncles and cousins had migrated, together with much of the East End Jewish population, a few miles to North-West London. My brother and I and our parents lived in cramped accommodation in a modest semi-detached house in Golders Green with our grandmother and my mother's maiden sister, who, as my father always said, enjoyed poor health. My aunt continued to enjoy her poor health, outlived all four of her siblings by many years, and finally died early in 2014 at the age of ninety-six.

And here's something that I remember from when I was a very small child: my mother and her brother and sisters scrimping together a little money every two weeks to send to Amsterdam to help support their sole surviving Dutch cousin, an elderly lady who had returned in 1945 from Bergen-Belsen, blind, infirm and penniless, to live out her few remaining years.

With this particular memory and with this family background, it was especially important to me to be sure that my statue of Saint John wasn't one of those many objects looted by the Nazis before and during the Second World War. Fortunately, there are online resources where you can check lists of artefacts that are known to be missing, or whose location is known (for example in museums and private collections) but their ownership is in dispute.

> "No one believes that restituting art will undo any of the horrors inflicted by the Nazis, but most believe that restituting valuable property to those from whom it was stolen because of their race is right. Most people don't realize that one core component of the Nazis' Final Solution was to steal Jews' art collections... The Nazis stole more art than any regime in history... It is widely accepted that over 100,000 significant art objects stolen in the Holocaust era remain unaccounted for. Some were destroyed, but the... art market is infected with Nazi-looted art."[5]

The Nazis of course weren't the only people who have ever used the looting and destruction of cultural property as a way to exert political power. As we have seen, our Calvary group had suffered in the French Revolution two centuries earlier, and it's easy to think of many other more modern examples, such as the work of Islamic State jihadis in Syria and the Taliban in Afghanistan – not to mention the wilful failure in recent years of Allied invaders to protect ancient monuments and antiquities in Iraq.

This is a huge and highly controversial subject, and gives rise to much heated argument. How can you tell if an object is a legitimate prize – the spoils of war – or loot? Can it still be defined as looting if the seizure of cultural artefacts is carried out under the decree of a government deriving its legitimacy from popular revolution (France in 1794) or democratic election (Germany in 1933)? If a work of art has been on public display in a secure air-conditioned museum for sixty years, why should it be returned into the private and unregulated hands of a distant descendant of someone long dead? For every argument that says a museum piece should be restituted to its original owners, there's another one that says it's better off to stay where it is.

But it isn't my purpose here to describe all that is being and has been done (and not done) throughout the world to restore looted pieces of art to their rightful owners. My purpose is much narrower – to tell you what I did to ascertain that The Saint didn't fall into the category of looted art. The truthful answer: I didn't do very much. To be fair, I did make a start on what could have been a very lengthy and expensive process by looking at a number of public online databases – you can find these on very helpful websites such as *Looted Art* and *Lost Art*[6]. I spent some time searching for mediaeval religious wooden sculptures listed as missing. And there were indeed some such statues on the lists – but none resembling my Saint John closely enough to give rise to doubt.

I could have used up much more time on doing this exercise thoroughly, or alternatively I could have commissioned someone else to do the research for me. But instead I gave up searching early on, for precisely the same reason that I also gave up trying to find out if The Saint had been recently stolen. Why? Because I got lucky. I was able to get a simple and, to me, fully satisfactory account of where the statue had been for a great many of the missing years.

Meet the Auctioneer

Before re-selling the statue, I wanted to be comfortable about three ownership issues. The first two of these were covered in the previous two sections: could it be stolen property? Or could it be looted property?

The third issue was: had The Saint been consigned to the Edinburgh auction in which I bought him by a bona fide seller who had good title to his ownership? All sorts of scenarios were possible. Could he have been brought into the auction room by someone who was trying to sell him on behalf of someone else and who didn't have full authority to do so? Or could he have been technically an asset of a business which the seller was consigning for auction as a private individual? Or could he have been previously bought but not fully paid for? Or was he being sold from a dead person's estate where probate had not yet been granted?

As we have seen, it is difficult to check up on these matters in a context where data protection law may prohibit the auctioneer from disclosing details of the seller. However, too much can be made of this point. In a High Court case in 2005 involving the provenance and ownership of the original manuscript of Rachmaninoff's Second Symphony, the Judge said this:

> "There is a dark side to the confidentiality surrounding the identity of an auctioneer's principal… The less the legal risks involved in committing a work for auction, the more attractive the market in works of art and manuscripts becomes for criminals. The policy of the law… is to look more sceptically than would have been proper in the past upon those who have very valuable property for which they have no provenance."[7]

For reasons which should be becoming clear by now, I'm not going to reveal the real name of the firm of auctioneers who sold me The Saint, but they figure largely in this story and it will be useful to call them something, so let's say they are called Johnson & Andrews Auctioneers. Their proprietor and chief auctioneer is Malcolm Andrews.

Malcolm has known me for many years. I'm not his personal friend but am one of his regular bidders. He knows that I'm interested particularly in studio ceramics, and that if I see something I really want I'll go out of my way to win it. He knows that I pay and collect my goods promptly. I'm by no means one of his biggest customers (those are all dealers), but I'm among the bigger spenders in the private collector category. He doesn't want to lose me as a bidder.

On my side, I know that Malcolm runs a decent business which is very handy for my home. As far as I'm aware he sources his goods for sale honestly and legitimately. He knows enough about most general items to be able to value and catalogue them adequately. But as the proprietor of a hard-pressed small business he works fast and under pressure and can sometimes make a mistake by failing to identify a valuable object, particularly if it's out of the run of his usual ranges of goods. Malcolm operates just the sort of congenial small auction room that I like to spend time and money in. I don't want to do anything to jeopardise the relationship.

But I still needed a way to learn how The Saint John statue came to be offered for sale at Johnson & Andrews. There was no alternative – I had to ask Malcolm Andrews directly.

Ask the Auctioneer

This seems a blindingly obvious course of action. If I ask Malcom, he'll either tell me how the statue came to him, or he won't. He might take offence and plead his duty of confidentiality to the seller. Or he might think it preferable not to offend me, and give me a clue about provenance in general terms: "it was from an executry sale" or "an old chap who lives around here brought it in". Or (since I finally went to see him some four months after the sale where I bought The Saint), he might simply say, truthfully or otherwise: "sorry, I really can't remember a single lot out of the thousands that we sell, and we don't keep records of provenance".

But I was reluctant to ask. It seemed to me a breach of etiquette to expect the auctioneer to risk transgressing the Data Protection Act by divulging details of the origin of an item. Any private collector who's a regular customer in a local auction house might feel equally diffident – or perhaps not. Perhaps it's just me being super-scrupulous.

I wouldn't expect a dealer to worry in same way: the dealers who frequent Johnson & Andrews are a hard-boiled lot, not much concerned with the niceties of etiquette. In the unlikely event that any one of them might care one jot about the provenance of an item, he or she would simply ask straight out, at maximum volume, in the open auction hall, without a second's thought: "Hey, Malcolm – see this old statue, do you know for sure that it isn't a bit iffy?"

O, what wouldn't I give to be able to address an auctioneer with such freedom! But no, I must screw up my courage, make a special mid-week journey to the auction hall, and beard Malcolm in his inner office. As I hover on the threshold of his sanctum, let me ponder why it is that I – a reasonably successful, fairly self-confident retired businessman – should feel as nervous as I did decades since, when going into my first job interview?

A private buyer might be a friend or close acquaintance of the auctioneer and/or might regard him or her – often the sole proprietor of the auction business – as a powerful figure who holds the key to the supply of the antiques and art objects which the buyer/collector craves. In the same way that another type of addict might not wish to cause offence and jeopardise a long relationship with the neighbourhood crack cocaine dealer, you might not want to upset your auctioneer by seeming to question if an item you've just bought has a dodgy provenance.

You can also fall out with the auctioneer if you reveal that an item you bought was misdescribed or misidentified in the catalogue and is in fact enormously more valuable than the price that you have just paid. Such a revelation could make the auction house look foolish and amateurish and put other sellers off consigning their goods. Worse still, if the seller subsequently discovers that a major error has been made, there could be a claim against the auctioneer for failing in the duty of care owed to the vendor.

If you can get over your worries about upsetting the auctioneer, there's a further and perhaps yet more significant consideration – upsetting yourself. If the news gets out that you have bought something that turned out to be the bargain of the century (and once you've told one person it *will* get out, because auction halls are terrible places for gossip and rumour), you'll immediately become a marked man or woman. When you are identified by the regulars as a bidder with an eye for a good object and for a good profit (I'll have something to say about The Eye later on), you instantly lose a large element of your bidding advantage. And at the same time you may lose a little of your auction enjoyment.

The Joys of Anonymity

In the upper strata of the auction world, anonymity has become easy to maintain in recent years with the wide availability of telephone and live online bidding. Many higher-end auction rooms tend nowadays to be half-empty of bidders while the auction is taking place. Alongside the mostly unoccupied seats set out for the audience, you will often see serried ranks of auction house employees manning telephones and laptops to take new bids as they come in from absentee bidders.

But that does not hold true for my regular haunt in Edinburgh, nor for dozens of other owner-operated provincial auction businesses up and down the country. Johnson & Andrews hold weekly general sales of lower-grade second-hand and antique objects, including ceramics and glass, metalware, collectables, pictures, carpets and rugs, and furniture. Sometimes there are electrical items like lamps, hi-fis and televisions. Usually there are some lots of costume jewellery and silverware. Occasionally vintage toys. They save up the better grade stuff for quarterly antique sales. At the bottom end of the spectrum they have a weekly uncatalogued cash-only sale of – well, it's mostly unutterable junk, although sometimes remarkable finds emerge from the trash. Once there was a coffin (unused).

Unlike at the upmarket auctioneers in the city centre, every sale is crowded with bidders and onlookers, who turn up week after week, month after month, in search of a bargain, an addition to a collection, or simply an object that they think they can turn a bit of a profit on. If you prefer not to attend in person, you can leave a commission bid for the auctioneer to make on your behalf – but commission bids can sometimes get lost, and some auctioneers (but not Malcolm) tend on occasion to encourage bidders in the hall to outbid the absentee. Or you can arrange for an auction employee to call you on the telephone just before your lot comes up for sale – but what if they take your number down wrong or your phone's battery has run down? You don't have an option of online bidding, because Johnson & Andrews only uses a live auction bidding platform for its occasional better-class and specialist sales.

So one reason that you go in person every week is because if you're a buyer it's the best way to make sure you can get the things you want.

But that isn't the main reason that you go. The main reason is that *you love going to auctions*. Why do so many people still go to the cinema or to football matches or to live concerts when they can sit at home in front of a high-definition screen in real time and get a much better view, a much less interrupted experience, no jostling, and no nasty smells? Because people love to congregate in crowds, even when they don't need to.

It's the same with the Johnson & Andrews regular bidders. They attend in person (not that in this particular case watching remotely on a screen is an option) for the addictive theatrical experience of being at an auction, for the drama, the entertainment. They go so they can interact with other members of the audience as well as watching the auctioneer. They go because bidding at an auction gives you a remarkable opportunity to participate as a principal in a dramatic performance in a way that you can regulate yourself. When you bid, you and the other bidder are locked in a direct competition, umpired by the auctioneer and with everyone else in the room looking on.

If you're not willing to pay as much for your lot as the other bidder, you can stop at any time you wish, without consequences, without shame, and at nil cost. There's no downside, because you haven't lost – rather you've won because you have had the good sense not to overpay.

On the other hand, if you win the item, then you get not only the collector's or dealer's satisfaction of coming into possession of the thing that you want, but also the joy of having beaten the other bidder(s) in a fair and open tourney. This satisfaction is a quality which increases exponentially with the amount of financial risk that you take to win the object, and the amount of emotion that you have invested in it since you first saw it yesterday at the auction viewing.

Conversely, you lose some of your satisfaction if you believe that even although the item is worth much more than you have ultimately bid, you might still have been able to get it for less. This can happen if prices are forced up not by the intrinsic merit of the object but by your personal reputation as an expert or a lucky buyer.

An Ugly Brown Bowl

Here's an example. Until such time as any of the auction regulars read this book (which might well be a very long time) I don't expect to gain a reputation as the bloke who made a bundle from the re-sale of The Saint. But I have been known to them for a few years now as the bloke who made a bundle from the re-sale of The Jug (we'll get to The Jug).

This means that at the auction viewings some of the other bidders keep an eye on me to see which ceramics in the upcoming sale I'm looking at most closely. And then they have a good look at those pots themselves. In many cases, they might think: "that chap's mad to be thinking of bidding for that – he just can't stop himself", but in other cases they might think, "I don't quite know what's so special about that old brown bowl he's looking at so closely, but if he's going to bid for it, I'll try to outbid him".

It happened to me at the Johnson & Andrews weekly junk sale a couple of years ago. No, it's not paranoia, I can prove it.

This event is held on a Thursday morning, outdoors in the forecourt of the auction hall. Stuff for sale is mostly low-value (often zero-value) residual contents brought from houses being cleared by relatives or executors after an old person has died. It's not unusual to see dressing tables with underwear and make-up still in the drawers, and wardrobes stuffed with hanging clothes. Smaller items include china tea sets, drinking glasses, ornaments, metalware, pictures, books, pots and pans, letters and photographs, the detritus of a lifetime. Some people find the whole experience pathetic, distasteful, nauseating, ghoulish, too close a reminder of their own mortality.

But not me. Whereas I have qualms and emotional uncertainties about many things – enough in fact to fill a whole chapter later on in this book – I have no problem at all about looking for interesting and valuable items amongst the residual possessions of the dead. The deceased have no more use for them. Their heirs and executors have taken what individual items and keepsakes they wish to retain. What remains is available for re-use, re-sale, recycling or disposal for the benefit of the estate. I can think of no better or more efficient way to achieve these ends without disrespect to the departed than through the public auction process. Whilst I'm sure that I fear death just as much as the next person, I feel no present unease about eventually having my own possessions exposed for inspection and distribution in this way.

So I and the rest of us get stuck in without a second thought – because lurking in amongst all the dross there might be a gem. There's no catalogue. The goods are set out by 9.30 on the morning of the sale, the smaller items on trestle tables, everything else lying on the ground loose or in cardboard cartons. If it's raining, we all get wet and much of the stuff gets ruined, but the sale still proceeds. By the time the sale starts at 11.00, there are maybe 100 of us in attendance, mostly regulars, and over the next three hours or so, we follow Malcolm the auctioneer around his forecourt bidding for items as we go.

The item in question on the day in question was an old brown earthenware bowl, big and chunky and very poorly made, and in almost all respects an unattractive piece (See **Illustrations**, **Picture 2**). But when I turned it upside down – and you can learn at least as much from looking at the base of a ceramic piece as you can learn from looking at it the right way up – I saw two impressed seal marks. One of these was clearly and obviously a version of the very recognisable SI mark used from about 1920 until today by the St Ives pottery in Cornwall. The other mark had been unevenly stamped by the potter into the wet clay and was indecipherable.

My train of thought ran roughly as follows:

Here under this pile of old plates is a pretty horrible brown bowl. It's crudely made and unattractive, but I'll just turn it over to see if it's marked because I can't stop myself.

Ooooh, that's a surprise... there's an early St Ives mark here and another mark that I can't decipher.

But it's such an awful bowl, with a sludgy brown glaze, a rough burned area on the top edge and two serious firing cracks from shrinkage in the kiln – how can it possibly be from St Ives?

Ahhhh yes, now I remember reading a story about the early days of the St Ives Pottery. They were having trouble with their three-chamber climbing kiln and were rapidly running out of money, so they had to sell off anything they possibly could, even the most substandard wares that came out of the kiln in one piece. This bowl might just be one of the rejects.

But wait a minute – if it's one of those objects, then it can only have been made by one of the two potters working at St Ives in the early 1920s during the very birth-pangs of the studio pottery movement.

That means that the mark must be either the personal seal of Bernard Leach, the god of studio potters, or the personal seal of Shoji Hamada, the god of Bernard Leach. The bowl has to be made by one or the other of them, there's no alternative.

Hmmm... must try not to look excited, must try not to look excited, must try not to look excited.

Now, when Malcolm arrives at this table and asks for bids for any items on it, how much will I bid? If it's a Leach piece it would fetch at least £500 in a decent auction, if it's by Hamada maybe twice as much.

Even though I rarely pay more than a fiver for an old pot at this auction, this bowl is quite special and I'll probably want to keep it in my collection, so I'll push the boat out on this occasion and bid up to around £300.

After I had looked at the bowl I put it back as unobtrusively as possible, hoping that no-one else would spot it. Between then and the moment that Malcolm reached it on his route around the tables, I kept my eye on it, and saw it being looked at and discussed a few times. So I was expecting a fair bit of competition.

In the end, the competition was stronger than usual, but I got the bowl for £65, bidding against a dealer. Here's the dealer's train of thought:

There's that quiet chap having a close look at an old brown bowl. He made a packet from that old jug a few years ago so he knows his stuff when it comes to studio pottery. Better wait until he moves on and have a look myself.

God! It's an awful bowl, with a sludgy brown glaze, a rough burned area on the top edge and two serious firing cracks from shrinkage in the kiln.

Hmmm… I see it's got a couple of marks on the bottom. One looks like the St Ives seal. Maybe it's a second from their standard ware range, or maybe it's something else that looks similar.

It could be worth a punt at a tenner, but I'll wait and see if he goes for it. If he does I'll maybe give him some competition to see how much he thinks it's worth.

OK, perhaps that wasn't precisely his train of thought, but he must have seen that I was on to something although he didn't know exactly what it was. So his final bid of £60 represented the point at which he lost his bottle, and I gained my bowl.

I considered the hammer price of £65 to be a great bargain, but a very odd amount to pay. If the dealers know it's a bowl by Leach or Hamada, it's a given that one of them will pay several hundred pounds for it and still stand to make a good profit. But if they don't know the maker, they wouldn't pay more than a couple of pounds for such an ugly and ill-made object.

Which leaves only one logical explanation. It was my reputation as an expert on old brown earthenware pottery that pushed up the price. If I could have stayed anonymous, I think I'd have had the bowl for a fiver.

When I got it home, I studied the indistinct second mark on the base using a strong light and a magnifying lens, comparing it with internet images of other early St Ives pieces. And sure enough in an hour or so I was certain that I had an early piece bearing the personal seal of Bernard Leach. I also emailed some photos to a specialist studio pottery auctioneer with whom I've had contact in the past, and she confirmed my attribution and gave an auction estimate of £600 – £800.

I've still got the bowl. It's on display in my dining room. It's still ugly and ill-made, but the more I look at it, the more I consider it has a certain presence and a certain distinction. And (although I may be kidding myself) I don't think that my perception of this presence and distinction is merely a patina conferred by my knowledge of the bowl's maker and its market value. However, there's still that small niggle that if I wasn't known to the other bidders as the studio pottery bloke, I could have won it for much less.

The Auctioneer's Answer

A couple of sections ago, I left myself hovering nervously on the threshold of Malcolm's office, about to ask him what he knows about the provenance of the statue of Saint John.

I'm nervous because I am aware that if he asks me why I want to know, and if I tell him the whole honest truth of what I have discovered about The Saint, then I might make him look professionally inept, or get him into hot water with the seller, or, worse, I might find out that the statue isn't mine to re-sell, or lose my anonymity when it comes to bidding for future saints (not that I can ever expect to find another saint of the same distinction as my Saint).

But I'm on a mission and I can't put it off any longer, so in I go.

Malcolm is busy. He is the owner-operator of a small auction business, so he's always busy. It's a two-minute conversation.

ROGER: Hi Malcolm, just wondering if you can spare me a minute?

MALCOLM: Hi Roger, what can I do for you?

R: I don't know if you remember, but a few months ago I bought a wooden statue from here?

M: Yes I do remember. Arts and crafts? Or maybe sixteenth century? Even fifteenth century? Don't think I looked at it closely.

R: That's the one, and I also bought the oak bracket that it had been standing on. I think they are quite early and I'm trying to do some research into them. Just wondering if you can tell me how they came to you?

M: Oh yes – they came from MacGregor's of Edinburgh. Remember them? Johnnie MacGregor came in with them and asked me to sell them for him.

R: Yes, I remember MacGregor's. Wouldn't they have been sold in their big auction a few years ago?

M: I think Johnnie said they belonged to the family and not the business.

31

R: Right. Well, er, thanks Malcolm. That's a great help. See you on Saturday. *(Withdraws).*

M: Yeah. Bye Roger… *(Returns to his busyness before I leave the room).*

That's it. I went in nervously expecting a reluctant, generic sort of answer, possibly with offence taken. Moments later I came out cheerfully with a complete – and completely convincing – provenance for the statue.

You might legitimately ask me some tough questions. Why was I convinced so quickly and so thoroughly by this very brief conversation? How was I so sure that Malcolm instantly remembered that particular statue, which he had sold to me several months previously? Why would he be so frank with me, risking upsetting his vendor by breaching confidentiality? How did I know that he wasn't just making up a random tale to get me out of his office so he could get on with his work? Was I grabbing on to this story without further enquiry because it would be a good simple provenance to pass on to my selling auctioneer's expert in France? Why didn't I stay on in Malcolm's office and try to get from him some more detail and (better still) some documentary evidence?

No need. As soon as Malcolm uttered the words "MacGregor's of Edinburgh", I was completely satisfied that he knew exactly which statue I was talking about, and that his recollection of its provenance was precisely correct. It was almost as if The Saint himself, and the cheery mediaeval oak face built into the corner bracket on which he stood, were both affirming it in person: "yes, sure, that's exactly where we've been for all these years".

If you've hung around auction rooms in Edinburgh for a few years or decades, you get to be able to recognise infallibly when a piece of furniture has had the MacGregor's treatment, whether made by them from their own stocks of seasoned hardwoods, or restored and finished in their workshops. True, I had never before closely examined any mediaeval woodcarving treated by them, but the moment Malcolm mentioned the name of the firm, a penny dropped.

Ah! That explains the very subtle restoration work on the statue and its superb patination! And it explains how the sixteenth century misericord fragment has been set so successfully into an early twentieth century shelf bracket! And it explains how a fifteenth century statue and a sixteenth century carved head could be easily mistaken on cursory inspection for early twentieth century work (because one of MacGregor's specialities was making church furnishings in the arts and crafts taste, and after they had scrubbed off the mediaeval polychrome decoration from the statue, that's the kind of finish they gave it).

Malcolm's brief account also explained why the statue and bracket hadn't been dispersed when the residual stocks of the business were sold (because they were pieces kept in family ownership), and how they came to be offered for sale at Johnson & Andrews Auctioneers (because the current Mr MacGregor, a descendant of the last owner of the firm, was a personal friend of Malcolm Andrews, owner of the auction house).

My two-minute meeting with Malcolm also enabled me to construct in a more or less informed way my six-stage conjectural story related at the end of Chapter 1 about how the statue might have come into MacGregor's hands, and what happened to it thereafter.

So I needn't have worried about going to see Malcolm. He seemed content with my story of how my interest in the statue was for personal research, so he thought it acceptable to be a little bit indiscreet and to tell me, as one of his regular buyers, the name of the seller. He didn't think my questioning especially significant, so I didn't expect it would gain me a reputation as someone to bid against for old woodcarvings. The information I got from him was entirely credible, and provided a clear account of former ownership (so the statue was indisputably mine to sell), and circumstantial proof that the object had been in Scotland for many decades (derived from the early twentieth century MacGregor's style of the finish to the statue and the manufacture of the bracket) – which, of course, dispelled any doubts that the statue could be Nazi looted property.

Now I had a good, clean story to tell my Paris auctioneer about provenance. Later, in her catalogue notes she wrote this:

"Provenance:

- The private collection of an antiques trader, in activity from 1807 to 2004, Edinburgh (Scotland), then from 2004 to October 2012 in the possession of a descendant of this family of antiques traders.
- Private collection Edinburgh (Scotland)".

All highly satisfactory. Until, that is, Malcolm reads this book…

3

THE JUG, 1926–2007

Meet The Jug

In chapters 1 and 2 I attempted to provide a more or less coherent history of my statue of Saint John the Evangelist from its creation around 1426 until it came into my possession in late 2012. I had a lot to say about its origins, its disappearance during the French Revolution, its sojourn in Scotland, and its re-emergence in my local auction room.

You know that I bought The Saint, but somehow I've managed to leave out anything about how and why I came to buy it, and how I found out that it wasn't just any old statue but a fifteenth century Burgundian masterpiece. I'll return to these matters in later chapters, but for now, it's time to step gingerly into the arcane world of studio pottery and meet The Jug.

The term "studio pottery" might be unfamiliar to some readers. It's not at present a very popular field for collectors. Those few of us who are *aficionados* are ambivalent about how popular we want it to be. On the one hand we are pleased to see that some prominent makers such as Lucie Rie and Hans Coper (both dead) and Grayson Perry and Edmund de Waal (both very much alive) are gradually being accepted by the art establishment as important mainstream artists alongside painters and sculptors, conceptual artists and street artists. On the other hand we are worried that these growing reputations will soon lead to work by many other leading potters, currently affordable, being priced well beyond our means. It's difficult.

So, what is studio pottery? Here's a pretty basic definition from Wikipedia:

"Studio pottery is pottery made by amateur or professional artists or artisans working alone or in small groups, making unique items or short runs. Typically, all stages of manufacture are carried out by the artists themselves. Studio pottery includes functional wares such as tableware, cookware and non-functional wares such as sculpture."[8]

Studio pottery can be formed or modelled or thrown or built from many different types of clay using a variety of techniques. It can be decorated or left plain, glazed or unglazed, a functional vessel or a decorative sculpture. What makes it studio pottery is that each piece is individually and deliberately made by a named maker in his or her workshop or studio or pottery. It doesn't matter if you call the maker an artist or a craftsperson. Whichever, studio pottery is the opposite of large-scale factory production, and most people who know about studio pottery agree that it all started with Bernard Leach.

We are in St Ives, in West Cornwall in the very far south-western corner of England. It's 1926. Bernard Leach (whom we have already met as the maker of the ugly brown bowl described in Chapter 2) has been running his pottery on the outskirts of the town for about six years, since shortly after his return from a prolonged stay in Japan and China. He is regarded as a "curiosity"[9] among the thriving St Ives artists' community, and it will be many years until he fully establishes his reputation as a Grand Old Man and "the Father of Studio Pottery". His Japanese colleague Shoji Hamada has returned home after an extended stay in Cornwall, and so has the technician Tsuronosuke Matsubayashi, who had visited from Japan to rebuild the problematic kiln.

Three years before, in 1923, Leach took on his first apprentice, the young Michael Cardew, some fifteen years his junior. Decades later, Cardew too will become a Grand Old Man, perhaps second only in influence to Leach himself in the world of studio pottery.

During his three years at St Ives, Cardew learned a great deal from his master and mentor, and it also has to be said that Leach had much to learn from his apprentice. It is known that they collaborated on the making of many pots, but as far as I can ascertain only one pot has been discovered that bears both of their personal signatures. It's a big brown jug, and it turned up in January 2007, unidentified and miscatalogued, at Johnson & Andrews, my local auction house in Edinburgh. I bought it.

The Master

Bernard Leach was from an upper-middle-class colonial background. In his patrician way, he was charming, patronising, opinionated, bombastic, and bursting with ideas and enthusiasms. Imbued with arts-and-crafts notions absorbed from his nineteenth century heroes including John Ruskin and William Morris, he abhorred mass production and, like them, believed in a form of democracy where objects used in everyday life are handmade by traditional craftsmen. As with those same heroes, he didn't feel the need to consider or explain the precise economic and cultural mechanisms whereby his individually crafted, aesthetically superior, easily damaged and expensively priced drab brown pots would in an idyllic future time come to replace cheap-and-cheerful mass-produced hard-wearing colourfully-decorated Staffordshire crockery on the dining tables of millions and millions of low-paid working men and women.

During Leach's years in China and Japan he had immersed himself in the study of ceramic making and decorating techniques. He developed his own personal philosophical, almost mystical, vision in which eastern arts and English folk-craft traditions were to be combined and synthesised into a Bernard Leach-inspired ideal.

A great many books and articles have been written about Leach. Most of them are adulatory, some verging on hagiography, while a few dare to be more critical. Every writer remarks on his charm and force of personality, and no-one doubts the importance of his seminal and profound influence. As a teacher to numerous apprentices and pupils, and as a writer of many standard works on pottery, his mark is on everything that has happened subsequently in the rather esoteric and inward-looking world of studio pottery. As to whether this influence has been in overall terms benign or malign, there continues to be much debate amongst potters, dealers, collectors, connoisseurs, curators and critics.

It's a very technical and rather diffuse debate, embracing any number of more or less meaningful distinctions between form and function, between art and craft, between progress and ossification, between tradition and innovation, between utility and aesthetics, between democracy and elitism, between factory production and the work of individual craft potters, between ethical pots (made by Leach and followers) and fine art pots (made by everyone else). This is not a debate that I propose to get involved in. Suffice to say that

Bernard Leach, who died aged 92 in 1979, remains a controversial figure, part-god and part-demon, and still exerts a huge influence over many of the best studio potters working today throughout the world.

Bluff, charming and charismatic, Bernard Leach was excellent at persuading rich patrons to part with their money. With a characteristic unworldly and idealistic approach to his work, he was constantly short of funds, but invariably managed to find someone who would willingly supply some cash so that the effort could carry on. It was only much later when his eldest son David, and then his third wife Janet took over the management of the St Ives pottery and started to operate it as a business that they began to make ends meet. Throughout the 1920s, starting with Michael Cardew, the apprentices taken on at the St Ives pottery either funded themselves or paid Leach a fee for the privilege of being his pupil.

There is no doubt that Leach was a wonderful graphic artist. Before discovering the fascinations of ceramic art while living in Japan, he was a painter and engraver, and throughout his long life he produced two-dimensional work alongside his pots. With a few simple strokes of his brush or palette knife, he had an unrivalled and instantly recognisable ability to capture on his pots the very essence and movement of a bird in flight, a running hare, a weeping willow or a leaping salmon.

In the early St Ives years, Leach was strongly opposed to the division of labour. He taught and emphasised in his writings the importance of the individual craftsperson producing his or her pots from beginning to end – throwing, decoration, glaze and firing. The "first aim should be to throw to a standard; to be able to execute repetitive work accurately. Only when this was achieved, said Leach, could a potter call himself a thrower rather than an improviser"[10].

But there is reason to doubt the consistency and quality of Leach's own throwing – the process of forming lumps of raw wet clay into ceramic shapes on the potter's wheel. In practice many of the largest and best pots bearing Leach's personal seal were not actually thrown by him.

Evidence for this was provided by Harry Davis, who arrived at the St Ives pottery in 1933. He was engaged as a paid worker, not an apprentice. His status as an employee gave him a much lower position in the strict social hierarchy imposed by Leach than that occupied by the gentleman and lady apprentices who paid their own way. However, Davis was an outstandingly talented thrower, and

"Bernard Leach soon became aware of this, deciding that Davis had the ability to interpret his ideas. Davis states that it was he who made most of Leach's larger thrown pieces at this time 'with him looking over my shoulder and suggesting a touch here or a push there, sometimes giving the touch and push himself'. These pots 'were then signed with the master's seal or a brushed on initial'."[11]

The Apprentice

It had been a similar story a few years earlier when Michael Cardew was taken on as Leach's first apprentice. Like Leach, Cardew was from a patrician background. He had just achieved a poor third-class degree in Classics from Oxford University, and was destined by his education, class and family tradition for a gentlemanly profession in public service. But his heart wasn't in it: what he most wanted to do was to make pots, and to this end he had taken lessons in throwing, decorating and glazing from William Fishley Holland, the current presiding member of the long-established Fishley family of North Devon, artisan makers of slip-glazed country earthenware.

At this early stage in his career, Cardew was as much in favour of doing everything the hard way as was Leach. He railed against machinery and the use of industrial processes, but later on in their long careers and in their different ways, both Cardew and Leach began to understand that machines and large-scale production were key to making profits – or at least key to generating enough income from standard ranges of pots to finance their overriding interest in producing individual exhibition ceramics and commissioned pieces.

Leach and Cardew had much in common. We can picture Cardew "described by Leach as a 'young Apollo', a 'young man... as handsome as a Greek god, with forehead and nose all in a straight line, vivid eyes, golden curly hair, and a strong good jaw'"[12]. In return, Cardew described Leach at this time as "a perfectly preserved example of an English Edwardian, formal in manner, favouring collar and tie, plus fours, tweed jackets and brogues rather than casual dress, to all intents and purposes a gentleman potter"[13]. Both men were physically impressive, full of opinions and certainties, conscious of their class superiority over their workers and artisans, independently minded, artistic and somewhat bohemian in inclination, clever and highly talented.

With such similarities and such strong personalities, it might seem surprising that the two worked closely together for as long as three years without seriously falling out with one another. But in fact their collaboration was in general terms a successful exchange: Cardew at this early stage in his career felt he had much to learn, and Leach felt that having a self-financing gentleman thrower in his pottery was a godsend.

They also had their differences. Cardew, with his focus on reviving the joyous and exuberant English slipware tradition using earthenware clay, was unappreciative of Leach's yearning to synthesise Eastern and Western ceramic traditions by producing cool, contemplative stoneware vessels influenced by Chinese pottery from the Song dynasty. But Leach was also fascinated by English slipware, and a meeting of minds – and hands – was possible between them.

The results of the collaboration between Bernard Leach and Michael Cardew have been exhaustively researched and written about. To learn about Cardew, you can't do better than reading Tanya Harrod's masterly biography *The Last Sane Man*[14], which provides a vivid picture of a brilliant, charismatic, chaotic, confused, self-punishing, cruel and almost exquisitely egotistical figure, half-monster, half-genius.

In 1926, presumably not long after throwing The Jug that I later bought, Cardew left St Ives and set up his own potteries at Winchcombe, Gloucestershire, and later at Wenford Bridge, Cornwall. Abandoning earthenware for stoneware, he spent the following decades producing remarkable pottery and training local potters in Africa, travelling the world teaching and demonstrating, and establishing his reputation as a hero of modern art and a rather unlikely guru of the counterculture. He died in 1983.

In the Pottery

Unlike with Claus de Werve's fifteenth-century sculpture workshop in Dijon, Bernard Leach's pottery at Higher Stennack, St Ives doesn't need to be re-created in the imagination, because it's still there. After Janet Leach's death in 1997, the pottery passed into private hands, and by the time of its closure a few years later it was semi-derelict. But the building and its contents were rescued by the local council and carefully reconstructed and preserved. Then it was handed over to the Bernard Leach (St Ives) Charitable Trust and re-opened in 2008 as a museum, gallery, exhibition area and shop, with up-to-the-minute studio spaces for young and established working potters to produce new one-off pots and standard wares in the Leach tradition.

Similarly, there's no need to conjecture what it was like to be a member of the St Ives pottery community, because Leach, Cardew and many other potters wrote and spoke extensively about life and work at the pottery.

Visiting the reconstructed pottery gives a good idea of working life there. You can see the Clay Room, where clay was mixed with water and prepared for the throwers. Then comes the Pot Room, with space for up to eight potters to throw pots at Leach-designed kick-wheels. Then the Drying Room, with its ranges of shelves holding part-made pots and its large fireplace. And then you can see the famous three-chamber climbing kiln, now sadly cold and unsafe for use, but which in its heyday held more than 1,000 pieces for a single firing and could be heated to 1,300°C.

> "The heart of the pottery is the fireplace in the Drying Room, to the left of which is an old cast-iron three-legged cauldron topped by a wooden board. There, as an old man, 'Leach used to hunker down… examine the apprentices' work, teach, using pieces of found medieval pottery (still on the shelf above), and talk about the philosophy of potting: "He'd come down for crib [tea break] and sit here holding court: sometimes serious, sometimes not"'[15].

The potter and writer Emmanuel Cooper provides another entertaining description from earlier in Leach's career:

> "Break and meal times at the pottery were not only functional but instructive. Leach talked about pots, waved his arms about, drew on the blackboard, described shapes in the air in a great miming act, sometimes made pieces on his Japanese wheel and smoked endless cigarettes."[16]

On the day that Frances and I visited in July 2009, we were the only visitors to the pottery and I asked the guide nicely if I could be permitted to sit in the place from where the great man had handed down his gems of wisdom. To my surprise, she said yes, and I'm now proud to have a photograph of myself sitting upon the cauldron pretending to be Bernard Leach (See Illustrations, Picture 3). Sadly, my two minutes there didn't inspire me to any profound thoughts or utterances.

"A Rare Pitcher"

While working as Leach's pupil in St Ives, Michael Cardew spent part of his time on large-scale throwing and production of small items for sale to the tourist trade, but he also threw large one-off pieces for Bernard Leach to decorate. One day – we don't know which day, or what prompted it, or at whose instance – the collaboration resulted in the production of a remarkable and unlikely Jug (**See Illustrations, *Picture 4***). Tanya Harrod writes about this very Jug:

> "Most of these joint ventures only bore Leach's seal and that of the pottery. But unusually they both signed a heavily decorated stoneware pitcher, made in 1926. Michael certainly threw the robust shape and probably incised the inscription in Cornish round the shoulder of The Jug, Leach would probably have added the images of fish, a fire-breathing cat, the arms of St Ives and landscape with a tin-mine. Decoratively speaking, this pot was a muddle..."[17]

The best way to provide a visual description of The Jug is by quoting in full the entry in the catalogue from when it was re-sold by Bonham's auctioneers:

> "Bernard Leach and Michael Cardew, a rare Pitcher, 1926. Stoneware, the form thrown by Cardew and decorated by Leach, the design carved through slip includes inscriptions 'ONE & ALL', in Old Cornish 'EVEVGH TOS DHO GERNOW', in Latin 'SIGILLVM BURGH ST IVES IN COM CORNUBIA 1690 SIGILLUM', a row of three Mackerel, a row of three Seabass, a landscape with a Tin mine, stylised Wave motifs, the St. Ives town crest, a bunch of Grapes and a fire-breathing big Cat, the base with impressed MC and Leach Pottery seals, BL and 1926 date carved into the slip Height 26.5cm (10½ inches)."

To this fulsome and detailed description, the auctioneer added a footnote as follows:

> "As if this extraordinary and important Pot required placing in any additional historical context it also appears to have a mild saltglaze effect found on only a few other early Leach Pottery pieces. At the

time of the firing the local landscape had been stripped of mature trees as these had largely been used to make the props needed to support the tin mines. Consequently there were very few trees left in Cornwall that would have been suitable as a source of wood to burn in the newly built climbing kiln at the Leach Pottery. Without fire there could be no production so Leach managed to purchase a number of old railway sleepers for the purpose. These sleepers had been soaked in salts to prevent rot and when they were burned as fuel for the kiln they became volatilised and this produced an inadvertent saltglaze effect. Leach was surprised and apparently very pleased with the results, he later wrote about the firing in a number of his publications."[18]

You'll gather from this that my Jug was no ordinary jug. It was special enough to be signed by both potters. It was expertly thrown by Cardew. It was heavily decorated by both potters using unusual designs and motifs not seen on other more typical Leach or Cardew pieces. It was among a number of pots given special mention by Leach for the surprising and pleasing results of the firing. But unlike many other famous individual Leach and Cardew pots, this particular jug does not appear to have been exhibited, or to have featured in a collection, or to have been documented or recorded in either potter's writings. Which confers a touch of mystery upon it and perhaps adds further to its allure.

The Jug was unique. It was remarkable. It was historically important as an example of the collaboration between two founding figures of a significant and long-lasting and international art/craft movement. But was it beautiful? Hmmm. Tricky. Certainly beautiful in parts. Cardew's robust throwing was ruggedly handsome. Individual elements of Leach's incised decoration were as clean and elegant as in his best work. The glossy, treacly brown glaze with its inadvertent salt-glaze iridescence was rich and deep and very tactile. The whole emanated a striking and commanding presence. So yes, I think it was beautiful. Messy, difficult, but beautiful.

The Jug's Provenance

Whilst some six years later I was very anxious to find out about the provenance of The Saint, I felt no similar imperative in 2007 after I had bought the Leach/ Cardew Jug.

When I bought The Saint, I wasn't up against serious competition and my relatively modest winning bid of £340 didn't cause much of a stir in the saleroom. Nobody noticed. By contrast my purchase of The Jug caused a ripple in the room because I had bid for it in such a determined way and had bid so very much more than any sensible person might be expected to pay for an old brown pottery jug. Naturally, Malcolm Andrews the auctioneer was aware that I (and the underbidder) considered The Jug to be of significant value; and later he knew that I had sold The Jug on for a very large profit. But I never asked him about provenance, and he never offered any information.

Why the difference? A number of reasons.

First, Bonham's auctioneers who agreed to re-sell The Jug for me didn't ask about provenance. I simply told them that I had picked it up at my local auction and that was all they wanted to know.

Second, I didn't have any concerns about having good title to ownership of The Jug so that I could re-sell it. It was a British-made object, so the question of wartime looting didn't arise. To the lay person it might have appeared an unremarkable piece of household bric-a-brac, so it seemed hardly credible that it could have been stolen property.

Third, an item such as this Jug might be subject to some of the anti-provenance effects which I tried to describe in Chapter 2. When selling it on through a specialist auction targeted at high-rolling and obsessive collectors, gaining ownership of the object will be of infinitely greater significance to the successful bidder than knowing its provenance. The less you know about where it came from the better – just in case it turns out to be dodgy and you risk losing it. The same can't be said of The Saint, which was altogether too esoteric and extraordinary to be re-sold without some attempt being made to explain where it had been and how it re-emerged.

An Exception

My fourth reason for failing to ask Malcolm about The Jug's provenance was that there's nothing out of the ordinary or surprising about an old pottery jug turning up at an auction where many of the goods for sale come from house clearances and executries. I challenge you, readers, to spend a few moments searching (in life or in memory) through the kitchen cupboards and sideboards of your parents and grandparents. Somewhere towards the back, you'll find a ceramic jug – or more than one – that belonged to Granny, or to Granny's Granny.

This is axiomatic. I know it to be true. We have a jug in our kitchen that belonged to Frances's Great-Great-Grandmother, one of only a very few objects in the house which we can trace back through either family to the nineteenth century. It's a one-pint earthenware jug heavily decorated in the mid-Victorian majolica revival taste, probably made at the Alloa pottery in Scotland. It's of little value, not least because it has a huge crack, but it is indeed a genuine heirloom, commended to our care by my late mother-in-law.

I concede that there is a wide gap between this one instance and an axiom, but I have much more evidence. The bric-a-brac shelves of charity shops invariably have several old pottery jugs. So do low-grade auctions. The few surviving junk shops and antique shops are overloaded with them. And today, as I write, there are 22,680 listings on the eBay auction website under the heading "Pottery Jug".

We can safely assume that most of these objects are available for sale because they have been cleared out of old (often dead) people's kitchen cupboards and sideboards, dusty and disused. This might have occurred immediately before consignment for auction, or alternatively at some indeterminate date in the past when they have entered circulation via the antiques trade. But either way, there are lots of them. For the most part they are deeply unfashionable and in modern homes have probably been replaced by something brighter and more modern. Or – heaven forfend! – perhaps some people have no use for a jug at all, but *place the milk carton directly on the breakfast table!*

The great majority of dull old pottery jugs on the market comprises cheap factory-produced everyday tableware devoid of artistic merit. But from my extensive ramblings around the second-hand haunts of Edinburgh and further afield, I can confidently assert that a fair few of the emergent jugs are interesting and often beautiful objects falling into the category of studio pottery.

Here's a list of just some of the potters whose pots I have bought cheaply in Edinburgh charity shops and at Johnson & Andrews auctioneers in the last couple of years:

Richard Batterham
Alan Caiger-Smith (Aldermaston Pottery)
Emmanuel Cooper
Harry and May Davis (Crowan Pottery)

Mike Dodd
Ray Finch (Winchcombe Pottery)
Janet Leach (St Ives Pottery)
Sophie MacCarthy
William Plumptre
Alan Wallwork

In these days when only a very small number of studio potters have a wide public profile, I would expect most readers to look at the ten names above and say "Who?". But if you are a collector, you will know and respect all of the names.

The low prices asked for these pieces indicates that over the course of a few years or decades, they have somehow come adrift from identification with their potters, and have degraded into anonymous junk, random treasure fit only for the charity shop or the local auction.

In an assemblage of pots by these makers, a work by Bernard Leach or Michael Cardew is exceptional, but not all that much of an exception. It's an outlier, well out of the ordinary, but not so far out of the ordinary that it's off the end of the scale (as The Saint clearly was). Remarkable as it is, The Jug might indeed have come out of the back of Granny's sideboard.

So you might justifiably ask me: where was your famous Jug between 1926 and 2007? How did it get from being an outstanding exhibition-class piece of work made in Cornwall by Leach and Cardew, into a local auction in Edinburgh? Sadly, I have absolutely no idea.

4

THE BUZZ

Viewing: Friday at Johnson & Andrews

Johnson & Andrews hold their weekly sales on a Saturday morning. There are usually between 200 and 300 lots. They put the catalogue online on their website on the Thursday afternoon, and viewing is available all day Friday and on the morning of the sale from 9.30am. until the sale starts at 11.00am.

On Thursday evening, I look through the online catalogue. Each lot has a photograph and a rudimentary description. Occasionally something will catch my eye, and I'll make a mental note to have a close look at it when I go to view.

On Friday I go to the viewing. I buy a catalogue. Then I wander around the room, taking my time, trying to look at and think about every lot that's coming up for sale. Sometimes I'm there for 45 minutes or even an hour. While I'm there, I invariably see a small crowd of other viewers, mostly familiar faces, mooching around in very much the same way that I mooch. And I'll chat in a desultory sort of way with the members of staff in the office or on the floor of the saleroom.

Some Fridays I don't see anything of interest to me, and I decide that I won't bother to attend the sale tomorrow. Other Fridays I might see a few bits and pieces that are of interest. I make a note in my catalogue as a reminder to research the item during the evening and decide if I'm going to bid, and if so, how much.

Here's an example. The Johnson & Andrews quarterly antiques sale in October 2013 had 292 lots offered for sale. This was a rather more upmarket sort of auction than the regular weekly sale. The catalogue entries were slightly more detailed than usual, and included estimated prices. When I went to the viewing, I marked these seven lots in my catalogue:

Lot 59. 18th/19th century Persian pottery tile with glazed lotus leaf and floral lattice design (a/f), 34cm x 31cm (£200-£400)

Lot 61. 18th century delft ware pottery slipware decorated plaque, the central vase and floral [sic] enclosed within a sponged ware style border, 42cm diameter (a/f) (£30-£50)

Lot 70. 18th century Bible of the Old and New Testaments with later leather binding, 34cm long (£50-£100)

Lot 88. Wallet containing a collection of Victorian and Edwardian letters, postcards, etc (£80-£120)

Lot 106. After Burne Jones, lithographic print with allegorical scene in relief carved contemporary oak frame, 37cm x 20cm (£50-£70)

Lot 192. Cold painted bronze figure of an Arab riding a camel, 18cm high (£150-£200)

Lot 221. Bokhara rug, the centre panel with ten octagons enclosed within a scrolling diamond shaped triple floral border on red field, 292cm x 250cm (£200-£400)

So what was it about these seven objects that caught my eye at the viewing?

For starters, the pottery tile was lovely, probably from Iznik in Turkey, probably earlier than eighteenth or nineteenth century. Nice to have, but I expected it to be more expensive than I could afford. The delftware plaque was in fact a large plate or charger. It wasn't terribly attractive and was badly chipped (as signified by the "a/f" warning in the catalogue, which indicates "as found"), but it was big and interesting and I agreed with the estimated eighteenth century dating in the catalogue. It didn't have any pottery mark or other identification, but I was looking for a good reason to do some research into delftware, so I decided to use some of my evening on researching it.

Lot 88, the wallet containing a collection of Victorian and Edwardian letters, looked interesting. Most of the letters were still in their stamped envelopes, and I could see postmarks ranging from the 1880s to the 1930s. I didn't have time or leisure to look carefully through the contents of the letters (mustn't look too interested or other viewers will stick their noses in!), but many letters were addressed to people with the same surname, so I assumed that this was a family collection. Questions quickly followed: was this family documented? Were any family members famous or distinguished? Might the letters contain any interesting historical or social commentary? Might they hang together in such a way that transcription and publication might be worthwhile? I memorised the name of the most frequently occurring addressee so that I could Google him in the evening.

The Burne-Jones print didn't look to me like a lithograph, but more like a form of early photographic reproduction. And it was in a superbly carved arts-and-crafts frame. A fascinating piece, but my expectation was that the picture dealers would go for it and I wouldn't get a look-in at a price I was ready to pay.

I was interested in the cold-painted bronze camel (probably Austrian) because Frances has a small collection of camels and I'm always on the lookout for additions. But it was a good quality piece and would be easy for a dealer to re-sell, so I expected that the hammer price would be higher than the estimate.

The Bokhara rug was of fairly recent manufacture and superb quality. In my judgement it wasn't the type of Pakistan-made rug usually described as Bokhara, but a much more exotic Turkmen-type rug made by the nomadic peoples of Central Asia. I tend to fall head-over-heels in love with Turkmen rugs, as a result of which there is no space on the floor of my house for more of them. So, sadly, I have to use extreme discretion in buying them and will only buy if I think I'm getting a real bargain – which rarely happens because there are plenty of buyers at Johnson & Andrews who know a good rug when they see one.

That accounts for six out of the seven objects that I marked in my catalogue. When I came away from the viewing, my intention was to do some research into the delftware charger and into the portfolio of letters, in order to decide whether and how much to bid. And if any of the other items on my list didn't seem to be attracting much interest, I might pop in a bid or two in the hope of getting them cheap.

You might note that in no case described above was it my intention to buy any object that caught my eye with a view to re-selling it at a profit. That does happen sometimes but not on this particular occasion. If I do decide to sell an item, it's a decision that I usually make independently of my decision to buy it.

To complete the story of this auction, here are the results:

Lot 59. Persian pottery tile, estimate £200-£400, sold for £560. A fair price for a beautiful object, sold to a regular bidder, a collector with exquisite taste and deep pockets.

Lot 61. Delft ware pottery plaque or charger, estimate £30-£50, sold to me for £40. That's about what it's worth, but I've had enormous enjoyment trying to find out more about it. After emailing photos to a couple of museum experts and getting helpful replies, I now think it's French faience ware, late 18th century, but from an unidentified and probably unidentifiable pottery. Currently it's on display high up in a corner of my kitchen, standing atop the mediaeval corbel or misericord made into a corner bracket by MacGregor's of Edinburgh to support The Saint. Looks very nice there.

Lot 88. Wallet of Victorian and Edwardian letters, postcards, etc, estimate £80-£120, sold to me for £65. By the time the auction started I had discovered that the main addressee of the letters was one of the founding fathers of Manchester University, and a member of a prominent Quaker family. After I got them home, I realised two things:

1) The letters were, frankly, quite boring, and of themselves could never make an interesting research project for editing and publication;

2) One of the envelopes contained seven extra-boring letters, but one was dated 1840 and stamped with a good Penny Black stamp, while the others were all from later in the 1840s and were stamped with early imperforated Penny Reds.

So I won't get to write a monograph about the letters, and have decided to offer to donate them to the archives of either Manchester University or the Society of Friends, should either body be interested. I will however get my money back because I intend to sell the stamps at the local philatelic auction. Sadly, none of the Penny Reds were from Plate 77, of which much more much later.

Lot 106. Print after Burne Jones, estimate £50-£70, sold for £110 to a picture dealer. No surprise there.

Lot 192. Bronze figure of an Arab riding a camel, estimate £150-£200, sold for £280. No surprise there either.

Lot 221. Bokhara rug, estimate £200-£400, sold for £460 and now almost certainly gracing the floor of an elegant Edinburgh drawing room.

Bible-spotting

In the last section I told you about a fairly typical viewing session at Johnson & Andrews. I listed seven lots that caught my eye, but then I only followed up six of them. I have left the seventh, a Bible, until last, because it represents a recent experience of what happens to me when I first see an object on view in an auction that **I MUST HAVE**. I'll try to describe the feeling in detail in the next section.

But first, the Bible. You will recall that it was catalogued as:

Lot 70. 18th century Bible of the Old and New Testaments with later leather binding, 34cm long (£50-£100)

Now, I like old Bibles, and I know a bit about them. To say why, I need to provide another snippet of autobiography.

As a schoolboy I had a precociously-developed aesthetic sense, an appreciation of beautiful things, and a rather acquisitive turn of mind. My earliest collecting obsession was with coins, and I'll write more about this in a later chapter. But for now, you need to know that in the mid-1950s, when I was still a small boy, my parents left their house in suburban Golders Green and moved to Central London to follow their own parents' and grandparents' trade and become licensed victuallers or, more commonly, publicans. Naturally my elder brother and I accompanied them.

After two years in our first pub in a quiet street in Marylebone, we all moved in 1959 to a much busier establishment in about as central a position as it was possible to be – in Charing Cross Road, in the heart of London's West End, surrounded by theatres, on the edge of sleazy Soho, just off Leicester Square, and just a few hundred metres from Trafalgar Square. I was ten when we arrived, and sixteen when we left (and indeed left London altogether for a pub in Berkshire). But those five years are among the most formative of any child's life, and they were certainly formative for me.

Now in those mid-twentieth-century days, Charing Cross Road was celebrated for three things: its theatres, its surgical appliance shops, and its bookshops. I enjoyed the first, had no use for the second, but became obsessed with the third.

> *"Long before the American writer Helene Hanff immortalised the street in 84 Charing Cross Road (1970) – an account of her twenty-year correspondence with a buyer at the antiquarian booksellers Marks & Co – the area enjoyed a storied association with the city's literary scene and its accompanying book trade. In its 1950s heyday, denizens of the nearby drinking dens of Soho, from Dylan Thomas to Auberon Waugh, would stagger from shop to shop, scanning the heaving shelves."[19]*

If any of the aforementioned literary luminaries happened to tear their eyes from the books and look down, and just happened to notice a small pubescent boy with thick glasses in a black school blazer browsing the lower shelves – that was me. If I just happened to look up and notice that the browser next to me was a scruffy, red-nosed old bloke with leather patches on the elbows of his tweed jacket, well, that seemed kind of normal to me, because during opening hours my parents' pub at number 37 Charing Cross Road invariably had a few characters answering to that description sitting at the bar drinking the cheaper brands of gin or whisky. We didn't have a separate front door, so I had to pass through the Saloon Bar on my way to our living quarters above the pub. If Auberon Waugh or Dylan Thomas was sitting there haranguing my Dad, I wouldn't have known him from any of the other old boozers. It's by no means certain that my Dad would have known either.

I don't know what other (normal?) boys of my age were spending their pocket money on, but I was spending all of mine – and then some – on antiquarian books. My tastes in books are marginally more sophisticated now than they were half a century ago, but back then, my two criteria for buying books were that they must be *old* and *cheap*.

It's an incontrovertible fact that if you focus on buying books solely on the basis that they must be the oldest and cheapest you can find, you end up owning a large number of religious books, particularly bibles and prayer books. This is partly because there are many more of them than there are of other early books, partly because there is less demand except for those of the best quality and in the best condition, and partly because so many of them are in very poor condition resulting from hundreds of years of frequent handling.

I still own most of the religious books that I bought from the cheap racks outside the second-hand bookshops of Charing Cross Road, and for the most part I'm still very glad that I do, because they are interesting and beautiful artefacts. A by-product of my fairly indiscriminate purchasing policy was that I did a fair amount of reading in the public library about different translations and editions of the Bible. Admittedly this was perhaps not the most normal and healthy way for a teenage boy to be spending his time. While my grammar school mates were in the boy scouts, or tinkering about with their bikes, or chasing girls or hanging around on street corners foolishly stirring up trouble with the much tougher kids from the nearby secondary modern, I passed my time holed up with a pile of books comparing editions of the Bible. It seems a bit odd to me now. Perhaps it even seemed odd to me back then.

However, a lasting result of this – well, let's not mince words but let's come out and call it *weirdness* – is that for the last fifty years I've been able to spot an interesting and desirable copy of the Bible at 100 metres.

The Good Book

Now to return to Lot 80 in Johnson & Andrews sale in October 2013. Any book dealer or collector or specialist librarian will be able to date most books fairly closely from the style of binding, and so will know a lot about the book before looking inside. The Bible in question looked from the outside like any other early nineteenth-century folio-sized Bible that you might find in any auction or any second-hand bookshop anywhere. A plain hide binding, rather worn and scuffed, with the front hinge splitting at the top and bottom. Seemingly a very typical Church or Family Bible from around 1820. Nothing of interest there.

I opened the book and got a shock. The text started from Genesis Chapter III, verse 17 – which meant that the title page and the first dozen or perhaps twenty pages including the title page and prefatory material and the beginning of Genesis were all missing. But the binding was tight and there was no sign of pages having been torn out. Instant conclusion (also instantly obvious from the typeface and layout of the page): this is an earlier edition of the Bible which has been rebound around 1820.

It's never a surprise to find that an early printed Bible has its first few pages and last few pages missing and has been given a new binding. A Bible was often the only book in the house or church. It was expensive to buy, and exceptionally precious to its owner. But as it was also in constant use for private reading and for prayer service, it inevitably suffered from extreme wear. After the binding disintegrated and fell off, you would have to hold the book by its front and back pages, which over further decades of use would in turn erode and wear away. By this time the book would have acquired additional preciousness due to its antiquity, and it would be carefully and expensively re-bound, but minus its beginning and end. One of my teenage Charing Cross Road purchases, a 1612 first octavo printing of the 1611 King James Bible, had suffered precisely this fate, having been beautifully re-bound in suede pigskin around 1900 minus its beginning and end.

On opening the front cover of Lot 80, it was immediately clear to me that this was another instance of the same familiar treatment. But if you are faced with a book with no title page, how do you know what you're looking at? Fortunately, most early bibles are quite helpful here, because they invariably have a full second title page at the start of the New Testament, which hasn't suffered the same wear and tear as the outer pages of the book and is often well-preserved. Usually the New Testament title page contains much the same information as the main title page at the front of the book (which strictly speaking only pertains to the Old Testament section), and this generally includes the name of the printer, and the date and place of printing.

I waited until no other viewers were looking over my shoulder and turned to this second title page, after the Book of Malachi, before the Gospel of Saint Matthew, hoping to find a nice early date. Then I saw the imprint:

EDINBVRGH
Printed by Andro Hart, and are to be solde
at his Buith, on the Northside of the gate, a litle
beneath the Crosse. ANNO DOM 1610.

I'll say a bit about the bibliographical and historical significance of these few words later on, but for now I want to focus on the thunderbolt of realisation that what an instant ago was merely a dusty old book on display amongst a cluster of forlorn objects in an auction viewing, is in fact something quite extraordinary, a piece of random treasure.

From a View to a Buzz

It's a feeling I have experienced on a number of occasions. Although I'm writing about it in the context of a 1610 Bible, I got the same sensation on first encountering both The Jug in 2007 and The Saint in 2012.

I'm not certain about this, but it might be that this feeling engendered by that tiny moment of realisation is at the very heart of what I enjoy about auctions. It might be the reason why I keep going. Physiologically it could be similar to the effect of some drugs, and it could be addictive.

I have tried but failed to find an analysis of it in scientific publications. I note in passing that there's a new academic field of study called neuroaesthetics,

THE
NEVV TESTAMENT
OF OVR LORD IESVS
Chriſt, Tranſlated out of
Greeke by *Theod.Beza*.

WHEREVNTO ARE ADIOYNED
briefe Summaries of doctrine vpon the Euangeliſts
and Acts of the Apoſtles, together with the methode of the
Epiſtles of the Apoſtles, by the ſaid
THEOD. BEZA.

And alſo ſhort Expoſitions on the phraſes and hard places, ta-
ken out of the large Annotations of the foreſaid
Author, and Ioach. Camerarius, by P. Loſ. Villerius.

Engliſhed by L. Tomſon.

❡Together with the Annotations of FR. IVNIVS
vpon the Reuelation of S. IOHN.

EDINBVRGH,
Printed by Andro Hart, and are to be ſolde
at his Buith, on the Northſide of the gate, a litle
beneath the Croſſe.   ANNO DOM. 1610.

Cum Privilegio Regiæ Maieſtatis.

New Testament title page, Andro Hart's Geneva Bible, Edinburgh, 1610

which gives rise to learned articles in its journals employing this sort of discourse:

> "Viewing art is popular, pleasurable, and for the most part an unsolved puzzle when it comes to the neurological mechanisms underpinning this experience. Much of the pioneering work on the neurology of art tended to focus on what has been called 'neuro-esthetics' and has aspired to tell us why we find something beautiful. This broad-brush approach tells us little about the complex mechanisms that shape an individual viewer's response to a specific work of art…"[20]

…and so forth. But as far as I can tell from my less-than-exhaustive scanning of the literature, the physiology and psychology of this moment of realisation hasn't yet been subject to rigorous academic research.

So I'll try to describe how it feels in an entirely subjective and unscientific way. For this exercise I'll need appropriate terminology. What I'm looking for is the best word to encompass this particular essential element of the alchemy of antiques.

*It's an **insight**…* but no, the Oxford online dictionary defines an insight as "an accurate and deep understanding", and that's not what I'm talking about. Suddenly you know something you didn't know before, but that doesn't necessarily mean you have accurate or deep understanding. You might need to do hours of research before you even have a clue what it is that you have perceived.

*It's an **intuition**…* defined as "a thing that one knows or considers likely from instinctive feeling rather than conscious reasoning". A closer description, but too cool and unemotional. It doesn't take in the physical manifestations of the feeling: instantaneous total alertness and focus on the object, extreme excitement and arousal, probably accompanied by increased heart rate, faster breathing, changes in blood pressure, release of adrenalin and/or dopamine and the-Lord-knows-what other hormones, the kinds of things you would need to be wired up to several high-tech instruments to measure. But which will likely remain unmeasured until such time as it's possible to attend an auction viewing attached to an MRI scanner and ECG machine.

*It's a **frisson**…* no, it's much more extreme than that.

*It's a **jolt**...* no, because you get a jolt and then you get over it. But this feeling lasts and lasts, at least until you buy the object. With the statue of Saint John, it lasted almost undiminished from the moment I spotted it until I re-sold it seven months later, and then a bit longer after that. In fact, I still have it.

*It's a **revelation**...* no, there's nothing mystical or spiritual about it, and until you have done your research you might not know what has been revealed.

*It's an **epiphany**...* no, it isn't a religious experience.

*It's a **hunch**...* no, a hunch is a maybe, but this feeling is one of absolute certainty, even if you don't know what it is that you're certain about.

*It's an **inspiration**...* not really, because inspiration is "the process of being mentally stimulated to do or feel something, especially to do something creative". Inspiration is a precursor to action rather than to knowledge.

*It's a **premonition**...* no, it isn't to do with suddenly knowing what's going to happen next. You might well have no idea.

*It's a **hit**...* this could be a good one. A hit of crack cocaine is described by Wikipedia thus:

> "[It] affects the brain chemistry of the user: causing euphoria, supreme confidence, loss of appetite, insomnia, alertness, increased energy, a craving for more cocaine, and potential paranoia... Its initial effect is to release a large amount of dopamine, a brain chemical inducing feelings of euphoria".

That sounds quite like it. However, the hit from crack cocaine wears off in 5–15 minutes. But one hit of an exceptional object viewed in an auction room can last and last and last.

*It's a **rush**...* see **hit** above.

*It's a **point**...* now, I hesitate to compare myself with a dog. A pointer dog is the embodiment of everything that is sleek, elegant, superbly proportioned, fit, muscular. I, on the other hand, am slightly overweight, not very tall, well past middle age, bespectacled, bearded, balding. But:

> "The classical point is a dog very intense, standing motionless, with the nose thrust forward at the strongest scent, with one front foot bent up and tail (if it has one) directed toward the sky."[21]

> "Pointing for a dog is a natural instinct... [It] is the rigid posture of the dog's body and the passionate expression on his face. A dog with an intense point will have his eyes bright and focussed, his muscles will quiver and his whole body will be rock solid"[22].

These seem to be helpful descriptions of my appearance and demeanour on spotting an extraordinary object in the saleroom. But the dog's point only endures until the quarry – a game bird, a rabbit, a hare, a fox – is flushed. Thereafter, there's the chase, but the chase isn't what we are concerned with in this chapter.

*It's a **buzz**...* since I lack ability or imagination to coin a new word, perhaps buzz is the best word I can find, although it seems inadequate to carry the significance with which I am investing it. When I first viewed The Jug in 2007 and The Saint in 2012, I felt more of a roar than a buzz, and it's a buzz that keeps on buzzing and buzzing. But I'll stick with the term Buzz to describe what I mean, and hope that readers will understand that it's a small word which I'm loading with a very large quantity of meaning.

Buzzing

I got The Buzz when I saw the imprint on the New Testament title page of the 1610 Bible. Unlike with The Jug and The Saint (which Buzzes we'll come to in due time), on this particular occasion I knew well what I was looking at.

Andro Hart was by far the most important and prolific printer, publisher, bookbinder and book importer and seller of the early seventeenth century in Scotland. Among other distinctions, he was the first publisher of the poetry of William Drummond of Hawthornden, and of the scientific works of John Napier of Merchiston, the inventor of logarithms.

"His first major printing project was his great Geneva Bible of 1610, the second Bible edition to be printed in Scotland, which was so accurate it became the template for numerous editions printed in the Low Countries."[23]

The Geneva translation of the Bible into English first appeared in 1560 and remained in use in the Kirk of Scotland until several decades after first publication of the Authorised or King James Version in 1611. From 1610 onwards, the Andro Hart edition of the Geneva Bible was definitive in Scottish Churches.

Because of healthy sales, Hart printed a relatively large number of copies, but of course they were well used, and, having fallen out of favour by the 1650s, many were left to moulder. Thus, four hundred years later, this Bible is very rare – although not nearly as rare as some of Hart's other publications. The English Short Title Catalogue (ESTC, a wonderful online list of over 460,000 books published between 1473 and 1800, mainly in English, held in the British Library and over 2,000 other libraries) lists nineteen major libraries where copies are held. Some of these libraries own multiple copies, so I'd guess there are maybe around fifty copies of the book still in existence. Six are in the National Library of Scotland in Edinburgh, of which at least three are imperfect and incomplete, and two copies are in Edinburgh University Library.

Books as rare as this Bible are mostly held in major academic and national libraries or in the very privatest and most exclusive of private collections. Perhaps you can begin to see why I got The Buzz on spotting a copy in the local saleroom. At the auction next day, I bought it for £45. As an imperfect copy in a later binding, it isn't fantastically valuable. I know this because by a strange coincidence, another copy in similar condition was sold in an Edinburgh auction in May 2015 for £550. But I'm not selling my copy. It stays with me as one of my treasures.

The reader might be wondering how it was that on first seeing the Andro Hart Bible, I already knew quite a lot about it. If tasked to name a subject more dry and abstruse than Scottish printers of the early seventeenth century, you might think for a long time before responding. Or you might cast doubt on whether the possessor of such arcane erudition should be permitted to mix in society.

In actual fact my knowledge wasn't on this particular occasion the result of nerdiness or geekiness. I happened to know about Andro Hart because I happened to have spent a considerable time quite recently in researching him and his work. The reason for this is that I had bought another of his books, a very much rarer one, at a Johnson & Andrews auction a couple of years previously. That is a different story, which will be related in a later chapter.

The Wrong Buzz

Experiencing what I am calling The Buzz at an auction viewing does not necessarily mean that a fortune in profit is in prospect. I'm quite as happy with the discovery of my modestly valuable Andro Hart Bible as I was with the very valuable Jug and the almost obscenely valuable Saint. The Buzz was and has remained equally strong.

So too with occasions when The Buzz has been followed not by huge success and enormous satisfaction but by disappointment. Three recent and rather embarrassing examples come to mind, involving objects with widely varying backgrounds, all dismissed as inauthentic by experts. In each case, the difficulty from my personal point of view has been my perception – almost certainly erroneous – that the acknowledged authorities who I have consulted are too obstinate / too blinkered / too unimaginative to recognise the genuineness of the exceptional objects on which I have asked them to pass judgment. By contrast, from the personal points of view of those world-class authorities, the difficulty has been having some ignorant unknown geezer in Edinburgh sending them unsolicited emails attaching photos of obvious copies, reproductions or fakes.

Case 1. A tattered folio album, probably assembled by an amateur art-fancier in a Scottish country house around 1850. It contains more than fifty pages of pasted-in and loose artworks mostly from the eighteenth and nineteenth centuries. They are either engravings cut from printed publications, or original but undistinguished pencil drawings. All very pedestrian and yawn-inducing except for one Buzz-generating sheet. On it are pasted four small engravings, the largest about 10cms by 9cms. They are printed on old heavy laid paper, with the edges cropped. Each sheet features a group of between two and six studies of heads, male and female, old and young, handsome and grotesque. And each sheet is signed in the plate with the initials Rt and the date, in two sheets the year 1641, and in two the year 1651.

At the Johnson & Andrews Friday viewing The Buzz tells me: Rembrandt etchings!!! So after a little research online that evening, and thinking to myself that even if the etchings aren't "right" I could still break up the whole album and frame and re-sell much of its contents, I bought it at the next day's sale. I'm embarrassed to tell you how much I paid, but since I could see that I was bidding against a well-known picture dealer I didn't think I could go far wrong.

I emailed photos of the etchings to Sotheby's, and got a very helpful reply from their specialist Petra Kwan:

"Thank you for contact us regarding your group of etchings. We have looked through Hollstein's catalogue raisonné of Rembrandt's printed work, but have not found them recorded there. They do not look as if they are by Rembrandt's hand. As these are not signed by an artist, it is difficult to trace clues to the authorship of these sketches of heads. Perhaps these are from the School of Rembrandt, in imitation of his style, since

One of four small etchings of head studies or tronies,
maybe by Rembrandt, maybe not.

they are dated during the later years of Rembrandt's life. I understand why you thought they could be by Rembrandt, as he famously depicted sketches of figures' heads ('tronies'), subjects shared by your four etchings."

You can't expect a clearer and more reasonable expert opinion than that. No-one but a fool would argue. But, looking at them again as I write this passage (naturally I haven't done anything about breaking up the album and it sits today accusingly beside my desk), I still have The Buzz. I still think they might be by Rembrandt, that the experts might be wrong and I might be right.

Case 2. A small, steep-sided pottery bowl with a flattened flared rim, made of reddish-brown earthenware, covered inside and outside with a white slip. The upper surfaces have sgraffiato decoration incised through the slip, with a fantastical

An earthenware sgraffiato-decorated bowl, maybe mediaeval
Port St Symeon or Aghkand ware, maybe not

bird in the centre. Green and brown glazes are applied in patches of colour and large dots, the whole covered with a transparent glaze. It looked old. It looked middle eastern. I hadn't seen anything quite like it before. It was beautiful. Could it be mediaeval? I got The Buzz.

An evening's internet research revealed similar (but not identical) items described as Aghkand Ware (Persia, Azerbaijan, Georgia, twelfth century) or Bamiyan Ware (Afghanistan, 11th/12th centuries) or Port Saint Symeon Ware (Turkey, thirteenth century), or Nishapur Ware (Persia, tenth century). Alongside The Buzz, I had A Niggle. If the bowl was genuinely mediaeval, it was in remarkably (or perhaps suspiciously) good condition for its age. But if it was a modern reproduction, why did it have areas of glaze loss, and some seemingly age-related white deposits on the glaze? Could it be a fake that had been deliberately distressed? But if so, who would deliberately fake an obscure pottery bowl which wouldn't be enormously desirable even if it was the genuine article?

The next day at the sale, I discovered that A Niggle doesn't trump The Buzz. I found myself bidding against a dealer, and ended up paying much much more than I had planned. Afterwards I reflected that he might have been bidding only because I was bidding – another of those unfortunate incidences where one isn't served by gaining a reputation as a bit of an expert. An unmerited reputation in this particular instance.

I had very helpful replies to the emails and photos that I sent to the experts at Sotheby's and Bonham's. Alexandra Roy and Edward Gibbs of Sotheby's were encouraging:

> "based on similar stylistic models, your bowl has the characteristics of both Nishapur and Aghkand sgraffiato ceramics. It is difficult to be certain, based on the photograph, of its date, but it is possible that it is from the 10th/12th century."

Bonham's were sceptical. Their specialist Oliver White wrote:

> "You are right in thinking that the bowl bears resemblance to Persian incised pottery of the 11th/12th century known as Garrus and Aghkand ware. I am afraid, however, that the glaze and colours don't look right in our opinion and the shape itself is also a little strange. We are therefore more inclined to believe that is a later copy, probably made in the 20th century."

To settle the debate, I wrote to Professor Oliver Watson, the I. M. Pei Professor of Islamic Art and Architecture at Oxford University, a world authority on Islamic mediaeval pottery, and also on fakes and forgeries (and also, by the way, a world authority on modern studio pottery). I told him about my worries. Thinking that he might consider an unsolicited enquiry from an amateur upstart to be beneath his notice, I didn't really expect a reply. But I was delighted to hear back from him almost immediately, polite and helpful but not encouraging:

> "From the photographs I can see why you describe it as "worrisome". It purports to be a St Symeon type, but in all aspects – shape, material, drawing style, the stippling and its condition – it gives me concern."

That should be that. But as I look at the bowl on the table next to my desk while I type these words, there's still something about it that gives me The Buzz. What if the experts are all wrong?

Case 3. A brooch spotted in a box of nondescript 1950s costume jewellery. In Scotland (and I daresay in many other parts of the world) auction-goers are accustomed to seeing lots and lots of cheap-and-usually-nasty jewellery based on the designs of Charles Rennie Mackintosh and his circle. It has almost invariably been produced in the last forty years or so, oafishly designed and executed, and mass-produced in inferior materials. We dismiss it scornfully as "Mockintosh".

But this item looks different. It's a brooch or pendant about 5 cms square, clearly hand-made in beaten and engraved pewter, with a central rectangular panel cut out of the metal and filled with a white mother-of pearl plaque. Suspended from the lower edge on a silver wire is a small slightly irregular fresh water pearl. The back is fitted with loops in the upper corners for wearing on a chain or ribbon as a pendant. As an alternative a brooch pin with safety clasp has been soldered (possibly later) to the top edge of the rectangular opening so that it can be worn as a brooch.

The design is delicate and beautifully executed, subtler and more convincing than might be expected of modern producers of Mockintosh jewellery. Many of the archetypal motifs developed by the celebrated Glasgow artists known as "The Four" are present. The patination of the metal, the presence of the loops for a ribbon or chain, the clear evidence of hand-crafting, and the degree of apparently age-related wear, all seem to me to point to a distinctly different origin and a considerably earlier date than any of the tacky Mackintosh reproduction stuff which has appeared since the 1960s.

Glasgow style pewter brooch modelled on the Honesty Mirror,
maybe by Frances Macdonald McNair, maybe not.

The Honesty Mirror, definitely by Frances Macdonald McNair,
in the Kelvingrove Museum and Gallery, Glasgow.

64

I got The Buzz. Unbidden, the name Frances Macdonald McNair came into my head: sister of Margaret Macdonald Mackintosh, sister-in-law of Charles Rennie Mackintosh, wife of Herbert McNair, one of The Four. I rushed home to start on my internet research.

Sure enough, I quickly came upon an image of The Honesty Mirror of 1897, a large metal-framed mirror currently on display in the Kelvingrove Art Gallery in Glasgow. This was designed by Frances Macdonald McNair, and it had clearly been the model for my brooch, which was a scaled-down version of the Mirror, but with a minor re-interpretation of the design, in my opinion much too delicate and tasteful to be the work of a modern copyist. I bought the brooch cheaply along with the rest of the collection of costume jewellery, and decided to consult the experts, who, as usual, responded helpfully to my doubtless ignorant and presumptuous emailed approaches. Dr Elizabeth Cumming, curator of the most important exhibition of the Arts and Crafts movement in Scotland staged in recent times, said:

> *"It's an attractive piece, and as you already know, the design is close to Frances Macdonald's 'Honesty' mirror… It's very difficult to reduce such a design to the size of a brooch without losing much of the detail, and I don't really think Frances would have done so. Her designs were intended to be for a particular size and worked in one medium rather than adapted. Also, her jewellery (which is quite rare) is extremely linear and delicate… So, I personally don't think it is by her."*

That, of course, should have been enough to silence me. But no, then I wrote to Pamela Robertson, Senior Curator and Professor of Mackintosh Studies at The Hunterian Museum, Glasgow, who said:

> *"The brooch as you say is based on the Honesty mirror, a work executed in the 1890s in Glasgow. Frances Macdonald's known jewellery dates from the later Liverpool years i.e. post 1899, and tends to be finer, in silver, and often with semi-precious stones or enamel… It is always hard on the basis of electronic images alone to come to a confident opinion, but on the basis of the information provided, I do think this is likely to be a hand-crafted copy after the mirror by a later hand."*

The brooch is here on the desk in front of me. It still makes me Buzz. Frances Macdonald's style of work changed and developed over her short career. Only a very few pieces of her jewellery are recorded, and these were all produced later in her life after she had moved with her husband to Liverpool. It is known that she produced jewellery earlier on in Glasgow around the time that she made the Honesty Mirror, but there are no surviving items or illustrations. Most of her output was destroyed by Herbert after her death in 1921. How can the experts be so sure?

These three examples demonstrate, I think, that once you get what I'm describing as The Buzz in relation to an object spotted at an auction viewing, it's very difficult to shake off, even when confronted with good solid authoritative opinion and evidence that the object isn't what you thought it was.

I know I'm wrong sometimes. Quite often, in fact. But experts can be wrong too. And I do get slightly sceptical if I'm told, "It can't be genuine because it isn't listed in the *catalogue raisonné*", or "The condition is too good for it to be the real thing", or "None of the artist's work from that period is known but this piece isn't in her style".

However, in what might be a rare moment of self-insight, I'm beginning to wonder if the reason why I have in this chapter related detailed accounts of these three failed Buzzes is more complex than simply an attempt to illustrate how The Buzz is not infallible and is not a guide to future saleroom success.

Could it be that I have included these anecdotes with a secret ulterior motive? Perhaps I'm hoping that a knowledgeable reader will see the illustrations and descriptions of these three intriguing objects and contact me to say, hang on a minute, you're absolutely right, it *is* a genuine Rembrandt etching, it *is* a genuine mediaeval Islamic bowl, it *is* a genuine Frances Macdonald brooch.

If you're out there, I'm waiting for your call…

5

BUYING AND SELLING THE JUG, 2007

Jug-Viewing Credentials

In Chapters 2 and 3 I gave myself airs as an authority on twentieth century studio pottery in general and on Bernard Leach and Michael Cardew in particular. In fact I have no claim to real expertise. I have been interested in the subject only in recent years since being hooked by The Jug, and my interest has manifested itself in a rather slapdash and non-systematic sort of way. I can recognise work by some of the major potters, I have some small knowledge of clays, glazes and techniques, I've done some reading, I've handled and looked at a large number of pots, and I've amassed a smallish collection of a hundred or so pieces including work by an assortment of well-known and significant potters. But an expert? No.

As I have tried to show, this has not stopped me getting a minor reputation down at Johnson & Andrews as the studio pottery chap, but this is because of one known success, and because I tend to snap up most of the small number of lots that appear in successive auction sales. My pots tend to be in shades of brown and many people think them dull and ugly and out of date. I think them beautiful, but there's no doubt that they are a minority taste. So, in a milieu where almost everyone else is both ignorant about and indifferent to my area of interest, it's easy to be thought of as an expert.

In January 2007, however, I wasn't even aware of the term "studio pottery". It's difficult to recall what one knew at a precise moment, but here (I think) is what I did know:

- I had heard the name Bernard Leach and knew that his pots were desirable and valuable;
- I had heard the name Michael Cardew, and for some inexplicable reason I remembered watching a black-and-white television documentary about him in the 1970s;
- I remembered a family holiday in the Gwel Marten Hotel in Carbis Bay, Cornwall in the late 1950s when I was perhaps eight or nine years old. We arrived after a long and tedious journey in our uncomfortable and unreliable Hillman Husky. One of the outings to keep the children amused was to a pottery in nearby St Ives where my brother and I were shown clay throwing by a rather stern and whiskery old man. Might it have been Leach himself? It's possible.
- I might have had a dim awareness of what the St Ives Pottery seal looked like, but I have no idea where this awareness came from.

Thus far, unimpressive credentials for identifying one of the most remarkable and important pieces of studio pottery ever made. If I had had a good look around my house before leaving it to view the Johnson & Andrews sale, what ceramics would I have seen?

- Miscellaneous dinner ware and tea sets, mostly in the Victorian taste;
- A collection of Royal Doulton character jugs, inherited from Frances's late father, sitting unloved in the back of a cupboard;
- A Clarice Cliff plate (see Chapter 6);
- A pretty Copeland Spode transfer-printed fruit set of two dishes and eight plates, lent by a customer for display in my parents' pub and never reclaimed;
- A quantity of assorted oval meat platters (or ashets as we call them in Scotland), bought in a job lot from a closing-down wet fish shop in Edinburgh;
- A Sevres coffee can and saucer and a Meissen figurine (damaged) inherited from Frances's Aunt who had been manager of a china shop and had collected a number of interesting bits and pieces;
- A Meissen chocolate pot and lid (damaged) bought in the 1970s on a whim at an auction because the decoration matched Auntie's Meissen figurine;
- A few "art pottery" bits and pieces, including jugs, vases and jardinières;

- Two pieces of Wemyss ware: a lidless jam pot from a jumble sale, and a lovely "dog roses" pattern tankard, a present from Frances;
- An oxblood red Burmantofts two-handled vase, bought for me by my daughters as a fiftieth birthday present. They chose it themselves, knowing somehow that an elegant monochrome pot would appeal to me. They were right.
- A large celadon green glazed stoneware bowl from the Keramischen Werkstatt Margaretenhöhe in Essen, Germany, made by the wonderful Korean potter Young-Jae Lee. I had admired this in a gallery in Edinburgh some years before and Frances had bought it for me as a surprise. Perhaps my first and only item recognisable as a studio pot.

Although this list included a few bits of quite good stuff, it's obvious to me now that it was an assemblage of objects and not in any sense a collection. It was the result of opportunistic and whimsical buying of the "I don't know much about it but I know what I like" variety, supplemented by some well-chosen gifts, and some legacies of decent-quality items.

By contrast, I (and in many cases Frances and I) had been more systematic about the acquisition of many of our other belongings: furniture (mahogany, Georgian where affordable, otherwise mostly Victorian); pictures (mostly Scottish, modern, tending towards landscape and/or abstraction); rugs (eastern, hand-made, preferably nomadic, preferably Turkmen); books (Scottish interest, modern fiction, first editions, bibles); coins (British silver); jewellery (modern, silver, Scottish or Scandinavian), and so on.

It was not unknown for me (with spousal support and approval) to pay a few hundred pounds, even a thousand pounds, for a desired object – a chest of drawers, a picture, a brooch – in a category where I knew what I was buying and what its market value was. But in the area of ceramics, I don't recall ever having paid more than £50 for anything.

I left work a little early on Friday 12th January 2007 (these were still pre-retirement days) for my customary preview of the auction. Having herein demonstrated an utter lack of credentials as a connoisseur of modern studio ceramics, what might be the likelihood, as I locked up the office, that on the following morning I would find myself spending more than £1,000 on a pottery jug?

Viewing The Jug: Friday

With this background in ceramics – or rather with no background in ceramics – here I am, on the freezing late Friday afternoon, arriving to view the Johnson & Andrews sale to be held on the following day. I have with me the auction catalogue, which I had printed out from the auctioneer's website. In those days Malcolm had not yet commissioned a website which included photographs of the lots, so the catalogue has only brief typed descriptions of each lot.

There are 243 lots in the sale. I begin my circuit of the room, as usual clockwise, working fairly fast to see what catches my eye. It would be normal for me to go around once fast, once slowly, and then a third time looking closely at the objects that I've selected for close inspection. When Frances comes with me to a viewing, she's often out of the room and waiting patiently in the car before I have finished my second circuit. I'm alone today, and come quickly to the conclusion that pickings will be slim.

I note lot 43, a pair of mahogany candlesticks, and lot 153, a rug. On my second revolution, I stop to look more closely at the lots arrayed on the long trestle table in front of the auctioneer's podium which include items of pottery, metalware, treen ware and other bric-a-brac. The catalogue tells me, as I scan the jumble, that amongst other miscellanea before me there's: a reproduction Italian brass mantel clock (Lot 38); a damaged Cantigalli pilgrim flask (Lot 40); a crystoleum depicting a lady by a chair, in gilt frame (Lot 45); a treen money box (Lot 46); an Edwardian brass rise and fall light fitting with etched glass shades (Lot 47); a Masons Ironstone blue and white bowl (Lot 48); a metal figure of a terrier (Lot 49); a collection of four Hummel figures (damaged) (Lot 50); a pair of Adams jasperware vases decorated with sprigged figures (damaged) (Lot 51); and a continental pottery jug with incised fish and motto decoration (Lot 52).

I look at The Jug. It's big and brown, its surface crowded with images and words. I pick it up to read the inscriptions. Some words are clearly in English. Some are in a language I don't recognise (I don't subsequently blame myself for this failing – you don't come across the Cornish language all that often). Below the spout, around the edge of a shield bearing what appears to be a stylised tree, there's an inscription that I immediately recognise is in Latin. It begins "SIGILLUM BURGH ST IVES…"

I stop.

ST IVES?

The front of The Jug showing the Latin inscription

That isn't continental! It's in Cornwall. I've been there.

ST IVES?

There's an important pottery there. I watched a programme about it years and years ago. A thin chap at a potter's wheel. The voiceover said his pots sold for a fortune. Can't remember the name.

I get The Buzz. Ten years later, I still have it.

I turn the pot over. There are two impressed marks on the base. One looks like this: ⊞. The other looks like this: Ⓜ. The first mark I think I might have seen before. Could it be the letters SI crossed? Is this the symbol for the renowned St Ives Pottery? The second mark has me mystified. What does CM stand for?

It's a difficult sensation to describe, but when I start Buzzing, it is as if the object of my attention inflates in size to absorb my entire consciousness. I become alert. I become furtive, believing that I'm being surreptitious as I scan the room to see who's near me, who might be noticing that I'm taking an interest in a particular item. There's hardly anyone else present, and those who are there are absorbed in their own viewing. I look as hard as I can at the object from all sides, attempting to etch two- and three-dimensional images into my memory for later retrieval. I try to take a mental photograph of the maker's marks on the base. I lose interest in every other lot on view in the saleroom. I scurry home as fast as I can, fixated on getting to the computer to start googling St Ives pottery pictures without delay.

I work through the evening. It's slow and painstaking, mainly because this is taking place in the era before cable broadband arrived in our street, and we have a snail-like internet connection crawling through our telephone line. But it doesn't take me long to discover that the SI monogram is indeed the badge of Bernard Leach's St Ives Pottery, and that the CM stamp should in fact be read as MC, and belongs to Michael Cardew, who worked there as Leach's first apprentice from 1923 to 1926.

So far, so exciting. By further searches on variations of the terms "Leach", "Cardew" and "St Ives", I piece together a little more of the story. How Cardew left St Ives and started up potteries at Winchcombe, then at Wenford Bridge, then his years in Africa, his steadily growing reputation throughout his long life. Since this jug is from the St Ives period, it must be from early in Cardew's career.

Now that I have some clues, I start looking for auction records of Cardew's pots, and find records of several sales of large later pieces at Christie's and Bonham's. Prices seem to be in the range £2,000 to £3,000.

This is all very encouraging as far as it goes, but since I have never seen or handled anything like this jug before, how do I know that it really is what I think it is? Since the other Cardew pieces which have turned up in auctions and have sold for high prices don't look much like this jug (they are mostly from his Wenford Bridge or Abuja periods, much later), how do I know what would be a reasonable price to pay?

[Note. Readers might here be thinking, entirely reasonably: "hang on a minute, this chap has set out his stall in the first chapters of his book as a collector and a would-be connoisseur. He sees himself as a gentleman amateur putting the finishing touches to his Cabinet of Curiosities, but here he is finding a special piece and thinking about how to turn a profit before he's even bought it. Despite all his pomposity and pretentiousness, he's just like the other barrow-boy dealers in his back-street auction room, only distinguishable by his snobbery and his affectation of intellectualism". I can see why you might think that, and I'll try to analyse it

in more detail later to ask if it's wholly or partly true. But for now, please be kind enough to accept my assurances that even when you get The Buzz and feel that you MUST HAVE an object, you still need to consider what price you might be willing to pay for it. That price will inevitably be influenced, at least in part, by research into what others have paid in the past for similar items.]

I don't make much more progress with my pre-sale research during the Friday evening, but I think about nothing else, and worry and fret and Buzz constantly. I daresay I rabbit on and on (and on) about it to Frances, and to our elder daughter Sarah, who is staying with us that night before returning to her then home in London on the Saturday. As always with my enthusiasms, my family are very understanding, but they don't quite manage to achieve my extreme pitch of excitement and anticipation, as indeed I wouldn't expect them to.

Before retiring to bed, or possibly during a sleepless night, or possibly early in the morning, I come to the conclusion that I'm ready to bid up to £200, or maybe at a pinch £300, which seems a safe enough figure to risk – giving me, as I think, a good chance of winning The Jug (which I now refer to in my head with capitalised initial letters), while avoiding looking too much of a fool if it turns out to be worthless.

Viewing The Jug: Saturday

With the auction starting at 11.00, I arrive as usual around 10.30 to register and collect my bidding paddle (it isn't anything like a paddle, it's a rectangle of laminated card with a number printed on it. I don't believe I've ever been to an auction sale that's sufficiently posh to issue proper bidding paddles. Not even certain that such things exist outside Hollywood movie depictions of auctions). Frances and Sarah are beside me, partly because I've spent the last several hours droning on incessantly about The Jug and they want to see it for themselves, but mainly because we have promised Sarah a lift to the airport, and we have to leave by 11.30 to meet her check-in time.

The saleroom is always busy at this time, with potential bidders arriving early for a first viewing, or, like me, to get a second look at their coveted lots. With so many observers leaning over you, you try your best to study your target items fixedly, thoroughly and intensely, while at the same time affecting total indifference and lack of interest. You also try to divert other viewers' attention from yourself and your object by feigning equal fascination with adjacent lots in which in reality you have not the slightest interest.

However, it's important that I try to examine The Jug one last time in order to see if I can learn anything more about it in the light of my findings from last evening's internet research. I approach the section of the table where it sits, and peer closely at all of the objects around it, attempting to prove that I'm just as interested in the clock and the pilgrim flask and the crystoleum and the wooden money box and the dog statue as I am in the old brown pottery pitcher.

I pick up The Jug again (casually, casually) and look at its bottom. Yes, now I have no doubt about the St Ives mark and very little doubt about the Michael Cardew mark. Encouraging. I turn it the right way up and notice for the first time below the handle some numbers and symbols incised beneath the glaze in a sort of cartouche arrangement. At the top and bottom and at each side are four numbers: 1,9,2,6. After a moment's thought, I assume this to be the date 1926, which I know to be the final year of Cardew's apprenticeship at St Ives. More encouraging. In the centre of the device is this mark: 23. It might be the number 23. It doesn't really look like letters or initials. I've no idea what else it might be. It's neither encouraging nor discouraging, merely a mystery to be solved.

I put The Jug back down on the table. The auction is about to start and I can get no more information from peering at it. But this last-minute inspection has made me Buzz louder and harder than ever, and it's conceivable that my second look might influence me to increase my bidding limit. I find my seat beside Frances and Sarah and near to our auction friends Mary and Ron.

My belief (like most of my beliefs entirely unsupported by empirical evidence) is that while everyone tries to feign indifference to their desired objects in their own individual ways, everyone fails equally to pull it off. In any auction room, if you were to study the CCTV footage, I reckon you'd be able to foretell pretty accurately from the immediate pre-sale body language who's going to bid for which lots, and who's going to win.

During those last few jostling minutes as viewers begin to take their seats before the sale starts, it's probable that the salience of any Buzzing viewer trying to keep a poker face diminishes at the same rate as his or her *perception* of the salience of doing so increases. The closer it gets to the start of the sale, the more vital it is to me that I am not noted by anyone to be paying special attention

Device with Bernard Leach's monogram and 1926 date below the handle of The Jug.

to The Jug. I pointedly try to look like I'm looking in every other direction, while at the same time taking covert glances towards The Jug to see who else is examining it. What I overlook, of course, is that at this late stage all the other potential bidders in the room are much too fixated upon the particular objects upon which *their* desires are focussed, to take the slightest notice of *me* trying to appear as if I am not looking at *mine*.

Buying The Jug

Since Malcolm conducts his auction sales at a rate of about 120 lots per hour, we expect that he'll get to Lot 52 at about 11.26. But only if he starts the sale on time. This matters because we must leave the saleroom for the airport not later than 11.30. What's more important – my Buzz or Sarah's flight? Frances and Sarah and our younger daughter Hannah are all incredibly tolerant and understanding of my foibles and eccentricities. Within reason, Sarah won't mind if we stay on to bid for The Jug and then have to drive like maniacs for the airport. But it might be a close-run thing.

Malcolm starts with Lot 1 at around 11.05. The sale proceeds as usual. The first fifty-one lots sell, with no surprises and no spectacular prices. The candlesticks which I had noted on the previous day come and go for £72. I'm no longer interested in them. The highest price paid is £190 for the Masons blue-and-white bowl. I become increasingly nervous, and perhaps increasingly determined to win The Jug against all opposition. I watch the clock. Will he get to Lot 52 before we have to dash off? It's freezing in the saleroom. I start on one of my painful bouts of Reynaud's syndrome, caused by cold and stress, which stops the blood supply from getting to most of my fingers and toes and makes them go white and numb.

"Lot 52, a continental pottery jug. Sixty pounds?" Malcolm, as with many auctioneers, likes to start the bidding at somewhere near the price which he expects the item to sell for. If he had published estimated prices in the catalogue (which he didn't on this occasion), he would probably have estimated The Jug at £50 – £80.

Noting that one of the office staff is standing beside the rostrum with a mobile phone in hand, I realise that there is a telephone bidder interested in The Jug. But not I, nor the telephone bidder, nor anyone else in the room, make a bid of £60. This is as expected. It's normal behaviour for experienced (even highly excited) auction bidders to fail to respond to the initial invitation to bid, because the lack of response forces the auctioneer to reduce the opening price. There's always the possibility that you are the only interested person, and you might get the object for less.

"Forty pounds? Thirty?" These matters must be finely judged, because if there's no-one else interested in making the opening bid, and if you hesitate too long before doing so yourself, Malcolm might think that there is no demand for the object and pass it as unsold. With his fast selling rate, he doesn't have much time or incentive to work the crowd in order to drum up interest in an object which might eventually sell for just a few pounds.

I decide to strike first and bid £30. I do this by raising a hand to catch Malcolm's eye. Incidentally, there is no truth in stories that you might hear about people attending auctions as observers who move a hand or an eyelid and find that they have accidentally bid for and bought a lot. It just doesn't happen that way. The auctioneer has a good view of everyone in the room and has direct eye contact with those present who are bidding for a particular lot. He or she knows precisely who's a bidder and who isn't. There's invariably a considerable level of chat, badinage and gesticulation going on amongst the dealers, collectors and other habitués of Johnson & Andrews, but there's no way that Malcolm is going to mistake someone waving his arms about to make a point, for someone making a small controlled movement to indicate a bid.

After my initial bid, there's an immediate response from elsewhere in the room and bidding rapidly increases in £10 steps. From around £100, there's a long passage of bidding between me and another bidder who's somewhere in the room behind me. I've never found out who this was, but I suspect it might have been the regular bidder and private collector whom we encountered in Chapter 4 buying a beautiful Iznik tile on the same day that I bought my Andro Hart bible. It's worth noting in passing that professional auctioneers will usually only take bids from two bidders at a time. If there's anyone else wishing to bid (including the telephone bidder) then they will have to wait until someone drops out before joining in the contest against the bidder who's still in the game.

Bidding continues in £10 increments and I soon find myself teetering on the edge of the abyss. Overnight I had thought about bidding up to £300; confirming my research findings on the second inspection this morning had allowed me to flex the budget somewhat. But here we are at £500, and – good Lord! – I'm still bidding! I look at Frances to gauge how she's feeling about the whole business. She whispers, "If you want it, go for it – your call". I glance at Sarah, Mary and Ron, and see bafflement and bemusement in their faces, but no discouragement. Will I carry on or won't I? Of course I will – I haven't gone this far out on a limb just to back down and let someone else get it. If other bidders want the damn Jug as much as I do, then it must be an important and valuable item and I MUST HAVE IT! Marginally more rationally, I'm confident I can rely on a notional resale value of £2,000 – £3,000 in a specialist auction, so I've still got some headroom.

In the fleeting moments while I'm in (metaphorical) free fall as I drop from the end of the (proverbial) limb into the (symbolic) abyss and enter (figurative) uncharted bidding territory, I notice that a familiar phenomenon has occurred around me in the saleroom. I have occasionally been a participant in this phenomenon, but have rarely if ever before been the subject of it. It happens in any auction house at the moment when it dawns upon the generality of the audience that something well out of the ordinary is developing. Bidding for a particular lot begins to exceed the expectations of most of those present to a startling extent. The nattering and fidgeting stop suddenly. All faces turn to the actors in the drama – the auctioneer, the lot which is the subject of the bidding (usually these days represented by an image on a large TV screen above the rostrum), and the bidders. In this case the other bidder in the room has dropped out at £500, and the contest is between me and the telephone caller, whose bids are being conveyed by signals from the saleroom employee.

The room becomes silent. Thought becomes visible. "What have they noticed that I haven't noticed?" "They must be nuts to bid that much for an old brown jug." "How high is it going to go?" "I hope he wins / doesn't win." "Oh bloody hell – I can see why they're bidding it up. Wish I'd looked at it more closely." Many people go to the auction not to buy (or not only to buy). They go for the drama, and it doesn't get much more dramatic than this. Of course, in more upmarket auction halls the sums involved are bigger – it might be tens of millions for a painting rather than some hundreds for a brown jug – but the level of tension is the same. I feel it as I continue to bid, and it is just possible that the attention from the others in the room urges me on to a yet higher bid than I might otherwise have made.

The excitement is heightened by Malcolm, who for some reason best known to himself has in this instance abandoned his conventional auctioneering practice of widening the bidding increments as the price rises. Normally, when the price reaches £100 he would increase the steps between each bid to £20; then when the price reaches £500 he would increase again to £50 increments. Instead, he plods on with £10 steps between bids, which makes the whole bidding process interminably long for those involved in it (Malcolm, the phone bidder, and me; presumably The Jug itself is indifferent), but which adds to the palpable suspense now pervading the room.

It feels as if an age has passed since I made my first bid. Buzzing, worrying, hands and feet benumbed, fretful about Sarah's flight, I focus my entire being into winning The Jug. It's become a contest between me and the phone bidder which I must win. Who knows where I'll stop if he doesn't blink first? I certainly don't know.

Suddenly, my opponent folds. It's all over. The Jug is knocked down to me for £900. The room is stunned. My friends and family gape. No-one is more shocked than me. But then, no-one is more delighted than me. It's after 11.35. There's a risk Sarah will miss her check-in time. Frances, Sarah and I sweep immediately out of the room and head for the airport at speed.

If, readers, you have accompanied me to this point in this book still thinking that I'm writing a manual on best practice for buying objects at an antique auction, I trust by now that you are thoroughly disabused. What I have just described is surely the antithesis of good practice. I became obsessed with having to have The Jug and lost my objectivity; I was overcome by the emotion of the moment; I took too much of a risk with my and my family's money; I succumbed to a vicious competitive urge which I didn't know I possessed; I responded to the silent pressure of the crowd by insisting on giving them a result which they would remember. This latter remark is not mere self-aggrandising fancy: several years on, I am still sometimes accosted by people I hardly know and reminded of the occasion.

So, if you came to this book to get tips on how to conduct yourself at an auction, I'm afraid you have come to the wrong place.

The Jug Comes Home

Having duly dropped Sarah off in time for her flight, Frances and I returned to Johnson & Andrews and arrived back shortly before the end of the sale. I paid for The Jug (total £1,058.63 including buyer's commission at 15% and VAT on the buyer's commission at 17.5%), picked up my prize from the table where it still stood, and left the premises. On the way out, a few people (including Malcolm) asked me why I had paid so much for it. I answered, entirely honestly, that I didn't quite know.

My recollection is that we went to lunch in a café with a still-stunned Mary and Ron, where I told them what little I knew about The Jug. They hadn't taken any particular notice of it at the viewing, were interested in my story, and said that they would await further developments with interest.

Then home around 2.30 pm to start on my on-line research. Whereas my memories of viewing and buying are detailed and vivid, my recollection of what happened over the following days is slightly hazy, so I have had to go back to documentary sources in order to reconstruct the sequence of events. After all, I'm talking about several years ago, and my memory for dates and the order of things was never all that good anyway. My memory for makers' marks and seals on pots is better.

I see from my e-mail archive that at 3.48 pm on the following day, Sunday, I sent an e-mail to Ben Williams, then head of the (sadly now defunct) contemporary ceramics department at Bonham's auctioneers in London. It ran:

"Dear Mr Williams,

May I please ask your opinion on a jug which I picked up (against stiff dealer competition) at a local general auction in Edinburgh yesterday?

Several (not very good) photos are attached. I think The Jug may have been produced collaboratively by Bernard Leach and Michael

Cardew at St Ives Pottery in 1926. [There follows my best attempt at a physical description including size, decoration, etc.]

Beneath the handle is an octagonal design containing an arrangement of the numerals 1926, with what appears to be a stylised monogram in the centre.

There is a small and apparently old chip in the base of the handle, but otherwise The Jug is in nearly perfect condition other than a few minor firing cracks around the handle

On the base are two impressed marks, one that of the St Ives Pottery, the other apparently Michael Cardew's MC mark.

If (as I suspect) this is quite a significant piece, I may be minded to sell it as it may be better off in a collection or in the care of an expert than on my mantelpiece.

I shall be grateful for any advice that you can give me.

Yours, etc."

Reconstructing my activities in the twenty-five hours or so between arriving home after shocking friends, family and self by paying over £1,000 for The Jug, and despatching the email quoted above, it seems that I had made progress in four key areas.

First, I had become confident that it was made at St Ives by Cardew; had satisfied myself that it was an important piece; had examined its condition; and had learnt sufficient pseudo-art-critical jargon to enable me to provide a rudimentary description. I must have reached this point by trawling internet images and studio pottery websites for pictures and descriptions of related types of object. I think I must have had a suspicion that the odd symbols in the centre of the octagonal cartouche below the handle could just possibly be the stylised personal monogram of Bernard Leach himself, but wasn't confident enough to mention it in my email to Bonham's. I was uncertain because I didn't see how symbols which looked like the number 23 could be read as BL; and because I had had no success in finding any other pieces signed by both of the legendary potters (and nor have I seen images of any such in succeeding years).

Second, I had identified that The Jug could be categorised as an item of Studio Pottery, that Bonham's was the go-to auctioneer for selling this particular type of contemporary ceramics, and that the top person there was called Ben Williams. And I had traced his personal email address and decided that he and none other should be the first person from whom to seek advice.

I'll be saying more in Chapter 7 about the importance of selecting the most appropriate auctioneer to sell your object.

Third, I had photographed The Jug to the best of my ability from many different angles. This was not as simple as it might sound, because at the time I had a crude and underpowered digital camera, and no experience of uploading pictures onto my computer's hard disk and then cropping and condensing them for email.

Fourth, I had arrived at a provisional decision to sell The Jug if it could be sold. I'll be addressing the issue of selling and not selling later on in this book, so I won't say any more here.

To accomplish all of that, I must have done little else during those twenty-five hours – an illustration of how a dose of The Buzz can lead on to a bout of pure monomania*. Looking in my 2007 calendar to see what else I had on my plate at the time, I note that I should really have been spending the weekend hard at work preparing for the coming week of frantic office activities aimed at saving my ailing business. On the Monday I was scheduled for an important sales conference, and wanted to be present in the office for the delivery of our new photocopier. On the Tuesday I had a progress meeting in Motherwell for a major consultancy contract; then a quarterly meeting in Perth of the Tayside and Central Scotland Regional Transport Partnership, to which I was Clerk and professional adviser; then a working dinner to advise on the selection of new board members for a College in Glasgow. And so it went on for the rest of the week. Whatever else I should have been doing that weekend, I should *not* have been obsessing about a pot. But that's what I was doing.

Consigning The Jug

A couple of days after sending the email, the telephone rang. I was astonished when the caller introduced himself as Ben Williams from Bonham's auctioneers. He sounded quite excited, perhaps even moved. He reported that his then assistant Marijke Varrall-Jones had opened my e-mail and viewed the photographs, and instantly yelled "Ben, come and look at this!" From my blurred snapshots he

---

* *Monomania*: defined by Wikipedia thus: "In 19th-century psychiatry, monomania (from Greek monos, one, and mania, meaning "madness" or "frenzy") was a form of partial insanity conceived as single pathological preoccupation in an otherwise sound mind."

could confirm that The Jug did indeed bear the seals of St Ives pottery and of its thrower Michael Cardew, and that it was decorated by Bernard Leach, whose personal monogram was in the octagonal device below the handle together with the year 1926. It was more than a significant piece, it was important. From the photographs alone, Ben suggested a value of around £3,000–£4,000 at auction. Might he see The Jug, please, in order to advise me more fully, without any obligation to sell?

Ben was based in Bonham's headquarters in London, but the firm also have an office and saleroom in Edinburgh. There are frequent van deliveries between the two locations, and he proposed that I should take The Jug into the Edinburgh office, which would send it to him in London for examination. Thereafter he would get back to me, and if I decided not to sell it (or to use another auction house or to sell privately), he would have it transported back to me. That all seemed perfectly reasonable, so I agreed.

I took The Jug into Bonham's on Wednesday 24th January, on my way to a meeting in Glasgow. They had a receipt ready, which described it as "Bernard Leach and Michael Cardew, a rare Pitcher, 1926". And so it passed out of my hands just twelve days after I brought it home. I was sad to see it go. I still miss it.

Over the next couple of weeks I had one or two further phone conversations with Ben Williams, and the upshot was that I agreed to consign The Jug for sale at their next specialist auction of Contemporary Studio Ceramics on Tuesday 20th March.

Not many weeks later, a glossy catalogue arrived in the post. The forthcoming sale would comprise 284 lots of studio pottery, featuring a range of exceptional quality items from some of the world's most celebrated potters. The Jug's estimated price of £3,000–£4,000 was not the highest estimate in the sale; the biggest prices were expected for works by luminaries such as Lucie Rie, Hans Coper, Magdalene Odundo and Elizabeth Fritsch. But after checking carefully, I noted with childish glee that The Jug was the only lot in the sale that had been given a two-page spread of photographs and description all to itself. My goodness, I was proud!

Frances and I decided, just for the fun of it, to use the viewing and the sale as an opportunity for a jaunt to London. At the viewing in Bonham's' intimidating saleroom in New Bond Street, we had our last glimpse of The Jug, locked up in a display cabinet alongside many other exceptional pots, but rather browner, rather more squat, rather less elegant than most. I confess to feeling strangely unmoved by the whole experience.

In retrospect, I can see why this last-but-one episode in my story of The Jug was less satisfying than what had gone before. The viewing showed me that while I had been successful in spotting one very special pot amongst an assemblage of dross at Johnson & Andrews in Edinburgh, I still knew nothing about studio pottery. I could now recognise a St Ives pottery seal mark, but had so far failed to acquire any critical or aesthetic underpinnings to allow me to appreciate a pot in an informed way. I felt my inadequacy and was disappointed.

I wouldn't feel the same now. In the ensuing years, and entirely as a result of my experience with The Jug, I have become interested in studio pottery and it has become the principal, if unsystematic, outlet for my current collecting impulses. I consider myself lucky in having formed this particular collecting habit. As I tried to show in Chapter 3, there's plenty of studio pottery about. Because it's often brown, lumpy and to many eyes unattractive, it is easy to find good items cast out from people's homes and available for next to nothing in charity shops and local auctions. For the moment, it is a relatively non-competitive and cheap field in which to be a collector.

Back in 2007, viewing shelves full of outstanding pots at Bonham's, I couldn't really tell one from another, and had no knowledge of styles, techniques, materials, glazes or individual makers. But now, after having had the privilege of handling, examining, buying and selling many pieces, I think I'm beginning to be able to distinguish those I think good from those I think bad; I can recognise some makers without slavishly looking for their seal marks and rushing off to the reference books; I know which styles, materials and glazes please me most. I've begun to train my eye. If you put me back now in that 2007 Bonham's saleroom, I would expect not to be disappointed. On the contrary, I would expect to go from pot to pot, with some appreciation of what qualities about them make them beautiful, desirable and good. And I would expect during this process to arrive in front of The Jug and think: "wow, even in the context of this display of studio pottery wonders, this Jug, unlikely, brown, confusing and over-decorated as it is, is still a stand-out item!"

The Jug Sells

It was only while viewing the sale lots in Bonham's showroom that Frances and I realised that the auction itself was to begin on the following day at 6.00pm.

In our excitement we had simply assumed that it would be a daytime sale, and we'd failed to notice that it was scheduled for the evening. Our train home was booked for 5.30, and there was no way we could change our tickets. It was essential to get home that evening so that I could get into the office early to print and bind our younger daughter Hannah's dissertation, which needed to be submitted imminently for her LlB degree. And we had left painters and decorators in the house who we didn't trust one bit (with justification – one of them fell off a ladder and hurt himself after polishing off the entire contents of our drinks cupboard). So, sadly, frustratingly, we had to miss the auction.

In those far-off low-tech days I had a mobile phone with a very slow internet connection. Between tunnels, no-signal spots and repeated failures of the screen-refresh facility, I was able to keep up a sporadic online connection with the progress of the sale. It may have been somewhere between Peterborough and, perhaps, Repton that Frances and I were dumbfounded by news coming through the ether that Lot 16, our Jug, had sold for £12,000, three times its upper estimated price. I don't recall precisely what we did next, but I expect we texted our daughters, and then celebrated in our usual way with a cup of tea from the buffet car and an immediate attack upon on the Upper Crust sandwiches which we had purchased before leaving Kings Cross.

Ben Williams telephoned the next day just in case I hadn't found out the news for myself. He was astounded and delighted too. He reported that there had been two commission bids and around seven telephone bidders including two museums. The winner appeared to have been a holding company for a Mystery Buyer. Ben had seen the name before but didn't know who the buyer was. I haven't found out any more information since then, and haven't seen The Jug appearing as a new accession in any public collection, so I can only assume that it was bought by or for a private collector.

After adding buyer's commission, the Mystery Buyer paid £14,400 for The Jug, and this is the price which goes down in the auction records. Jointly with a pot made by Hans Coper, it achieved the highest price in the auction. As far as I'm aware, this was at the time a new record price for both Bernard Leach and Michael Cardew.

For me, it represented a multiple of almost fourteen times the amount I had paid just sixty-six days earlier. After deduction of commission and some other charges, I came out of the deal with a net profit of around £9,000 – a useful, but not a life-changing amount, but an amount which paled into insignificance by comparison with how absolutely and totally chuffed I felt.

Of course, if you get an unexpected success of this sort in a lifetime of buying and collecting and selling antiques, you naturally expect it to be a one-off. I didn't suppose that this heady experience would dim my enthusiasm or jade my palate for attending auctions and mooching around charity shops in the future. But at the same I knew that there was absolutely no way that I could ever discover another such amazing and profitable object as The Jug, or ever again get such a great big Buzz. It just couldn't happen again.

Or could it?

6

THE EYE

Eye with a Capital E

Before relating the story of the buying and selling of The Saint, I'm setting out on another digression into more reflective territory. Earlier in this book I tried to explain the feeling that I unimaginatively termed The Buzz. It seemed to me such an important concept that even its definite article deserved an initial capital letter, as did those of The Jug and The Saint. Now I'm going to introduce another momentous term: The Eye.

The Oxford English Dictionary contains multiple definitions of the noun "Eye". The particular one of interest here is definition number 7:

> "faculty of perception or discrimination of visual objects, either in general or in some special connection. Often in phrases: *to have The Eye of, with The Eye of (a painter, etc.); to have an eye for (proportion, etc.).*"[24]

We are familiar with phrases such as "an eye for a bargain" or "an eye for an antique". In circles frequented by antique dealers, collectors and enthusiasts, it seems to be a given that some fortunate individuals possess The Eye. But what does it mean? Who has it? How do you get it? Are you born with it or can you acquire it by education or experience? Is possession of The Eye a prerequisite for antiques alchemy?

Let's start out with a hypothesis that some people do indeed have The

Eye – that they possess some special quality or ability which enables them to be better than others at rapidly distinguishing, from among a random jumble of second-hand goods, those items which have significant market value. How do you demonstrate that it's true? How do you explain it? If you *can* prove the hypothesis, can you measure how much better some people are than others at this task? Can you use such information to help predict performance, or to select candidates with this particular aptitude, or to pass it on to others by way of education and training?

If you can indeed prove that The Eye exists in some people with reference to antique items of value, then what qualities or responses are involved in exercising it? Is it all about aesthetics? Taste? Beauty? Fashion? Desirability? Quality of making? Rarity? Age? Material? Colour? Is The Eye's response to an object of value an emotional one or an intellectual one?

The search for answers to these questions should doubtless involve a degree of scientific rigour. I'm not aware that this has been a subject of research study at all, but I can envisage that a number of academic approaches might be available. A psychologist might conduct experiments in controlled conditions to measure and compare how subjects distinguish between a common, ordinary sort of object and one of value. An art historian or theorist might wish to account for the phenomenon of The Eye with reference to aesthetics and connoisseurship. A philosopher might explain it using abstract notions of beauty or calibration against a Platonic ideal. An economist might develop an explanation linked to demand and market value. A sociologist might use a behavioural or societal model. A physiologist might seek a physical site within The Eye to explain The Eye. A neurologist might wish to analyse brain responses. An anatomist might look for the answer through scanning and dissection. And so on.

By contrast, I propose to take the lazy author's route – a combination of unsupported subjective opinions and assertions; regurgitation of citation-free ideas read, heard and plagiarised from third parties; examples drawn from personal experience; and autobiography. The implication, of course, is that I start out from a complacent and self-satisfied assumption not only that The Eye does exist, but that I possess it in considerable measure. The unsuspecting reader might well feel aggrieved at this point, seeking an approach which offers a little more scientific discipline and a little less authorial indolence and self-indulgence.

Be that as it may, let me begin by asserting that *The Eye does indeed exist and the fact that I discovered both The Saint and The Jug proves it conclusively.* Then let me cite my numerous other auction successes over many years to prove it more conclusively still. There, I've proved that I possess The Eye, and thus that it must exist as a demonstrable phenomenon. Job done.

But wait! There are manifold objections: you could argue that anyone who has been to as many auctions as I have over fifty years and more is statistically almost certain to have made a few good purchases in amongst any number of disasters. And I have foolishly shot myself in the foot by already owning up in Chapter 4 to some of those disasters —the dodgy Aghkand ware bowl, the iffy Glasgow style brooch, the doubtful Rembrandt etchings. So it's obvious that having The Eye does not imply infallibility.

Then again, if you speak to just about any dealer at an auction or a viewing or in an antique shop or market or fair, he or she will tell you about a fantastic success at some point in their career. Everyone's got a good story or two, of something spotted and turned into a big profit, or, more often, of something spotted but just missed by a hair's breadth. These stories demonstrate, of course, that by their own accounts, everyone has got The Eye. Which is precisely the same as saying either that no-one has got The Eye, or that The Eye isn't anything special. Because if we've all got the same talent, then it isn't exceptional and it doesn't deserve to have its initial letters capitalised.

However, it is an unarguably true, hard, measurable fact that over the course of a career some antique dealers are markedly more successful than others. If this isn't down to The Eye, then maybe there's another explanation. Perhaps they are more willing to take a risk? Or do they have more time or money to invest in the first place? Or is it nothing to do with having an Eye and everything to do with knowledge and experience? Or do they have better taste than their peers or a better feel for what's marketable at any given time? Or better visual memories? Or are they brainier? Or is it through hard work? Or is it just pure blind luck?

Clearly I need to put in more effort to explain The Eye. I intend to do so with three short autobiographical vignettes.

The Golden Egg

It is 1960. Here's another glimpse of that boy first encountered in Chapter 4 haunting the second-hand bookshops of Charing Cross Road. Aged eleven, he lives

with his parents and big brother Philip in *The Bear and Staff pub at Number 37,
on the corner of Bear Street which leads directly into Leicester Square. Next-door
to the south is the Cameo-Royal cinema with its policy of showing foreign-language
X-certificate films. The pub's still there today, updated and extended slightly, a small
but busy and thriving West End drinking spot. The cinema was demolished in
1988.*

*The boy is quite a brainy, bookish, swotty sort of boy, with thick spectacles and a
generally serious turn of mind. He isn't solitary or reclusive by inclination, and has
a few close-ish friends at his grammar school. But he lives a fair bus-ride away from
the school, in a direction in which very few others travel, and in an area inhabited
by very few other kids of his age or indeed of any age. But he doesn't need other kids.
In the otherwise austere and rather colourless world of the early sixties, the sounds,
images and smells of exotic life in the very centre of London are sufficient to feed a
lively imagination and a yearning for stimulus.*

*If the boy looks to his left down to the street at an angle from his bedroom
window, he can see on the opposite corner of Bear Street a shiny new branch of the
Golden Egg restaurant. This was the first restaurant venture of Philip and Reginald
Kaye, Jewish brothers from North London whose family later went on to establish
other popular dining brands including Garfunkel's, Zizzi, Ask and Prezzo.*

> "The most controversial use of colour in British restaurants has come
> from the Golden Egg chain where riotous colour schemes and brilliant
> opaline lights have brought a jazzy mood to eating in low-price popular
> restaurants."[25]

*The Charing Cross Road Golden Egg (see **Illustrations, Picture 5**) has an added
attraction that makes it stand out from every other café anywhere – a pair of
live monkeys (possibly green monkeys, chlorocebus sabaeus, but maybe some other
closely-related species) in a cage built into the corner window. Installed in a splash
of tabloid publicity when the restaurant opened, they don't do much and usually
look rather depressed. Their corner of the restaurant isn't much used by diners
because of an accompanying aroma. After a few months, they aren't there any more
and the cage is dismantled to be replaced by a different window display. The aroma,
however, lingers awhile.*

*When he isn't watching the monkeys hoping they will do something interesting,
the boy can look across the road to the crowds queuing outside Wyndham's Theatre,
or to his right where he can clearly see, over the rooftop of the National Portrait*

Gallery, the imposing figure of Lord Nelson looking back at him from the top of his column in Trafalgar Square some four hundred metres distant.

At his present age he doesn't know much about what's going on in the bar. But he does have a dim awareness that his parents' modest pub isn't one of the fashionable ones which attract the luminaries of the theatre world, such as the glittering Salisbury about two hundred metres away near the top of bookshop-lined Cecil Court. He knows that many of his parents' customers are drink-sodden past-their-best actors and music-hall performers, pantomime dames, drag artists, agents and backstage staff from theatres and cinemas, plus a selection of Soho poets and writers and hacks and myriad types of other more or less shady hangers-on to the fringes of pre-Swinging London's demi-monde.

It doesn't occur to him that the life he leads must be very different from that of any of his school friends or contemporary cousins. He expects not to see much of his parents after opening time at 5.30pm. There is no separate private front door to approach the family's apartment at the top of the building: he comes home through the main front door to the bar. During opening hours, he communicates

The Bear and Staff pub in Charing Cross Road, London, where I lived from 1959 to 1965. My bedroom was on the attic floor, right-hand window. This is a fairly recent photo: in my time the pub was unmodernised and considerably dingier.

with his parents mostly across the counter. At bed-time he either comes down to the bar to say goodnight to Mum and Dad and incidentally to anyone else who is sitting at the counter; or, if in pyjamas and dressing gown after a bath, he calls down on a primitive electric intercom system which he knows broadcasts his voice at high volume throughout the pub.

Normal life includes walking into the bar – in practical terms the main room of his home – and finding himself in the middle of a hilarious drunken harangue between larger-than-life characters such as Rex Jameson (better known as the drag comedian Mrs Shufflewick), Hylda Baker (catch-phrase "she knows y'know") and the young, up-and-coming cabaret performer Danny La Rue. One year, the family goes on its summer holiday to Guernsey where his parents spend most of their time partying with Shuff and his troupe of comedians who are doing a summer season of Olde Tyme Music Hall at the theatre in St Peter Port. Other years, Mum and Dad go on holidays to Malta with Danny. In those days, none of the London gay theatrical set are "out", and homosexual acts are still illegal. It's simply a bunch of flamboyant close friends, accompanied by a couple of respectable conservative-leaning, middle-aged, Jewish publicans plus their two serious-minded bespectacled sons.

Against this colourful backdrop the boy leads a normal, happy, untroubled sort of life. His parents are loving and generous, if preoccupied and inattentive. He attends school regularly and punctually, works hard at this particular stage of his schooling, and performs well academically. Outside school he reads comics (the Beano and Dandy on regular order from the newsagent's stall outside Leicester Square Tube station) and looks at Philip's Weekend and Reveille. He eats as many sweets and watches as much television as permitted. Uninterested in sport or outdoor activity, he tries to conform with his peers by joining the Jewish Lads' Brigade for a few miserable months. He goes to a judo club for several unbearable weeks with his school friend Bob Lyons. On Saturday mornings he goes to morning service at the synagogue. At age thirteen he has his Barmitzvah and then almost immediately quits synagogue attendance. His parents don't object. By this stage they have also stopped going to shul, even on the High Holydays.

The boy doesn't find the early years of secondary school very challenging. Homework is soon done and he has plenty of time and inclination to follow his own pursuits. Even at this early age, he is an experienced hand at the collecting game, having developed a passion for old coins at around six or seven. In five years at the Bear and Staff before moving on again, he keeps up his interest in coins, but alongside it he develops an even stronger urge to collect old books. As he says in adulthood "I don't know what other (normal?) boys of my age were spending their pocket money on, but I was spending all of mine – and then some – on antiquarian books".

The boy needs desperately to find extra money to satisfy his cravings to buy books from the shops that surround his house. His weekly income from pocket money is around ten shillings, the pre-decimalisation equivalent of fifty pence. This is fairly generous, and is enhanced by wages earned from a strenuous session of cleaning the bar every Sunday morning. But, if in any given week of browsing through the second-hand bookshops surrounding the house, he finds, say, an old Bible at 10 shillings, and an old Book of Common Prayer at 2 shillings*, where is the extra two bob to come from? At his high rate of acquisition, he rapidly uses up any residual savings, birthday money and odd half-crowns handed over by visiting relatives, in particular Uncle Reg, who is by far the most generous and consistent in this respect. But he needs more cash.

Fortunately he has a resource to earn extra money through a precocious combination of deployment of The Eye and engagement in trade. The 1960s licensing laws severely restrict the opening hours of public houses. Every pub in Central London is required by law to close between 3.00pm and 5.30pm. This is excellent for the boy's Dad, who gets peace and quiet for the mandatory afternoon nap required to set him up for his evening session as Mine Host, which will continue until 11.00pm. His Mum is also able to get some rest, do housework and prepare the evening meal for the family. For the boy, it means that he arrives home from school while the pub is closed. He can get his hands on his own personal Golden Egg – the cash register!

Unexcitingly, there is no crime or petty pilfering involved. His purpose is to carefully sort through all the coins left in the till after the lunch-time opening session, looking for rarities. When he finds one, as he often does, he simply removes it and, with scrupulous honesty, replaces it with a coin of equivalent face value from his own pocket money. Then, every few weeks, when he has an accumulation, he puts the family's bad-tempered black miniature poodle Pepe on his leash, and they march together round to one or other of the two biggest coin dealers in the country. Spink's is about twenty minutes' walk in one direction, Seaby's about half an hour in the other direction. There, he tethers Pepe to a lamp-post, enters, and negotiates a sale of his coins at whatever rate the dealer might offer. In that way, he is often able to turn a few pennies or sixpences into a couple of quid, which he almost immediately splurges on the purchase of antiquarian books.

---

* 2016 update: I still possess both books. The ten-bob Bible is an imperfect 1611 issue of the Geneva translation, interesting but unexciting and not uncommon, although it gave me The Buzz at the time of purchase and for many years afterwards. The two-bob Book of Common Prayer is a rare first issue of John Baskerville's printing of 1760, considered by some to be one of the most typographically perfect books ever printed.

An Incomplete Explanation

Thus I can say with some certainty that before I was a teenager, I was already a dab-hand at spotting a rarity, and was developing an accompanying facility for turning a rarity into cash. But simply telling this story doesn't explain the how or the why of The Eye. It's necessary to look a little harder to ascertain whether it was something that I was born with, or which simply emerged unsought, or whether I deliberately said to myself, "I'm going to develop The Eye". Or whether The Eye is merely a myth and doesn't exist as a phenomenon at all, and such talent as I had was nothing more than the result of a fortuitous combination of **behaviour**, **environment** and **circumstance**.

As to **behaviour**, I've already told the bare facts of what I did to generate some profit, but it's important to note that I had *prepared myself* for the task of combing the till for scarce change. By age eleven, I had been studying coins for some years. I had looked at and handled lots of UK and foreign specimens, had borrowed and pored over all the books about coins in the public library, and had formed my first collection. I knew what to look for and which dates and values and varieties of legal tender British coinage were of interest to grown-up collectors.

And of course I had *motivation*. It was important to me to get money to buy books. My unlimited access to bargain racks outside innumerable second-hand bookshops just a few metres from my front door meant that I was subjected to Buzz after Buzz after Buzz. My earnings from pocket money and trade were usually sufficient to enable me to buy the books that I wanted, but not always. Even after more than half a century I still feel the pain that I experienced on those few occasions when I simply didn't have enough funds to make an important purchase. I vividly remember a five-volume set of Vasari's *Lives of the Artists* with Thomas Carlyle's autograph signature on the flyleaf of each volume; and a book from the late eighteenth century about a voyage to Australia which contained incredibly early engravings of kangaroos and platypuses. Penniless when I spotted them, by the time my next instalment of pocket money came through, they were long gone. Asking the dealer to reserve a book for me, or going to my parents to seek an advance, would have been equally unthinkable.

I also had a specific *physical advantage* in being from a very early age extremely short-sighted. Even by age eleven, I had unusually high myopia of around minus 10 diopters, although my eyes were otherwise healthy.

This meant that I had to wear my glasses from the second I woke up in the morning until the second I settled down to sleep at night. Without my specs, I couldn't read a book or find my way around the streets. Still can't. Now, in what way could this have been an advantage to me? In two ways: first, it hugely enhanced my natural disinclination and ineptitude for sport and physical activity, giving me much more time than many other children to follow my main inclination to study books and coins. Second, it meant that by removing my glasses for close work I could focus my vision on an object at an extremely short distance away from my eye without needing a magnifying glass or loupe. Thus I could tell at a rapid glance the difference between a 1902 "high-tide" penny (common) and a 1902 "low-tide" penny (scarce: it's all to do with the level of the sea depicted behind the seated profile of Britannia).

As to **environment**, I had excellent *opportunity*. The pub till during afternoon closing hours was an available resource, easily accessed, and with no competition or jostling. Knowing that I was honest, my parents made no objections. I had time and leisure to pursue my interest.

And I had a *rich seam to mine* for my random treasure. Decimal currency wasn't introduced until 1971, prior to which the UK coinage hadn't changed much in appearance or design for the last 100 years or so. As a result, there were very large numbers of dates, denominations and varieties of coins in general circulation simultaneously.

Further, I was helped by an *affordability* factor. The ten shillings of pocket money available to me could be sufficient each week to purchase up to 120 scarce pennies (especially 1918KN, 1919KN, 1950 and 1951), up to 40 twelve-sided-brass threepenny bits (1946 was a scarce year), or 20 sixpences (1952). At the rate of one or two finds per week I could usually, but not invariably, rely on getting enough extra cash to buy more old books, while maintaining my regular expenditure on the other, less esoteric, essentials of pre-teenage existence: sweets and comics.

Next, I had a ready *market* for my finds, with the UK's two biggest coin dealers willing to do business and easily accessible to me and Pepe.

And then – and this is speculative – I wonder I benefited from some **circumstances** of a special nature? The possibility occurs to me that since the clientele of my parents' pub was so – how shall I put it? – non-standard, perhaps even the small change that they used to buy their essential supplies of alcohol and tobacco was also non-standard? Any bar attracts drinkers, and among these a substantial proportion will be alcohol addicts, with an uncontrollable need to spend their last penny on booze. Arguably this proportion might have been higher in a pub in the middle of London's theatre-land and on the fringes of Soho. Almost certainly the profile of the population was skewed far away from a representative cross-section of society in general. Is it fanciful to suppose that the coinage which passed from this unusual clientele into my parents' till was loose change of a looser nature than average, and thus more likely to include rarities than the average shop till? Was a substantial part of their negotiable currency accumulated from dodgy payments for transactions of unimaginable kinds with unimaginable people, sweepings from seedy theatre and nightclub floors, scrabblings down the backs of broken-down bedsit sofas, and hoards liberated from violated piggy banks and looted gas meters?

So, there you are. My analysis of my profitable adolescent sideline in spotting and selling scarce coins might suggest that it was all down to behaviour, opportunity and circumstance. But if you accept this as a full explanation of my youthful development of The Eye, then you have acquiesced in the removal of two important elements from the mix: *luck* and *aptitude*.

As for luck, I'll attempt to deal with that in my third anecdote later in this chapter. However, if you leave out aptitude, then it should follow that any likely lad placed in the same circumstances and environment might be expected to behave in the same way with the same level of success.

Now let me introduce you to my late brother Philip, my senior by two years and nine months, and two years ahead of me at the grammar school. Also of a studious turn of mind, also averse to sport and exercise of all kinds, also myopic, also in need of extra cash to boost his pocket money. You might expect him to take advantage of his seniority to erect a physical or psychological barrier around the cash register, where I have demonstrated time and again that untold riches lie hidden in the small change. But does he? Do I have to fight for access? Nope. He has his own pursuits and shows not a glimmer of interest in mine.

It isn't proof of anything, and isn't scientific in any way. But perhaps it shows that even given identical opportunities and incentives, people who are otherwise similar behave in different ways. So maybe there is an additional ingredient to the formation of The Eye after all. Let's keep looking.

The Cats, the Shed, the Cobra and the Plate

Five years pass. The boy is now sixteen. His parents, both in their early fifties, have had enough of the stress of working in the West End of London. What's more, they are fed up with working as managers for someone else's public house and want to run their own business. They take on the tenancy of The Queen's Head Water Oakley, a small pub in the middle of Berkshire farmland in the Thames Valley halfway between Maidenhead and Windsor, some 30 miles from central London. The boy is now a teenager, in the sixth year of secondary school, halfway through his A-level studies. Much more gregarious than at eleven, he has a wide circle of friends and regularly attends various synagogue youth clubs hoping eventually to get a girlfriend. Having up to now been a quietish compliant sort of lad, he is bursting with teenage resentment and anger at Mum and Dad's decision to move out of London at such a crucial moment in his development, which necessitates a three-hour daily round trip to and from school, and sounds a death knell for his burgeoning weekend social life. His brother Philip isn't much affected because the move takes place in the summer holidays of 1965, and he'll be off to Bangor to start at university in September. The boy is about to embark on an entirely wasted final year at school culminating in spectacularly poor performance in his A-level exams, but this fact is not relevant to this particular anecdote.

The Queen's Head is a small detached building, dating from the eighteenth century with later adaptations, and of no architectural merit whatsoever. Downstairs, a saloon bar, a snack bar, a family living room and a kitchen. Upstairs, three bedrooms and bathroom. The bars have modest pretensions to a Ye Olde Inne style, with exposed wood beams and an open fireplace. The boy's father, ever the perfect pub landlord, believes that the bar counter with the host holding court behind it must be the focus of attention, and he won't have any truck with new-fangled bar-room distractions such as fruit machines, pinball tables or juke boxes.

The regular clientele is a stereotypical home counties country-pub mix of local characters – farmer, butcher, knackerman, rat-catcher – with a contingent of professional and business people working in nearby Slough or doing the daily commute to London. But in bizarre addition it soon becomes apparent that the theatrical and entertainment industry has by no means been left behind in Central London. The Queen's Head is the closest pub to Bray film studios, less than a kilometre away. At this time in the sixties, Bray is the epicentre for production of the uniquely British cinematic phenomenon known as the

Hammer Horror Film. Casual passers-by arriving for a lunchtime beer and a ham sandwich would be dumbstruck to find Christopher Lee or Vincent Price sitting chatting familiarly with the locals, or a bevy of heavily made-up starlets quaffing gin and tonic while awaiting their turn to suffer such terrible on-screen fate at the hands of Count Dracula or Baron Frankenstein as the infallible Hammer formula might dictate. On occasions Dracula himself or Frankenstein's monster are present in full costume for a quick pint between takes.

Not, then, an entirely typical country pub. But one which the boy's parents are determined should look the part. Strictly traditional décor is the order of the day. They have taken on the lease of the premises lock, stock and (literally) barrel, which means that the inventory includes all the bar furniture and even the pictures and ornaments. They are pleased on moving in to find that most of the stuff already in situ is well-suited to their ideal image of what such a hostelry should look like, and are able to set up their business with only the bare minimum of change.

The Queen's Head, Water Oakley, near Windsor, my parents' pub from 1965 to 1979

Furniture – old, rickety, mostly nineteenth-century mahogany or country oak. Pictures – generic hunting and stage-coach prints. Horse brasses and bits of old saddlery. Some old green blown-glass wine bottles on a shelf in the Saloon Bar. On a high display shelf around all four walls of the snack bar, an assortment of china plates, mostly floral transfer prints or blue-and-white willow pattern.

One of two points in which Mum conforms to the archetype of a Jewish

97

mother is in her obsession with cleaning, the other point being her obsession with feeding people. On moving into the Queen's Head, everything must be cleaned until it gleams. One of the boy's jobs is to climb upon a bar stool and hand down all the plates from the high shelf in the Snack Bar for washing. When they are clean, a selection is made, but not by him, of which ones are to go back on display. Any item which doesn't meet his parents' specification of what a country pub plate should look like is ruthlessly banished. The boy is directed to take to the shed a small pile of plates which haven't made the cut.

The shed is a slightly picturesque creosoted timber structure with a red tiled roof, about five metres square. At the rear is a much smaller and decidedly tumbledown annexe with a rusty corrugated iron roof. One of Dad's early and, as ever, misguided attempts to improve the appearance of the enormous and unkempt pub garden is to plant a fast-growing creeper with the objective of concealing this unsightly but useful excrescence at the back of the shed. The plant is a Russian Vine (Fallopia baldschuanica).

> *"Russian vine, aka mile-a-minute, is a devil of a climber. Traditionally people have lobbed one into the ground when they want to rapidly obliterate a view of an ugly shed or border fence. Only when it's too late – this plant being virtually unkillable – do people realise what they've unleashed."*[26]

Turning to the interior of the shed, we find a huge chest freezer, where Mum stores her frozen food supplies; Dad's stocks of soft drinks for the bar; sundry discarded bits of broken furniture and household effects, now including the rejected decorative plates; and a company of outdoor cats whose job is to keep rodents under control and to provide a never-ending supply of kittens to be given away to more or less receptive pub customers. At peak production level, the shed contains eighteen such felines, some cute, some deeply disreputable.

One other interesting item found in the shed on the family's arrival at the Queen's Head had been an AC Shelby Cobra sports car in British Racing Green, being stored there for a friend of the former pub tenant. This was really something to catch The Eye of a sixteen-year-old boy, but sadly it was removed after just a few weeks*.

The space vacated after removal of the Cobra is soon enough filled with other junk, none of it of any interest to this story. No, it is that small pile of

---

* The first Shelby Cobra ever produced was sold in August 2016 for more than $10 million.

plates, now consigned to a shelf in the farthest and dingiest corner of the unstable and malodorous rear annexe, which interests the boy. Or rather, one plate in particular.

It is a dinner plate, octagonal in shape, with a black rim. In the centre is painted a castle in a landscape in cream and black against an orange and yellow background. It is brightly coloured, garish and crude, but at the same time stylish and attractive. He doesn't know why, but it gives him The Buzz. On the back is stamped the name Clarice Cliff, which means nothing to him. All he knows is that he likes it (See **Illustrations**, *Picture 6*).

The Eye Further Observed

The plate stayed at the back of the shed for the next fourteen years. Whenever I was visiting, first from university during vacations, then from my adopted home in Edinburgh a couple of times a year, I'd check that it was still there. One time I was shocked to find that the weight of the Russian Vine on the rusty corrugated roof had – as could have been predicted – caused a collapse which had resulted in breakage of several plates in the pile. Others were broken by other causes, notably the unrestrained antics of a coven of heavily pregnant tortoiseshell cats. But my plate remained miraculously intact. In 1979 my parents retired and sold the pub business lock, stock and barrel to the next tenant. I visited for a few days to help with their move to a new flat. Long since abandoned as rubbish, the plate didn't feature in the inventory of chattels included in the sale, so there was no objection when I liberated it to bring home to Scotland with me.

The plate has been with me since, sometimes in a spring-tensioned plate hanger on a wall, sometimes in a cupboard, at present on a display stand on top of the bookcase opposite my desk. At some early point I became aware that Clarice Cliff was a big name with collectors and the plate must have a significant value – perhaps a hundred pounds or more for a standard pattern. But it was only two or three years ago that I finally bestirred myself enough to check it out. And blow me down if that sixteen-year-old boy in 1965 hadn't spotted one of the very rarest and most coveted of all of Clarice's designs: Appliqué Lucerne Orange! The highest price on record for a single piece by her was for a large plate or charger in this pattern. And the last octagonal plate like mine to appear at auction sold at Bonham's in London in 2009 for £1,320. But my plate is undamaged, whereas the Bonham's one was cracked.

I don't think it is only the rarity of the Appliqué series, Lucerne pattern, orange colour palette that makes it so highly prized among the world's collectors of Clarice Cliff ceramics. There's something else about it, perhaps to do with the intensity of colour, which in fact meant that the Appliqué range was more expensive to produce than other Clarice ware and thus costlier to buy new. I wonder if I would have been so struck with it at age sixteen if it had been in one of her more standard patterns?

Bearing in mind that I'm only relating my exploits in spotting rare and valuable objects in order to provide an explanation for the phenomenon of The Eye, the question now arises of whether in my case The Eye is nothing more than a magpie-like quality of attraction to bright shiny objects? I think I can dismiss this notion quite quickly by reference to The Jug, which my friend Mary described as being one of the dullest objects she had ever seen. Her description: "painted with mud". Nothing bright and shiny about it whatsoever.

Is it then perhaps to do with a sympathetic response to the simple vulgar tastes and fleeting fashions of the common people? No, because the very brightness and shininess of the plate, brought about by heavy application of strong colours, made the Appliqué designs *un*common. They failed to catch the public Eye. They didn't sell well and were withdrawn early – accounting for their rarity.

To the contrary, is it maybe a matter of spotting objects that appeal to those with a heightened aesthetic sensibility? This theory might conceivably apply to The Jug, produced as it was by two upper-middle-class aesthetes obsessed by romantic notions of reviving a mythical, mystical arts-and-crafts tradition. But certainly not to the Clarice plate, which, like her other ware, was aimed at a strictly petit-bourgeois aspirational market.

Perhaps, then, The Eye lights on special objects that may be dissimilar to each other but have close conformity to some indefinable Platonic ideal of beauty or value or beauty-and-value combined? The Saint might come into this category, but by no means all of the objects that I'm writing about in this book. Indeed, it appears that aesthetics – in any kind of high cultural sense – might not be involved at all. My third vignette in this chapter of autobiography and speculation is a much more recent one and is about a different type of artefact altogether.

The Magic Lamps (1)

It is 2012 and I am no longer a boy. I am retired and live with my wife Frances in a semi-detached Victorian house in the suburbs of Edinburgh. We have had a summer house built in our garden. It's not nearly as grand as it might sound, actually little more than a garden shed with double doors and some extra windows*.

After the shed-erectors leave, I promise Frances that I will run an electrical cable from the house and rig up some lights. I describe this as a ten-minute job. We both know perfectly well that it is never going to happen, and sure enough, it doesn't. My patient wife diplomatically allows the elapse of a short period of inaction in the cabling department before making the following suggestion: "Why don't we get some kind of oil lamp that we can light in the summer house when we're sitting out there of a summer evening?"

A number of repetitions of this helpful suggestion elicit no further action, but it must have become lodged in my mind in some rudimentary fashion. Sitting one Saturday morning in my usual haunt of Johnson & Andrews saleroom, a bit dreamy, not too enthused with the sale, I hear Malcolm the auctioneer announce the next lot – a miner's safety lamp. Having no interest in miners' lamps, and knowing nothing about them, I haven't noticed this particular object when viewing the sale. However, the mention of the word "lamp", plus the appearance of an image of an oil-lamp-looking thing on the monitor above the podium, plus some smidgen of guilt at having thus far failed to provide lighting for the summer house, all combine to make me raise my hand and bid £12 to win the lot.

After getting the lamp home and starting to examine it, it takes perhaps 30 seconds for me to understand that there is no way in the world in which I can use this item for the purpose for which I have bought it. To the uninitiated, a miner's lamp provides very few clues as to how it's lit, how it's fuelled, how to trim its wick, or whether it is complete and in working order and not likely to cause rather than prevent fire or explosion. I decide it isn't useable as a source of light, but at the same time I can easily see that here is an elegant, finely engineered piece of kit. Could it be collectable? If so, perhaps I can get my money back by selling it on to a collector**.

---

*   Author's note: the recurrence of the shed theme in this chapter is purely coincidental and unrelated to the subject under discussion.

**   2016 update: at the time of writing, there is still no lighting in the summer house. No surprise there.

Time for some internet research. I soon discover tons of useful information from superficial skimming of the many websites dedicated to mining history and memorabilia. I learn that the scientific and engineering principles of the safety lamp were established by Sir Humphrey Davy, William Reid Clanny and George Stephenson around the year 1815. Working independently, but each trying to improve on the others' inventions, their developments initiated the manufacture of safety lamps by many makers in many countries in many different patterns over more than one hundred years.

Although long since replaced in deep mining by carbide lamps and then electric lighting, "Davy lamps" are still made in small numbers today and remain the only available method to transport a live flame safely over a long distance. Hence the everlasting Olympic Flame is still carried from country to country by aeroplane, using devices identical to those used by deep miners all over the world for more than a century.

Miners' safety lamps were objects of extreme significance in the safety and survival of their users. They were sturdily made, built to last, and jealously guarded and cared for by their owners. And of course, their association with a lost era of industrial history imbues them with a lustre of masculinity, muscularity and romantic mystique. These factors, combined with a profusion of makes and models and the longevity of production, naturally render these objects irresistible to collectors worldwide. Common ones are cheap. Rare ones can fetch astronomical prices. Because of international interest and the ease of classification and description of the various makes and models, miners' lamps are highly suitable for selling by internet auction.

Having established the basics, I then proceed to compare my lamp with thousands of drawings and photographs of other lamps which can be found online, and it turns out that my one is a bit special: a Best's Gauzeless. The very large majority of lamps used a sleeve of metal mesh or gauze to keep the flame separate from flammable gases in the mine. But the Best's design, introduced around 1886, unusually employed different – gauzeless – principles, so all collectors want to own an example of this type.

Not wanting to start my own collection, although tempted to do so, I list the lamp on eBay and a week later my £12 outlay elicits a winning bid of £387. The buyer is a Presbyterian pastor from a rural parish in New South Wales, Australia. He's delighted. Me too.

The Sequelae

The third anecdote above appears to describe a simple process. There's no Eye involved. No judgment. Just pure luck. There's an end to all the agonising and waffle about The Eye, and whether it exists, and what causes it and where it comes from. QED.

However, it's not simple at all, because there's a sequel. Actually two sequels, because in fact I'm only one-third of the way through the anecdote. At this point, if I were relating the story to Frances, I would become aware of her attention starting to wander and her eyes starting to glaze. If I can stop talking for a moment and start listening, I might hear her muttering something under her breath about the genetic influence of my putative Ashkenazi rabbinical forebears. But such a warning would not – and will not – deter me from pursuing the tale relentlessly to its conclusion. To continue…

The Magic Lamps (2 and 3)

A few weeks after the Best's Gauzeless is bought and sold, another lamp comes up at a Saturday auction. Thinking I can't go wrong, I fight hard for it and consider that I've bagged myself a bargain when I win it for £55. This one is more difficult to identify, but is eventually pinned down as a Marsaut-type lamp, probably made by Arras, a French maker, around 100 years ago. It is quite an early one, but not all that rare and not really special in in any way. However, I list it on eBay just to see what will happen, and it sells to a French buyer for £47.50, leaving me with a loss, after deduction of commission and charges, of around £15.

OK. You win some, you lose some. You can't expect to get lucky twice. Further support for the no-such-thing-as-The-Eye argument. As to the slightly separate question of why I paid £12 for a rare and valuable lamp in one week, and £55 for a less rare and much less valuable one just a few weeks later, I have no clue to the answer. Probably just to do with who turns up at the auction on a Saturday. Let us proceed.

Then, a few weeks later still, there is a cluster of about eight miners' lamps on display at the Friday auction viewing. Having had my fingers burnt with my second purchase (figuratively of course, since I know better than to try to ignite a lamp), I approach them gingerly. I see mostly types and makers' names that I recognise from images seen online when researching my first and second lamps, but I jot down in the margin of my catalogue what information I can glean from them. One lamp looks different from the others – heavier, sturdier, more complex in its construction, more of a precision instrument. Stamped upon it are three names: Ashworth, Hepplewhite and Gray (**See Illustrations, *Picture 7*).

On getting back to my computer, I quickly ascertain that all the other lamps are common models produced by volume manufacturers. After my most recent experience, they are of no interest as a source of possible profit. A little more research soon reveals, however, that there is nothing common or ordinary about the A-H-G lamp. While it isn't to miners' safety lamps what *The Jug* was to studio ceramics, or what *The Saint* will be to French late Gothic sculpture, it comes fairly close:

> "*The Ashworth Hepplewhite Gray (AHG) lamp [was] one of the best gas testers, being able to detect 2.5% firedamp. In use, hollow tubes direct feed air to enter the lamp through gauzed openings below the flame. A thin layer of gas against the mine roof can be detected without tilting the lamp by opening the cap shutter on top allowing air to be sampled and closing the tube ferrules on the bottom. In more normal operation, the cap shutter is closed and the tube ferrules are opened allowing air to be accessed to the flame. The lamp was in use from 1889 to 1920.*"[27]

It is an expensive, rather aristocratic sort of lamp, produced in small quantities for use not by coal-face workers but by mine managers and inspectors. A real rarity. At the auction, I buy it for £44, neither the most expensive nor the cheapest item in the small collection of lamps on sale. Once again, I offer it for sale on eBay. It attracts bids from ten collectors and eventually sells, again to a French buyer, for an astonishing hammer price of £1,711.

An Eye to an Explanation

I started out in this chapter with a hypothesis *that some people do indeed have The Eye – that they possess some special quality or ability which enables them to be better than others at rapidly distinguishing items which have significant market value.*

In the tale about the Golden Egg, where a boy finds scarce-date pennies and sixpences in the pub cash register, I argued that there might be no such quality as The Eye, but that it was all down to *behaviour, opportunity and circumstance*, with little or no place for *luck* or for *talent* or *aptitude*. But this explanation was incomplete and unconvincing.

In the second anecdote, about the Cats, the Shed, the Cobra and the Plate, I hinted that there might be some kind of inborn antennae or radar or sixth sense for detecting a good, rare or collectable object, and that I might possess this quality in some measure. But again this is unsatisfactory because I have no explanation for the origin of the phenomenon, or how in my own particular case it might operate culturally in terms of taste, fashion or aesthetics.

Finally, in the Magic Lamps story, I wrote about finding three miners' lamps in rapid succession, the first scarce and valuable (explanation: *luck*), the second common and of little value (explanation: *hubris*) and the third an exceptional rarity.

The conclusion which I seem to be arriving at is that, at least in my individual case, there are clues to the explanation of The Eye to be found in all three stories. It seems that I must possess some kind of aptitude or knack, which on balance guides me in a majority of cases towards good finds. In addition, I have a demonstrable and useful interest in old things of all kinds and in their stories. I am willing to make an effort to research the background of objects that catch my interest. I probably have a good visual memory for objects and details of objects, despite a terrible memory for human faces. I suspect I have a keener than average degree of discernment when it comes to judging quality in the making of an object. Perhaps I have always enjoyed good observational skills in relation to objects, which may in part be due to my extreme short-sightedness. Again this faculty applies more to things than to people: if you ask me to say what someone's thinking by looking at their facial expression, I'd probably be no help at all.

I think in the end the closest approach that I can make to defining The Eye is to quote Louis Pasteur, who said – in an entirely unrelated context – that *"dans les sciences d'observation le hasard ne favorise que des esprits preparés"* – "in the science of observation, fortune favours the prepared mind"[28]. Firstly, you must willingly enter into the science of observation, which implies an aptitude, or at the very least a degree of positive engagement. Then there's luck, but luck doesn't come looking for you: rather, you enormously increase your chances of getting lucky if you put in the hard work first. Which, again, might be saying exactly the same as "there's no such thing as luck". It's a circular argument and I'll leave it there.

7

BUYING THE SAINT, 2012

The Start of an Affair

It's Friday 26th October 2012, late morning. Now that I'm retired from regular work I can get to the Johnson & Andrews sale viewing earlier in the day. And now that Malcolm has a reasonable website I have been able to have a quick look through the catalogue for tomorrow's sale and a glance at the photos of the lots. True, it's a bit rudimentary – the descriptions are as ever sketchy and the pictures hastily taken in inadequate light, but at least it is possible to form some preliminary ideas about which lots might be worthy of close inspection.

The catalogue is underwhelming. Nothing has caught my eye. Naturally this hasn't stopped me from coming to view. I do my first rapid circuit to see if anything is going to throw itself into my eye line, or call out to me from across the room. I'm well aware that lots in this type of auction are by and large inanimate and can neither move nor speak, but sometimes it is almost as if an object deliberately demands your attention*. But not this time.

I commence my second circuit of the hall. On the table in front of the rostrum, in almost the identical spot where The Jug had stood nearly six years ago, perhaps a little to the right, stands a wooden figure about two feet high. I must have seen it in my peripheral vision the first time around, but

---

* Note for further enquiry: in livestock auctions where the lots are indeed animate, can it be shown that this phenomenon actually occurs? Might a cow be viewing you while you are viewing her? Might she moo in a becoming way or flutter her eyelashes if she wants to give you The Buzz? Might a sheep bleat, or a pig oink winningly in your direction? Perhaps I'll ask a farmer. Or perhaps not.

106

unconsciously dismissed it as being of no interest to me. I have seen religious statues before in auctions a few times. Although I'm a Jew, I am not an observant or orthodox one and I have no problem with graven images. Agnostic in belief, perhaps tending as I get older towards out-and-out atheism, I can yet see how religion can provide huge comfort and satisfaction to believers. Religious faith has inspired the creation of sublime beauty in art (as well as supreme ugliness and injustice in other fields), and I can understand how it might help a worshipper to praise his or her god through contemplation of an artwork.

I have been in many churches and cathedrals, and can catch a potent echo of the sense of holiness that comes with being surrounded by Christian architecture and artefacts. It doesn't make me feel religious; it is an aesthetic response, maybe tinged with slight envy of those who actually do feel that divinity is present and immanent.

But in the type of downmarket auctions that I frequent, you don't expect to get a spiritual frisson from a religious artefact (unless of course it's a 1610 Andro Hart bible). What you expect is a plaster saint or Virgin, poorly moulded, gaudily painted, cheaply made in either a large size to be contemplated in a niche in a Catholic place of worship, or a smaller size to be kept conventionally on the staircase landing or sideboard in a Catholic household. From the point of view of the cynical, hard-boiled, hard-pressed local auction viewer, there is no interest, no profit, no aesthetic or iconographical satisfaction to be gained from them. Seen one, seen 'em all.

But this statue is different. The catalogue says "Lot 32: Carved wood figure of a monk". All that this terse description tells me is that Davie has done the cataloguing this week, not Malcolm. No help there, then. It is made of bare wood, not painted plaster. I can tell that it's a saint, not a monk, although I don't at this stage know which one. I know enough about Christian iconography to know that saints are invariably depicted with their attributes for instant recognition by the faithful. I can even recognise a few myself: Saint Sebastian pierced by arrows, favourite of the S&M school of Italian Renaissance painters; Saint Agatha holding a plate displaying her severed breasts; Saint Jerome at the mouth of his cave accompanied by his pet lion.

I can't immediately see any attributes on this saint but I know he is one. There, look! I have started calling the statue "him" already, just seconds after noticing him. Because there is a person inside. I look closely. He holds his head at a slightly strained angle, looking upward to his right, and I can see the tensing of the muscles on the left side of his neck. And his face! The most extraordinary expression of thoughtfulness and sweetness that I have ever seen on a statue. His hands are clasped in prayer or supplication, and I note the veins in their backs. He is dressed in a long, heavy robe, the folds and drapes of which are incredibly realistic (**See Illustrations,** *Pictures 8 and 9*).

His wood glows. I realise weeks later that this isn't a good thing and that the loss of his original polychromy is little short of tragic, but MacGregor's craftsmen have made an outstanding job of stripping and polishing him, and he has a deep, rich shine. And I can see now that I look closely at him that he is old, old.

I get The Buzz. I have absolutely no idea what I am looking at, but I am looking at something very unusual and very special.

I pick him up. He is slightly lighter in weight than I was expecting, but clearly made of solid wood. I turn him upside down. No markings, but some age wear and a hole in the centre where he must have been fixed to a base. His square plinth with canted corners has a large chip out of one side, but the exposed surface has been worn smooth and polished, so it's old damage. Some other chipped bits are apparent now that I look more closely. His nose might have been skilfully repaired. I can see one or two inactive woodworm holes.

I put him back down, noticing briefly that beside him on the table is a corner bracket shelf, similar colour, similar wood finish, carved, looks early-ish twentieth century. The statue and the bracket must be related in some way. I finish my round of the saleroom cursorily looking at other lots, then go home, preoccupied.

Pre-sale Research

How do you find out about an art object if you don't have the smallest idea where to start? In olden days you went to the fine art shelves in the public library and spent hours browsing.

In the early 1970s I bought a small purple glass vase, less than three inches high. It cost me ten pence in a jumble sale, my then activity of choice on a Saturday afternoon. Sadly, since those far-off days the number of jumble sales available to the bric-a-brac devotee has decreased in inverse proportion to the increase in number of charity shops and the growth of online auction and second-hand sales websites.

The little ovoid vase was exquisitely delicate and beautiful, and appeared to have been made in layers, with sinuous floral decorations carved through a purple outer glass layer revealing lighter lavender-coloured glass beneath (See Illustrations, *Picture 10*). On one side, amidst the carving, was a squiggle. Initially I thought that this squiggle might be something written in Arabic script, and, since Frances was at the time a student of Arabic and Middle Eastern Studies, I thought she might like to have it as a present. She did like it, but it was instantly clear to her that the squiggle wasn't in Arabic.

So we thought it might be a signature. I could tell that the vase's style was art nouveau, but at that time this wasn't a period that I knew anything about. Intrigued, off I went to the public library. Knowing more or less where to start (glass, art nouveau, early twentieth century), it only took me half an hour or so amongst the art and antiques books to identify that the technique used in the making of my little pot was called cameo glass, and the squiggle was the signature of the celebrated glass-maker Emile Gallé of Nancy in France.

Here was another example of how an item of special rarity, beauty and value can come adrift from its identification and end up almost – but not quite – on the rubbish tip. The rest of the story of this pretty little vase is not germane to the point I'm trying to make here, but I'll come back to it in a later chapter.

In these days of the internet, the public library isn't the first port of call to find information about unknown or unidentified objects. If there are only a few hours between getting The Buzz and the moment when the lot comes up for sale, the library might not be an option. But the internet is there all day and all night, and that is precisely where I was for all of the rest of that Friday and part of Saturday morning too, scanning images and websites looking for statues with characteristics similar to those of The Saint.

I started with the simplest of search terms: "wood saint statue" generated more than 30 million results. I won't say that I looked at all of them, but I did scan a good number of images and website descriptions. Not being a church-going sort of person, I was amazed to discover that the production of religious statuary (especially of the Roman Catholic persuasion) has survived into the twenty-first century as a thriving global industry. Leaving aside questions of taste and quality, it was soon clear that a more specific description would be needed to get some more specific leads. I tried various combinations of searches using "saint" and "religious"; "statue" and "sculpture"; "wood", "wooden" and "woodcarving"; "mediaeval" and "antique"; "Gothic" and "Renaissance". Although I could tell that The Saint wasn't made of oak, I didn't know what type of wood it was, so I put "oak" into the mix to see if I could find anything similar. I had no idea where The Saint might have been made, but my instinct told me that he was more likely to be from the European mainland than from Britain. But I didn't have enough knowledge or information to specify any particular country or region.

After several hours of searching I had satisfied myself that many religious statues were carved from wood in the late mediaeval or late Gothic period, and that they mostly came from Northern Europe, particularly Germany, France and the Low Countries. I had also half-formed an impression that they shared a number of common characteristics. They were painted in polychrome colours. They had well-defined facial features tending away from realism and towards the idealised and conventional. They bore rather stern or sometimes almost trance-like facial expressions. They often stood or sat in rather unnatural poses. They were clothed in stiff draperies hanging in straight folds. In summary, I found that this general class of statue was long on convention and short on naturalism. By contrast, I felt that there was very little about *my* Saint that corresponded to any items on this checklist. But at the same time, I had a strong feeling that I wasn't all that far away from identifying an example which I could compare with him.

Turning to statues from the Italian Renaissance, I found that these tended to be very much more florid, ornate and expressive of violent emotion and strong movement than my simple, still, contemplative Saint. And Renaissance statues were mostly made in marble or bronze, with very few images of wooden ones available. I dismissed the Renaissance as a style and Italy as a possible place of origin.

Another consideration was that the wooden statues whose images I scanned on the internet were often in poor condition with major losses and worm damage. It was difficult to understand how The Saint standing on the table in Johnson & Andrews' saleroom could be both very old (as I still believed him to be) and yet so complete and so beautifully patinated.

After a late night and an early morning of searching and frustration, I reached a very tentative identification. By the exertion of copious amounts of optimism, imagination, and perhaps self-delusion, I had convinced myself that it was *just* possible that the statue *could* be from the sixteenth century, *could* be from South Germany, and *could* be carved from limewood.

In my wholesale trawling of images, the most frequently recurring names attached to the most similar (but somehow not similar) statues were those of Tilman Riemenschneider of Wurzburg (c1460–1531), Veit Stoss of Nuremberg (c1450–1533), Michel Erhart of Ulm (c1440–c1522) and his son Gregor Erhart of Augsburg (c1470–c1540). They all carved in limewood, a light-coloured wood from the lime or linden tree; their figures were realistic and individualised, with expressive features and flowing movement; some were carved in bare wood, polished but not painted; some had survived in stunningly original condition. The best of these statues were exceptionally graceful and beautiful, but the moods on the faces of The Saints and Virgins seemed all to be cool, distant, severe, somehow disengaged – how unlike the sweetness and humanity in the facial expression of my Saint! **(See Illustrations, *Picture 11*)**

Looking at auctioneers' websites, I noted with passing interest that good quality statues from these German sculptors had sold for high prices. A large and breathtakingly beautiful statue of Saint Catherine by Riemenschneider had sold at Sotheby's New York in 2008 for an astonishing price.

There were also many inferior works by contemporary imitators and followers of the best woodcarvers. Even I with an untrained and unfamiliar Eye could see that many of these were of poor quality, and in some cases decidedly amateurish, presumably made for local churches by village woodcarvers who might or might not have caught a glimpse of a carving by one of the masters. Yet, presumably because of their age and rarity, examples of these rustic works had sold for significant prices in the thousands and tens of thousands.

While still not at all confident that I had pinned my Saint down to a location or a style or a period, I nevertheless concluded that there was a sufficient level of confidence to risk a modest bid of one or two hundred pounds buy him. It seemed a safe enough bet that I would get my money back in a specialist saleroom – supposing that once he was bought I could ever bring myself to part with him.

A further quick look at him in the saleroom on the Saturday morning didn't tell me anything new, but made me a little more certain that he had some genuine age. At the same time I looked more closely at the next lot, a corner shelf bracket with a similar colour and finish, which must have supported The Saint in the vendor's house. It suddenly dawned on me that while parts of the bracket were of twentieth-century manufacture, the central high-relief carving of a cheerful clown's or fool's face was undoubtedly made in the Middle Ages, but then skilfully inserted into the bracket in more modern times. This realisation somehow made me more confident that The Saint was also of mediaeval origin.

Buying The Saint

I bought him. No fuss, no bother, no big build-up, no high emotions in the saleroom. Malcolm raced through the bidding in £20 steps until after not very many seconds the single underbidder dropped out. Lot number 32, carved wood figure of a monk, later identified as *un chef-d'oeuvre de la sculpture bourguignonne du XV* *siècle retrouvé: Le Saint Jean de Calvaire de l'église [de Saint Genest] de Flavigny-sur-Ozerain (Côte d'Or)*[29], was knocked down to me for £340 (total £403.92 including 16% buyer's commission and VAT on the commission). I also bought the next lot, the bracket, for £60 (total £71.28). As you might recall from Chapter 1, it's now on the wall in my kitchen.

I hadn't marked down anything else in the catalogue for bidding, but for interest (OK, because I'm an addict), I stayed on until the end of the sale, then paid for my two lots and brought them home.

Frances, Sarah, her husband Iain, and their small daughter Amy (then aged two-and-a-half) happened to be in our front living room. They waved to me as I reversed the car into the drive. How shall I describe their expressions as I unloaded The Saint and carried him past the window into the house?

IAIN: Oh for God's sake! He's surpassed himself this time!

SARAH: Oh for God's sake! What's he brought home now? Mum will kill him!

FRANCES: Oh for God's sake! Here we go again! More junk to clutter up the house!

AMY: Here's Grandpa!

The mood changed a bit when they got their first look at The Saint. They could easily see that here was something utterly unlike all the other junk and clutter. Whatever it might be – it was something special.

A Georgian mahogany dower chest stands in our downstairs hall. I moved a large studio pottery jug off the end of it and stood The Saint in its place. He presided. There he stayed until despatched to Paris for auction. During that time he was admired, ignored and wondered at by a considerable number of visitors to the house. I found myself saying good morning to him every day as I came downstairs. I even caught Frances once or twice doing the same thing. Our younger daughter Hannah and her husband Niall were captivated. Their four-year-old son Samuel learned to say, "Hello Saint John, how are you today?" in passing. Samuel's sister Eliza, less than a year old, was indifferent. Frances's elder sister Judith entered the house and stopped dead in front of him in astonishment. Our close friend Bob, a mountaineer and lover of wilderness, and thus more attuned to appreciation of the wonders of nature than of human-made artefacts, was fascinated by the emerging story but was apologetically unmoved by the object itself. Rob and Jane, our long-time friends from Fife, were enthralled. Mary and Ron, who had been involved step-by-step in the purchase and sale of The Jug, were just as excited by The Saint.

On the 21st January 2013, eighty-seven days after his arrival, he left our house, bound for Paris.

An Approach to Identification

During those eighty-seven days when The Saint graced our Edinburgh house, considerable work was done to identify him, and not a little anxiety was engendered.

First, identification. As you know, he was bought on the half-formed surmise that he might be from the mid-sixteenth century, made in Southern Germany and carved from limewood. It took several weeks for me to comprehend how spectacularly wrong I had been on all three counts, but at first I had very little to go on.

As with all problems of identification of an unknown object, the main challenges are knowing *where to look* and *whom to ask*.

Frustrated by continuing inability to find suitably matching images online, I decided to do it the old-fashioned way and resort to books, but here the normally trusty public library service failed me by offering nothing in its catalogue on the subject of late mediaeval German statuary. Not, I grant, a majority taste, so perhaps unsurprising. However, I did identify a couple of books online which might be useful starting-points, but neither was available to read in electronic format.

It turned out that one of them was stocked in Edinburgh University Library, and Frances kindly used her university staff ticket to borrow it for me and bring it home – no mean feat since it was a monster of a book, academically weighty but physically much more so. It was called *Carved Splendor: late Gothic Altarpieces in Southern Germany, Austria and South Tirol*[30], and contained many beautiful illustrations, some tantalisingly similar to my Saint – but none close enough for confident attribution.

The second book wasn't stocked in a local library but was available and affordable to purchase, so I bought it from an online book retailer. It was *The Limewood Sculptors of Renaissance Germany* by Michael Baxandall[31], a book which I later learned was considered to be a classic work of modern art-historical writing. The subject matter was broadly the same as in *Carved Splendor*, but its narrative was remarkably accessible and some of the illustrations seemed yet closer to my statue. A Saint Matthew by Riemenschneider with similar hair and detailing to the hands; two angels by Hans Multscher with flowing robes and steeply upturned faces; a Saint John by Nikolaus Gerhaert with a strongly individualised face wearing a highly emotional expression. Generally, faces were longer and thinner and sterner than on my high-cheekboned, round-faced, full-lipped statue, but I felt at last that I was getting warmer – but not warm enough.

It's an interesting thought that while Baxandall's book on *The Limewood Sculptors* has become one of the classics of art history writing since publication in 1980, the exceptional artist-craftsmen who form its subject matter remain practically as obscure in the present day as they were when Baxandall wrote so lucidly about them. Successful as his book has been – and it's now a standard text in many university art history courses – the names and works of Riemenschneider, Multscher and Gerhaert are scarcely likely to come to mind when thinking about fifteenth and sixteenth-century European sculpture. But were these "late Gothic" German sculptors inferior to their much more famous Italian "Renaissance" contemporaries such as Donatello, Michelangelo and Verrocchio working a few hundred miles to the south? I'll have a few things to say about quality, desirability and value in art objects and antiques in a later chapter.

In the meantime, back at my desk, I was beginning to feel that my superficial book-reading was at least helping me to learn how to look at this kind of object, and to gain a basic vocabulary to try to describe it. Now was the time to begin seeking expert help.

The attentive reader might have gathered from various anecdotes earlier in this book that when I find myself in possession of an object about which I'm unsure or (more often) totally mystified, I ask an expert. You might also have inferred that when I do so, I try to avoid an approach along the lines of *"Here's a picture of a something-or-other that I've got. Please tell me what it is and how much it's worth. By the way, wanna buy it?"* What I prefer to do is to work hard to get as far as possible by desk research, and then to work just as hard again to identify the best person to ask for help – if he or she is minded to be helpful. After all, expecting to get valuable expert advice for free might be thought of as being a bit cheeky. Here are these world-class scholars with their own work to do, and here's me, an unknown nonentity whom they don't know from Adam. And here's me expecting not only to get the expert's attention, but also to get him or her to write back with an opinion.

So, first I try to form a preliminary opinion or hypothesis about the object. Then I try to describe it using clear but simple language, stating its physical dimensions, identifiable features, and what I think I've found out about the material, style and technique of making. I might also say what my amateur researches have turned up as possibilities in respect of age, origin and maker, but if I say anything of this sort it will be couched in a self-deprecating "here's-what-I-think-but-what-do-I-know?" sort of tone. I might employ a touch of pseudo-art-critical terminology and idiom gleaned from my reading, but only sparingly, and only if confident that I'm using the terms correctly. I don't mind being thought an amateur but I do mind being thought a pretentious ass.

Then I photograph the object as clearly and from as many angles and aspects as my limited equipment will allow. Then I identify my first target expert. Then I send the photos with an email, which includes my description and a polite but not obsequious request for any advice or guidance. If I'm writing to a dealer or auctioneer, I'll sometimes say that consigning for sale is a possibility; but when it's a museum curator or an academic, I would represent my interest as purely that of a collector and would-be connoisseur. I wouldn't normally write to more than one expert at a time, in the hope that each reply received might (if incomplete in itself) furnish me with additional pointers to include in the next email to the next expert.

Since I have very low expectations of ever getting a reply, I'm always very pleasantly surprised when I do get one. In fact, overall, I find that my hit-rate is well over 50%, and moreover that I'm just as likely to get a helpful reply directly from a world authority as from a Poppy. A Poppy is the generic name that Frances and I use when referring to the charming, well-bred and immaculately-groomed, privately-educated art history graduates, usually young women but sometimes young men, who seem to get all the junior curator or intern or assistant jobs with all the best auction houses, high-end dealers, galleries and museums. In fairness, they aren't all called Poppy. Recently I've had dealings with a Theodora, a Lydia, a Lucianne, an Arcadia, and an Alexandra. If it's a boy, his name is Oliver, but we still think of him as Poppy.

The Expert View

I started at the top, and worked my way upwards from there. My first targets were two dealers. Not mere low-brow back-street antique and bric-a-brac traders, but the two top London dealers in mediaeval and haute époque artefacts. One, based in Mayfair, is "a specialist in the art of the European Middle Ages". He "has presented a series of exhibitions and publications, breaking new ground in the fields of medieval sculpture, stained glass, works of art, illuminated manuscripts... His clients include the world's major institutions as well as private collectors".

The other dealer, based in Westminster, "specialises in Haute Époque fine art with an emphasis on continental sculpture, works of art, furniture and complementary old master paintings dating from 1200–1700. We are driven by the search for objects of the finest quality, rarity and provenance. Inspired by the emotional response a work of art elicits, every piece is selected carefully for its capacity to enrich the lives of those who possess it. We seek to source the extraordinary for discerning clientele".

The term "haute époque" was used twice in the last two paragraphs in a fairly off-hand sort of way. After having spent many months in the company of The Saint and his expert admirers, the phrase comes easily to me now, but prior to October 2012, I can't recall having ever heard it. I'd guess that it might not be familiar to absolutely every reader, so it should perhaps be introduced into this narrative more formally. Unfortunately, perhaps because haute époque is such a rarefied and/or outdated and/or imprecise notion, I couldn't find a definition of it in English, so the quotation which follows is from the French language Wikipedia website:

"La Haute époque est le terme employé par les antiquaires pour désigner des meubles et objets d'art datant ou faisant référence au Moyen Âge, de la Renaissance et du xviie siècle. N'ayant aucune pertinence historique (car recouvrant plus de dix siècles) il n'a pas davantage de signification esthétique précise car il peut être aussi bien gothique, roman, byzantin, baroque, arabe, etc. Il englobe donc tout ce qui, authentique ou moins authentique, a trait au Moyen Âge, selon l'imaginaire de celui-ci propre notamment au XIXe siècle, période où le terme "Haute époque" fut inventé."

I tried rendering this into English using Google's auto-translate facility, but the result was more or less gibberish. So I have attempted my own translation which, if inaccurate, might at least give the gist of what seems to be a rather dismissive Wikipedia definition:

"'Haut Époque' is the term used by antique experts to describe furniture and works of art dating from or making reference to the Middle Ages, the Renaissance and the seventeenth century. Without any historical specificity (because the term covers more than ten centuries), the term no longer has any aesthetic significance because it can equally well mean Gothic, Romanesque, Byzantine, Baroque, Islamic, etc. It thus encompasses everything more or less authentic which has to do with the Middle Ages, as envisaged by experts, mainly in the nineteenth century, when the term 'Haute Époque' was coined."

Vague as it is, haute époque remains current usage in the exalted circles where The Saint mingles with his fellow mediaeval, gothic and renaissance artefacts. You're unlikely to find a haute époque shop down your high street or a stall at your local car boot sale, but my researches had turned up these two specialist London dealers, so I targeted them as first two experts for consultation. In emailing them I was knocking gently on the gates of a new and ethereal world, into which I entered more fully over the next few months.

The email ran as follows:

"Hi.

I wonder if you may be able to give me some advice about a carved wood statue? I know nothing about this object other than what I have found by looking at images online, but I think it might be mediaeval.

The statue, which is 69 cms tall, seems to be an unidentified saint. He appears to be carved in limewood, maybe German, maybe 16th century. I can't find any traces of polychromy.

Some photos are attached. If you wish to see it in person, I'll have to work out a way to get it to you from Edinburgh.

It will be a great help if you can tell me anything about the statue, and if it is likely to have any value.

Many thanks in anticipation."

I received prompt replies from both dealers. The Westminster one said "Hello. We are in Amsterdam preparing for the PAN fair which opens this weekend. I will consider this following the conclusion of the fair. Regards". Then, nothing. Nothing since. End of correspondence.

The reply from the Mayfair dealer's assistant Arcadia was more enthusiastic: "We would very much like to see this piece. Are you based in London? Is there any way you could bring it to the gallery? I look forward to hearing from you". I bridled. Since I had given my Edinburgh address in my email to her, it should have been perfectly obvious that I wasn't in a position to saunter down Bond Street with my statue under my arm on my way between the Wallace Collection and the Royal Academy. I sent Arcadia a don't-call-us-we'll-call-you sort of reply, and immediately decided that someone with such a London-centric outlook didn't deserve The Saint. We ex-Londoner adoptive Scots tend to get like that.

Time to spread the net more widely. I discovered that Wilkinson's auctioneers in Doncaster, South Yorkshire has a good record for selling mediaeval wooden artefacts, "specialising in Early Oak Furniture sales that include a rich variety of carvings, tapestries and paintings… With only six sales per year we are able to concentrate on high quality sales that attract buyers from all over the world". In response to my enquiry I received a nice note from Sid (not many Poppies or Olivers in South Yorkshire), who said: "It is so difficult to give a valuation on these sort of items as they often look so different in real life – however it does look as though it would be suitable for our next oak sale, but it really depends upon what sort of reserve you were wanting… have you got a price in mind?". But of course I didn't have a price in mind because I was so much more interested in identifying The Saint than in selling him.

Next, the Victoria and Albert Museum. I received an automated reply to my email, telling me to expect an answer within twenty working days. Four years later, I'm still expecting.

Then an email to Christie's. Again, no reply, so I moved on.

Then I had my first stroke of luck. Still fixated on a German origin for The Saint, I discovered the name of Dr Bernhard Decker of Frankfurt am Main[32]. His excellent and bilingual website informed me that he "specializes in European sculpture and Old Master paintings dating from the Middle Ages up to 1900. The extensive selection from these period fields includes a wide variety of choice works of European art, every piece of best museum quality... His main focus lies on European medieval and Baroque sculpture whereby – typical for these periods – religious themes prevail". I emailed him more in hope than expectation, and received an almost immediate reply:

"Thank you for your E-mail asking for my opinion on the figure. It is a St. John from a crucifixion group (Calvary), as it seems to me it could date from about 1400/20, being maybe of French or north Burgundian origin, not German. The salient point is: I cannot say anything about the authenticity of the piece from watching on the base of photographs only. Actually, I must see it to be able to be more precise."

I replied thanking him, and he came back with a little more:

"Let me give you an additional hint: Following all I could see on the photographs, the material of your St. John sculpture seems not to be limewood, but Walnut. This could be another confirmation concerning the assumed localization of the workshop: "Northern France, Belgium, or Burgundy"... In case the figure is old, it would probably be of interest to collectors and museums. You obviously did a very good catch! Let me know if you should decide selling it."

I wrote again, with fulsome thanks, but saying that I wasn't ready to sell yet. We weren't in contact again, and I'm not sure if he became aware of the outcome of the story before his death in 2015. But I'll be forever grateful to him for his expertise and his generous help.

Progress

So. Not German, not limewood, not sixteenth century, but French, walnut and fifteenth century. It took no more than about five minutes of looking at internet images of late Gothic Burgundian sculpture to comprehend that Dr Decker was absolutely on the button. I recommend readers to try it for themselves. If you search on "Burgundian Sculpture", you get over 5 million results. Then click on the images tab, and you are transported instantly into the self-contained world of the little alabaster Mourner figures parading around the arcaded tombs of the Dukes of Burgundy in Dijon. Searching for images of statues in the wrong country, wrong period and wrong material had inevitably led me nowhere. But one glance at the Mourners, and I knew I was on the right track.

An alabaster mourner carved by Jean de la Huerta and
Antoine le Moiturier for the tomb of Duke John the Fearless.

And not an anonymous saint but Saint John the Evangelist from a crucifixion or Calvary group. An hour or so of searching conventional mediaeval depictions in paintings and carved altarpieces of the scene at Calvary, explained the sharp upward turn of the head – obviously (as it now seemed) for Saint John to contemplate and mourn the crucified Christ above and behind him to his right, while the Virgin stands looking demurely downward at the other side of the Cross. As for his saintly attributes, he was, as convention dictates, bare-headed, clean-shaven and barefoot. All instantly recognisable if only you know what you're looking at.

I felt that I'd made huge progress, assuming, of course, that my statue was the real thing and not a fake or a later copy. I went back to my emailing. Next, Sotheby's.

With my newly-acquired expertise gleaned from Dr Decker in Frankfurt, I was now able to sound a little more knowledgeable. I wrote: "I now believe that the object is a St John from a crucifixion group, and may be carved in walnut. Stylistically it appears to be very close to the alabaster pleurant figures on the tomb of Philip the Bold, Duke of Burgundy, dating from the early 15th century, carved by Claus de Werve and successors".

I waited and waited and waited. A month or so later, after a reminder to Sotheby's, this helpful reply came back, not from a Poppy or even an Oliver, but from a Christopher:

"I have looked into your enquiry carefully. I quite agree with you that your figure is very similar to 15th-century Burgundian 'Mourners' such as those adorning the tomb of Philip the Bold. I wonder, however, whether your figure might be South Netherlandish as a number of similar St John figures (though with more angular and deeply undercut folds) were made in this region in the 15th century. If your figure does date to this period the value would be in the region of £5,000-7,000. However, we would need to view it in the flesh to come to a final decision on this".

Encouraging, but by the time this reply eventually arrived, the decision had already been made about what was to happen to The Saint, so Sotheby's missed out on discovering how wrong they were.

While waiting for Sotheby's (and also the V&A and Christie's) to come back to me, I carried on spending my evenings trawling the internet to find specialists in the French haute époque who might be able to help me to build on the invaluable information supplied by Dr Decker. By this time I was finding – not altogether surprisingly – that most websites were written in French. I also discovered that whereas the Google auto-translation facility might be able to give you a more or less meaningful French to English rendering in a subject area which employs familiar terminology (for example, information about holiday resorts), it doesn't do much of a job at translating the very formal art-historical language used by experts to describe mediaeval sculpture. Many hours of head-scratching and concentration were required until I suddenly realised that much of my grammar-school-acquired ability to understand literary French had come back to me. So much so that on thinking back to a website I had looked at yesterday, I sometimes couldn't recall if I had been reading French or English. My level of self-satisfaction and self-congratulation was however tempered by the absolute knowledge that if I ever had to write to someone in French, let alone speak to them in French, utter humiliation would result and all would be lost.

This phase of searching turned up trumps. I found the name of a Mme Laurence Fligny[33], an independent specialist on the haute époque, who worked as an expert adviser and consultant for many French auction houses, particularly for those which conducted their sales at the Hôtel Drouot in central Paris. I noted from her website that she was responsible for a number of highly successful discoveries and sales of Burgundian sculptures, including some pieces with apparent similarities to my Saint John. Might she be able to help me?

Here's what I wrote in my email on 27th November 2012, exactly one month after buying The Saint at Johnson & Andrews:

Dear Mme Fligny

I wonder if you might be able to give me any information about a carved wood statue which may be a St John from a crucifixion group? The statue is 69 cms tall and carved all round, possibly in walnut.

I know nothing about this type of object other than what I have found by looking at images online, but the style and appearance make me think it might perhaps be from Burgundy or the Netherlands, dating from the 15th century. I can find no traces of polychrome decoration anywhere on the piece, but have found behind one of the folds of the robe a tiny flake of what may be original gilding.

Some photos are attached.

I bought the statue recently in a local auction here in Edinburgh, Scotland. It is a long way outside my main collecting interest (20th century ceramics), but I thought it such an exquisitely beautiful object that I decided to buy it and see if I could find out more about it. If it is likely to be of interest to expert collectors or scholars, I would consider selling it. Or if not, I'll be very happy to keep it.

I found your name while researching on the internet, and I understand that you are an expert on this type of object, and will be grateful for your opinion on whether it might merit a full appraisal. I apologise for being unable to address this enquiry to you in French, but I look forward to hearing from you.

Yours sincerely"

The very next day, I came home in the evening to find this reply:

"Cher Monsieur Roger Stewart,

Merci pour votre mail. Votre sculpture de saint Jean est très intéressante et je vois vers quel sculpteur bourguignon on peut la rapprocher.

J'ai essayé sans succès de vous joindre par téléphone aujourd'hui et recommencerai demain.

Best regards,

Laurence Fligny."

Thanks. Your Saint John sculpture is very interesting and I can see how it could be attributed to a particular Burgundian sculptor. I have tried unsuccessfully to telephone you today and will try again tomorrow.

Gulp! This has happened to me before – with The Jug. If a high-end auction expert picks up the phone to talk to you as soon as he or she sees your photos, then you know you're on to something. A new chapter was about to start in the history of my statue. Accordingly, the next part of the story requires a new chapter of this book. Not the next chapter, but the one after next.

But just before moving on, I have some unfinished business to relate. You'll remember that I was still waiting to hear from the V&A and from Christie's. As for the former, I'm still waiting, but Christie's eventually came back to me weeks and weeks later. Suddenly out of the blue, this arrived from the Head of their London-based European Sculpture and Works of Art Department:

"I would like to express my embarrassment at the length of time it has taken me to respond to your message. Your email got lost in the deluge of emails that are currently in my inbox.

I would also like to thank you for sending them in the first place and I hope that my appraisal will still be relevant – and necessary.

I am rather excited about the figure of St John. I cannot [be] 100% sure in my judgment of it from the photos alone, but I think this might be earlier than you suggest. My gut feeling is that it is actually be [sic] French, second half 14th century. There are certain stylistic elements such as the carving of the hair and face as well as certain passages of the drapery that resonate with French gothic sculpture. On the basis that this is indeed old and not a clever fake (which I doubt) then this piece could be worth anywhere between £20,000 and £40,000. I think it would be a very good idea to have a closer look at it in order to be sure."

I read this email on my phone on returning to my car in a car park on an industrial estate in Motherwell, Lanarkshire. An uninteresting fact in itself, but the place from where I was returning is of slightly more interest. Moments before, I had dropped off The Saint, carefully rolled in a thousand layers of bubble-wrap, at the Scottish depot of Constantine, specialist removers of fine art and antiques. Too late for Christie's, I had just sent him on his way to Laurence in Paris for appraisal and possible sale.

1. Above: Oak bracket shelf containing a carved relief face from a mediaeval corbel or misericord, manufactured by MacGregor of Edinburgh as the support for The Saint.

2.Below: A stoneware bowl made by Bernard Leach in the early days of the St Ives Pottery.

3. The author occupying the favourite seat of Bernard Leach, St Ives Pottery, July 2009.

4. The Jug.

5. The interior of the Golden Egg Restaurant, Charing Cross Road, London, in October 1963.

6. My octagonal plate by Clarice Cliff in the Appliqué Lucerne pattern, colour Orange.

7. The Ashworth-Hepplewhite-Gray miner's safety lamp.

8. The Saint pictured from the rear showing the all-round carving.

9. The Saint

10. A Gallé vase. This example from the Hermitage Museum in St Petersburg is similar in shape, colour and decoration to my little jumble sale find.Photograph © The State Hermitage Museum. Photo by Yuri Molodkovets.

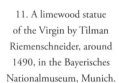

11. A limewood statue of the Virgin by Tilman Riemenschneider, around 1490, in the Bayerisches Nationalmuseum, Munich.

12. The Saint and the Mourning Virgin, photographed together on the occasion of their brief reunion in the church at Flavigny, February 2013.

13. A New York City policeman sifts through the junk in the Collyer mansion after the brothers' deaths in 1947

14. An imperforated Penny Red stamp posted on 16th September 1845.

15. Above: An 1859 cartoon by Honoré Daumier showing the auction crieur Père Jean in action.

16. Below: Another 1859 cartoon by Honoré Daumier showing an auction crieur working the crowd.

17. The Big Red Vase.

18. Not-The-Jug.

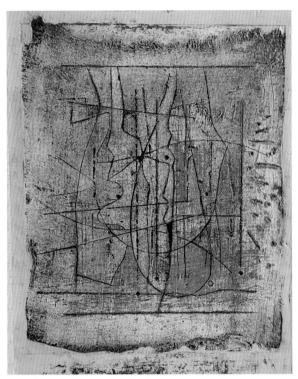

19. *Lambent*, oil on board, by R T H Smith, 1972.

20. A typical Wally Bird lidded stoneware jar by the Martin Brothers.

21. My split-pod-form stoneware vase by Alan Wallwork, found in an Edinburgh charity shop.

22. The Doucai Chicken Cup sold by Sotheby's in April 2014 for $36 million.

23. The diamond-encrusted golden egg made by in 1990 by the jeweller Paul Kutchinsky for the Argyle Diamond Mining Company of Australia.

24. The installation of eighty stoneware guinomis or sake cups which Frances and I bought each other for our 40th wedding anniversary.

25. The Satsuma Vase.

26. The Yaozhou Peony Bowl.

8

COLLECTOR OR DEALER?

What am I?

Before continuing the story of The Saint, I feel a need to deal with another matter which is troubling me and might perhaps be troubling my readers. In my Introduction I described myself as "a very ordinary and run-of-the-mill sort of amateur enthusiast and collector", and suggested, doubtless rather pompously, that "my story might help to explain more generally why so many of us love to spend so much time at auctions, or in charity shops or at car boot sales, up to our elbows in other people's cast-off stuff". But if I can't demonstrate that I am indeed very ordinary and run-of-the-mill, then I have been writing under false pretences and risk losing any credibility that I might have gained with readers.

Throughout this book, I've frequently referred to myself as a collector. I've focussed mainly on my collections of coins, books and studio pottery, but there are and have been others. So *collector* is the term which comes immediately to my own mind and tongue.

But the principal point of the book is to tell the story of two objects – The Saint and The Jug – which I *didn't* collect. I bought them and then very soon afterwards sold them. So what does that say about me? Perhaps readers will see not a collector at all, but a dealer or trader motivated by profit. If that is the impression that this book is giving, then there are three possibly significant implications. Firstly that being a collector and being a dealer are different sorts of occupations and can be perceived as being mutually exclusive. Secondly that dealing, with its associated profit motive, might be a lower-order occupation than collecting, inferior in both social and intellectual standing. And thirdly that I, your author, might be setting myself up as something that I'm not. That out of hypocrisy, dishonesty, self-delusion or self-aggrandisement, I'm an unreliable or dishonest narrator of my own story.

Another issue arises. If you don't think of me as an amateur collector, and I don't think of myself as a dealer, then perhaps some other descriptor applies. An alchemist? No, I think we've discounted that possibility already. So what else might I be? A hoarder? A connoisseur? A dilettante? Or, if my findings are that a combination of two or more of these terms applies, which ones and in what combination?

And yet another related issue, to be addressed in a later chapter. Once we have some findings, I want to look at the *dimensions* of my hobby/obsession/profession/trade of collecting/hoarding/dealing/whatever. Frances worries about the amount of time I spend buying, studying and selling objects, and the sheer number and physical volume of articles arriving in our house. I sometimes worry about it too. So I need to find out if I'm normal. Or am I obsessive? Is it getting worse? Does it adversely affect my functioning? Am I weird? Are others who are interested in art and antiques affected by the same worries? Will reading this book be time well spent for them? Or are the experiences and emotions related herein merely the ramblings of a one-off, an eccentric, whose behaviour and attitudes are too far beyond normality to exemplify anything at all?

At this early stage in my investigation, about the only thing that I can say for certain is that in reality I'm nothing like the self I see in a ridiculous but recurrent daydream. I picture myself as a gentleman collector, amateur, patron of the arts and connoisseur. Actually, I know someone like that, a friend of a friend. Hugh has a large estate in the Scottish Highlands and several lovely country houses, and he enhances and beautifies his land and property in a methodical, authentic, studious, tasteful, and excruciatingly expensive way. Inside: the best Georgian mahogany furniture, sporting pictures, porcelain and silver. Outside, several thousand acres of prime Scottish landscape including a Munro or two, and a picturesque herd of highland cattle. Sadly I don't possess the cash nor the single-mindedness nor the connections nor the taste to fulfil such a role.

Perhaps that sounds as if I have a great big British chip on my shoulder about social class. Maybe I have. But I don't delude myself that I'm like Hugh, and I don't truly want to be like him. However, I do persist in thinking of myself first and foremost as a collector, while at the same time with an awareness of a certain weight of evidence indicating otherwise. In the simplest terms, I submit in my defence (not that it's in any way necessary for me to defend myself), that although I have been selling my finds for profit from a very early age, I have always regarded such sales as incidental to my main interests. I've held to the view that most profits generated should be reinvested to improve, or at least to enlarge my collections. Until, that is, The Saint came along; he, as will become clear, was a very special case indeed.

I first became conscious of a perceived dichotomy between the collector and the dealer at a very early age. Let me commence my argument with a further short burst of autobiography.

The Sin of Ruby Buggins

It is 1956 and I am eight years old. I live with my parents and big brother Philip in a public house called the Harcourt Arms in a small street in Marylebone, Central London. An unremarkable boozer then, it remained so until well into the twenty-first century, when it underwent a makeover and, in 2016, re-emerged as a new upmarket "restaurant, bar and dining space", a "beautiful venue... dedicated to laid-back luxury and our signature stamp is our fun ambiance". Hmmm. It's a typical late-Georgian terraced house of five stories, configured during our time of un-made-over occupancy as: vaulted cellars and pub kitchen in the basement; saloon and public bars on the ground floor; a large function room on the first floor; family accommodation on the second floor with kitchen, unmodernised Victorian bathroom, living room and parents' bedroom. Then, on the top floor, four attic rooms, two available for Philip's use and two for mine. I have a large bedroom, with a utility-type bed and chest of drawers and not much else. And next door, my own private playroom, a small abandoned unheated derelict storeroom lit by a dormer window with a view over the back yard. In it I have installed two wooden orange boxes, one on end for my desk, one on its side for my chair. As far as I can recall, there is nothing else in the room.

There I sit between the end of school and bedtime (minus the evening meal time and Children's Hour on the TV), studying my coin collection. I don't remember how it started, or where my first coins came from, but by this early age I am already hooked on collecting. At some point around this time, my reputation as a budding numismatist having already spread throughout the family, I am given (I think by an aunt) a leather purse of old coins which had belonged to my late grandfather. It contains some interesting specimens, including a lovely 1679 silver crown. I think

I must have removed the crown from the purse and taken it next-door into my bedroom to continue admiring it after bedtime. This is fortunate because not very long afterwards the purse is stolen from my private sanctum with all its remaining contents and never seen again. The crown is the only survivor from the purse, and it remains with me throughout my life as one of the best pieces in my collection. I report the theft to my parents but as far as I know the offender, who might have been any one of the several members of the pub's bar, kitchen or cleaning staff, is never identified. My own suspicions fall on Ruby Buggins (yes, really), the charwoman.

The reason for relating this quaint, sub-Dickensian tale of central London life in the austere middle years of the twentieth century is not to seek the reader's pity on a small and rather lonely boy, and not even to heap accusation and contumely on the memory of Ruby Buggins. I'm telling it because I have a clear and very particular memory of my early days as a collector which is pertinent to my argument in this chapter. It's this: as I became more and more interested in collecting and studying old coins, and as my peer group of cousins and school friends came to hear about this preoccupation, their reaction was to attribute to me a uniform and unvarying motive. *He collects coins: therefore he loves money: therefore he must be rich.*

It was banter. I didn't take it too seriously. But I remember very precisely my feeling about how wrong they all were. It wasn't anything to do with money or value. Rather, my interest stemmed from the coins as artefacts and as symbols – small, almost perfect repositories of beauty and history. The elements that interested me were their aesthetics and their stories. Any market value that they might also possess was merely a pleasant and useful by-product.

The 1679 crown, then my most prized possession, and still to this day among my favourites, has a splendid profile bust of a bewigged, wreathed and toga-ed King Charles II on the obverse, and on the reverse four crowned armorial shields. Aged eight, I could have told you that the coin was made of silver and that its face value was five shillings sterling; that the King depicted on it had been restored to the throne in 1660 following the Civil War and subsequent demise of the Commonwealth; the meaning of the phrase *Decus et Tutamen* inscribed around the edge ("an ornament and a safeguard" – used for the very first time on the Charles II crown and still to be seen on the edge of English one pound coins today); and the heraldic significance of each shield (three lions couchant for the Kingdom of England, lion rampant for Scotland, harp for Ireland, and three fleurs-de-lys signifying the British sovereign's continuing claim to the throne of France).

The two sides of my silver Charles II crown coin of 1679, my most prized childhood possession

Yes, I know that's a bit geeky, but as well as telling you the bare facts about the coin, I could have told you (had I been sufficiently articulate) that the object produced in me a strong emotional response – to the beauty of its design; the colour, feel and heft of the old sterling silver; its historical significance as a reminder of a long-ago age when kings wore long curly wigs; its personal history bound up in the number of hands it had passed through over three hundred years and the transactions in which it had taken part; and the marvel of its survival in good condition to be finally passed on to me. What made it special was the whole package – the article itself and the story it embodied.

And so it has been with all of the other objects that I have accumulated over more than sixty years of collecting. The description of me aged eight is equally accurate for me aged sixty-eight and for all times in between. Antiques for me are things to provide interest and romance, and for delight and contemplation, and to adorn my surroundings.

Collector

Do these altruistic intentions mean, then, that I must be forgiven the sin of commercial leanings (if it's a sin and if forgiveness is required) and defined after all as a Collector? In recent years, academic researchers have studied collectors closely. The German psychoanalyst Peter Subkowski, in a detailed Freudian analysis, says that collecting:

> "1. refers to the seeking, selecting, gathering and storing of objects that have a subjective value for the collector, and in most cases includes some attempt at completion…;
> 2. in a focused way is systematic (in the sense of series formation) and, as a rule, limited to a definable and delineable area or topic, respectively, which can be outlined in, for instance, auction catalogues or through other collections;
> 3. is comprehensive and has depth, including an interest in secondary literature and background information;
> 4. tends to have an affective, passionate grasp on the person engaged in it;
> 5. is furthermore a relatively constant behaviour over time, and not just a short-term fad"[34].

Subkowski describes a number of different types of more or less nutty or obsessive collector, with whom I am pleased to find that I have virtually nothing in common.

But just to be sure, perhaps I need to look a bit more closely at each of his criteria to see how it might apply to me. I guess I only partially fit in with Criterion 1, because I don't feel any need whatsoever to complete any collection that I start. I tend to want to find a few good specimens of what catches my interest at any moment, and then move on to something else. As for Criterion 2, I don't think I'm systematic and have no real interest in series formation, unlike, say, a collector of Penny Red stamps, who might not be able to find rest until he (gender used advisedly) has added to his collection a specimen stamp from every printing plate used over several decades of production. I'll introduce the reader to Mr PennyRed in a later chapter of this book.

On Criterion 3, yes, I do have a keen interest in secondary literature and background information, as with my childish but enduring fascination with the 1679 silver Crown. But a collection which is comprehensive and has depth? No, I don't think so, because I'm always keen to move on. Criterion 4 – yes, my collecting does have a passionate grasp on me at any given moment. If you've read thus far in this book, you don't need any extra evidence in support of this one. And lastly, Criterion 5 – no, I wouldn't say my behaviour is constant over time. Over the years my interest in collecting as a pastime has waxed and waned frequently, and I've flitted from collection to collection with no regret and little nostalgia. Even now, I'm beginning to get an inkling that my preoccupation over the last few years with studio pottery could be finite in its extent. Even now, I find myself drifting in terms of my overriding interest inexorably towards early tin-glazed ceramics: towards Dutch and English Delftware, French Faience, and – ahh! – the wonder of Italian Maiolica!

With five boxes to tick, I find that I have one definite Yes, two half-Yes-half-No, and two definite Noes. Fortunately, I note that in amongst his descriptions of collector types, Subkowski has one who does not indulge in "collecting as a specific neurotic symptom" and thus is excused the attentions of the psychoanalyst. This "integrated, mature" type of collector

"is well aware that he will never achieve the perfect, complete collection... He nevertheless succeeds in restricting the time and money he spends on his passion in his daily routines, i.e. to integrate them into his lifestyle and relationships, and is also able to draw aesthetic enjoyment and personal pleasure from his own limited collection – which he knows cannot compete with big collections like those of museums – and after 'regression in the service of the ego' via his collection, to constructively attend to the demands of reality again. At this level of functioning, collecting is quantitatively speaking, as to the degree of fanaticism, limitable, with the collector being able to determine the dosage, and so does not necessarily have to end in addiction."

That feels like a comfortable fit. What's more, it makes my kind of collecting sound like normal behaviour. Not only can I avoid addiction, and not only am I "integrated" and "mature", but under this heading it looks as if I can provisionally, and subject to detailed statistical checking, which will be provided later, call myself a Collector, without embarrassment or shame or weirdness. But what else am I?

Hoarder

Frances tells me that in recent years, particularly since the episode of The Jug, and since my retirement from full-time work, she has become increasingly concerned about my tendency to bring steadily more and more stuff (mostly but by no means exclusively studio pottery) home from charity shops and auctions, filling and overfilling shelves, mantelpieces and other horizontal surfaces all over the house. If she's looked in the attic recently, she would be more worried still. Does that mean, then, that I should be defined as a hoarder?

The Diagnostic and Statistical Manual of Mental Disorders (DSM) is published by the American Psychiatric Association, and is often referred to as psychiatry's bible. It provides a common language and standard criteria for the classification of mental disorders. The 2013 edition of the DSM introduces a condition called Hoarding Disorder, newly separated out from its previous inclusion in the umbrella definition of Obsessive Compulsive Disorder.

It's worth quoting the description of Hoarding Disorder in full:

"Hoarding disorder is characterised by the persistent difficulty discarding or parting with possessions, regardless of the value others may attribute to these possessions. The behavior usually has harmful effects – emotional, physical, social, financial, and even legal – for the person suffering from the disorder and family members. For individuals who hoard, the quantity of their collected items sets them apart from people with normal collecting behaviors. They accumulate a large number of possessions that often fill up or clutter active living areas of the home or workplace to the extent that their intended use is no longer possible.

"Symptoms of the disorder cause clinically significant distress or impairment in social, occupational or other important areas of functioning including maintaining an environment for self and/ or others. While some people who hoard may not be particularly distressed by their behavior, their behavior can be distressing to other people, such as family members or landlords."[35]

A very interesting article by Ashley Nordsletten and David Mataix-Cols of King's College, London[36] provides a detailed comparison between a collector and a hoarder as defined in the DSM. The purpose of the comparison is to distinguish those collectors whose collecting behaviour is normal, from those hoarders whose hoarding behaviour is pathologised into a medical condition by virtue of its inclusion in the DSM.

Gratifyingly, it appears that my behaviour ticks scarcely any of the boxes that define hoarding. I don't have difficulty parting with possessions (viz. The Jug and The Saint); there are no discernible harmful effects (indeed there are beneficial financial effects); my home is not unduly cluttered (at least I don't think it is, although Frances sometimes thinks otherwise); my collecting or hoarding doesn't cause impairment or distress to myself or other people. So – clinically at least – I'm not a diagnosable as a hoarder.

Connoisseur

Connoisseurship is a subject that has been written about and discussed and analysed for centuries, and was fairly straightforwardly defined by Jonathan Richardson, portrait painter and art theorist, in his *Two Discourses*, first published in 1719. David Freedberg, Pierre Matisse Professor of the History of Art at Columbia University, summarises Richardson's position thus:

"For Richardson, as, probably, for most practitioners, connoisseurship had three basic aims: firstly, the making of judgments of quality ('the Goodness of a Picture' as Richardson put it), secondly the assignment of hands [i.e. attributing it to a specific artist], and thirdly the distinguishing of originals from copies (including of course, the identification of forgeries). In the second of the *Two Discourses* Richardson sets out why connoisseurship was a suitable task for a gentleman."[37]

Richardson considered that the science of connoisseurship was an entirely mechanistic process, insisting that it is a science only and does not rely on any inborn talent or special aptitude (which might be described as The Eye), and that "one Man may be as Good a Judge as Another if he applies himself to it"[38]. Dr Carol Gibson-Wood of the University of Victoria, British Columbia comments that "this is not to say that Richardson demanded no special qualities whatsoever of the would-be connoisseur. But these qualities... all relate to rationality, not innate taste."[39]

Later writers and critics, while sticking broadly with Richardson's three basic aims, thought that the key to being a connoisseur was the cultivation and refinement of taste, and that thus connoisseurship could only be attained by a particularly superior sort of person. This argument either caused or reflected the emergence in the art and antiques world in the nineteenth century of an exquisite elite group of art critics, curators, gallerists and dealers. They still exist today, and, although often heavily criticised, they remain dominant in matters of attribution, authenticity and judgment of quality, and are inextricably associated with value of art objects and the workings of the market.

As I have tried to convey in earlier chapters of this book, these high art issues are a world away from the lower end of the market where I and other small-time collectors tend to congregate. The Oxford English Dictionary defines a connoisseur as "a person well acquainted with one of the fine arts, and competent to pass a judgement in relation thereto; a critical judge of art or of matters of taste". At best I consider myself to be only superficially knowledgeable about any branch of fine art, and only competent to pass judgment for myself but not to advise others. As for being a critical judge of art or taste, I'm firmly of the school of thought that taste is a matter of personal opinion, and I wouldn't presume to impose my taste on anyone else.

Clearly, then, I'm no connoisseur.

Dilettante

Here's how the Oxford English Dictionary defines the noun dilettante:

"A lover of the fine arts; originally, one who cultivates them for the love of them rather than professionally, and so = amateur n. as opposed to professional; but in later use generally applied more or less depreciatively to one who interests himself in an art or science merely as a pastime and without serious aim or study ('a mere dilettante')."

Now I come to think about it, that sounds rather like me: an amateur or enthusiast or dabbler, with some superficial knowledge, a bit of an Eye, a smattering of appropriate terminology, a little spare cash at my disposal, some leisure to devote to the pastime, but with a short attention span and insufficient application or dedication to aspire to or attain any credible level of expertise or connoisseurship.

But naturally, since the dictionary definition goes on to say that the term has latterly been used pejoratively – who wants to be a *mere* anything? – I would like to find a way to avoid being categorised as a dilettante. Fortunately a handy disclaimer is available.

The term dilettante, while describing me fairly accurately in the above respects, embraces other connotations which aren't like me at all. The word came into common speech to describe members of the real-life Society of Dilettanti and their fellows. In order to join in this distinguished and elite group, there were essential qualifications which the present author does not possess: you must be *young, rich* and *posh*.

The Society was founded in 1734 as a dining club for young gentlemen who had returned from the Grand Tour of Europe, the purpose of which was "to finish their education, collect antiquities of varying degrees of interest and authenticity and sow some wild oats at a convenient distance from home"[40].

The Dilettanti were initially led by the dashingly-named and dashingly-behaved Sir Francis Dashwood, who later found fame as the high priest and principal blasphemer in the celebrated drunken orgies of the Hell-Fire Club, conducted at Medmenham Abbey beside the River Thames. Joining Dashwood among the Dilettanti were several dukes and any number of aristocrats and grandees, but not Horace Walpole, who described it as "a club, for which the nominal qualification is having been in Italy, and the real one, being drunk".

Some years later the Society attained respectability, with an aim to "correct and purify the public taste of the country" and to raise funds to back worthy highbrow artistic causes such as the establishment of the Royal Academy. With a maximum of 60 elected members including Sir Joshua Reynolds the painter, Sir Joseph Banks the naturalist and David Garrick the actor, the Society became (and remains to this day) strictly the hyper-exclusive reserve of the wealthy and the elite of the art world.

Me? A dilettante? I think not.

Dealer

In recent years, since retirement, with a bit more time on my hands, I have taken to selling much more than I have done in the past. It's an enjoyable and challenging pursuit and incidentally generates cash to spend on new items. I tried at first (honestly, I did) to pursue a strict one-in-one-out policy, but sadly this has broken down disastrously in recent months. This breakdown is not due to an incipient descent into hoarding disorder, but because I decided to divert my energies away from selling into writing this book. For the time being, I simply don't have time to sell. (*"But you seem to find time to keep buying"*, objects Frances. *"Ah yes, but that's different"*, I respond, definitively).

I quite like selling. Most of the items that I offer for sale are of low value and suitable for online sale by auction to other collectors and enthusiasts. So most of the selling is done using eBay. It's a time-consuming occupation, requiring the taking and uploading of photographs, researching the item and writing an accurate description, and, after the sale, packing and despatch. Initially the objective was to reduce the number of long-held bits and pieces in which my interest had waned somewhat. But after the first few months, I found myself occasionally spotting an object in an auction or charity shop which I thought might sell for a modest profit. I would therefore sometimes buy specifically for re-sale. For a couple of years (post-Jug and pre-Saint) this hobby occupied a few hours per week of my time, and produced a sufficient net financial surplus to enable me to buy a few new things for my own collections. It also gave me two other opportunities: firstly to buy a small number of slightly higher-value objects for re-sale in upmarket antique auction houses; and secondly to buy examples of various types of object with which I was completely unfamiliar, so that I could research them and learn from them prior to re-sale.

It's a hobby; I sell for enjoyment, because I like the process and as a way to handle and to learn about different types of object without having to keep them. Some of my sales are of items that have been in my possession for decades. Others are bought for research and rapidly either re-sold or given back to charity shops if I think they won't sell profitably. Quite often I decide not to sell or to give an item away, but to retain it as an addition to my collections. Overall, I've been making a small net profit of one or two thousand pounds per year which is all re-invested in more objects of interest.

Surely that harmless and peripheral pastime doesn't make me a dealer? Oh, but yes, indeed it does, according to the rules of Her Majesty's Revenue and Customs (HMRC). They have a list of nine criteria which are known as "the Badges of Trade". Here they all are for the reader's interest.[42]

1. **Profit-seeking motive:** If you have an intention to make a profit, this is an indicator that you are trading, but by itself is not conclusive.
2. **The number of transactions:** Systematic and repeated transactions will support the definition of trading.
3. **The nature of the asset:** If you are selling something that can only give enjoyment by being turned into a profit, this is trading. But if it can give 'pride of possession' and personal enjoyment, like a picture or an antique, this is an argument against definition as trading.
4. **Existence of similar trading transactions or interests:** If what you're selling is related to an existing trade that you are already carrying on, then it will count as part of that trading.
5. **Changes to the asset:** If you repaired, modified or improved the item to make it more easily saleable or saleable at a greater profit, then this counts as trading.
6. **The way the sale was carried out:** Are you selling in a way that is typical of other traders (= trading), or are you selling for another reason, e.g. to raise cash for an emergency (= not trading)?
7. **The source of finance:** Did you borrow money to buy what you are selling? Can you only pay the money back by selling it? That's trading.
8. **Interval of time between purchase and sale:** If you buy items with the

intention to sell them quickly, that's normally a sign of trading. If an asset is kept long-term, then it is much less likely to be trading.

9. **Method of acquisition** An asset acquired by inheritance, or as a gift, is less likely to be counted as trading when it is sold.

HMRC look at each case on its merits, and you don't have to fit into all nine categories to be classed as a trader. In my own case, despite the fact that I think of myself as a collector who sometimes sells one or two bits and pieces, the Tax people would almost certainly think differently. If I asked them, there's no real doubt that they would rule that I wear at least five of the badges (numbers 1, 2, 6, 8 and 9), and they would count me as a trader or dealer.

In actual fact, I haven't asked them. I have owned up. A couple of years ago I let HMRC know on my self-assessment tax return that I am a self-employed sole trader in antiques; so I have to declare my income from sales and pay tax on the profits, and had to pay National Insurance Contributions (up until my 65th birthday). This made very little difference to me when my profit was just a grand or two per year, but a principal purpose of this book is to tell the story of The Jug and The Saint, and these objects both resulted in significant net surpluses which must be accounted for both to HMRC and to you, the reader.

The Jug is easily dealt with. In 2007, when I bought and sold it, I was still employed full-time as a business consultant with my own firm. I hadn't sold an antique for a few years and had no intention of taking up the trade of antique dealer. My accountant advised that The Jug should be counted as a personal possession or chattel, and the profits dealt with under the Capital Gains Tax rules rather than Income Tax or (as it would have been if The Jug had been sold through my limited company) Corporation Tax.

In the event, I didn't have to pay a penny of tax (except of course VAT on the auctioneer's seller's commission). A lucky escape? Not really. In 2007, thanks partly to the oncoming economic recession and partly to my own ineptitude, my company was suffering serious financial reversals. I was propping it up with injections of capital from personal savings in order to keep staff employed just in case of a recovery, which didn't come. So I had a stonking loss to report to HMRC on the debit side of my tax return, which could be partially offset with the profit from the sale of The Jug.

As for the taxation of the profit derived from the sale of The Saint, that is another story, which will be recounted in Chapter 15.

The Story so Far ...

To sum up my argument so far, I have established that I am a collector (of the mature, integrated variety) and a dealer. But I'm not a hoarder or a connoisseur or a dilettante. Likewise, I imagine, are many of my fellow denizens of Johnson & Andrews saleroom on a Saturday morning, and habitués of other salerooms all over the country. Many of us buy mainly to collect but do a little selling on the side, using the money to improve our collections. Many others of us buy mainly to sell, but are knowledgeable and enthusiastic about antiques as objects and derive huge enjoyment from handling and possessing them, however fleetingly.

So most of us are collectors and dealers at the same time and see no incompatibility between the two occupations. Moreover, pursuing either or both occupations, provided that it coincides with the conduct of a more or less functional life within society, seems to fall outside the range of psychopathological illness.

The next stage of my investigation is to find out if my own collecting and dealing behaviour is indeed within a range which people generally would find acceptable, and which doctors would regard as non-clinical. Or to put it at its most simple: am I normal? There will be an attempt to answer this question in the chapter after next. But for now, I have ignored the fate of The Saint for too long, and must return to his story.

9

CONSIGNING THE SAINT, 2012–2013

A Chronicle of Anxiety

I had bought a statue. I knew from my own internet research and from my contact with Dr Decker in Frankfurt that it was perhaps an image of Saint John at Calvary, made in Burgundy, carved in walnut wood, fifteenth century. I knew that it was achingly beautiful. But I didn't know much else, and I was full of doubts and questions. How can something like this appear at Johnson & Andrews? If it's six hundred years old, how can it be in such exceptional, glowing condition? Is it genuine? Could it be a later copy? Is there anything dodgy about it or its provenance?

The reader already knows the answers to these questions, which, incidentally, didn't include "How much is it worth?", because I was far too interested in learning about the statue than in consideration of its value. After having The Saint in my house for more than a month, I didn't have firm answers about anything, and I still didn't know how I was going to get them. Day 33, 28th November 2012, was the date when everything changed, and events started moving forward in a totally unexpected and alarming fashion. I had emailed Laurence Fligny, an Haute Époque expert in Paris on the previous day. On Day 33 I received a slightly breathless email from her. She had been trying to phone me because *"Votre sculpture de saint Jean est très intéressante"*.

Chapter 7 ended with me in a car park on an industrial estate in Motherwell, Lanarkshire on Day 87, 21st January 2013. I was returning to my car after dropping off The Saint at the Scottish depôt of Constantine, the fine art removers, who were to transport him to Paris for appraisal. Now I need to relate in some detail the events of the eight weeks between my first contact with Laurence and the start of the statue's journey back to his native France after a sojourn in Scotland of many decades.

Day 34 (29th November 2012). A very short telephone conversation with Laurence, whose English is as poor as my French, followed by a slightly longer session with Benoît Bertrand, her assistant, marginally more fluent. I gather that they are excited by my photos of The Saint, they think he might relate in some way to the famous Burgundian sculptor Claus de Werve, but they would need to see him before passing judgment, and could I please send him to them for appraisal? Would I like to engage them to sell the sculpture through their Paris auction house? Could they please send me some catalogues of their recent sales so that I could see the kind of stuff that they advise on? Oh yes, and without seeing him they would suggest an auction value of at least €30,000. Huh? *Pardon?* Yes, that's right. *Au revoir.*

I put down the phone a little confused and more than a little stunned. It's a Thursday morning. Off I go to the Johnson & Andrews weekly outdoor junk and house clearance sale, where I'll rarely bid more than five or ten pounds for an object. I can't concentrate. I don't buy anything.

Days 34–37 (29th November–2nd December). A period of reflection and thought, alternating with nervous and frenetic trawling of the internet, punctuated by the arrival through the post of copies of glossy catalogues from Laurence's two most recent sales. For decision: could my statue be the real thing? Is Laurence the most appropriate person to advise me? If so, how do I get The Saint to her in Paris safely, and, if necessary, get him back? Am I allowed to send him overseas? How does the French auction system work anyway, since it seems immensely more complex than the UK system? And as for the suggested value – are they having a laugh?

So: what is it that I have bought? I find that I'm beginning to get my Eye in. Just a matter of days ago I was immersing myself in everything pertaining to the sixteenth-century limewood sculptures of Southern Germany. But now that I have studied online images of the alabaster Mourners on the tombs of Dukes of Burgundy in Dijon, I know how naïve and ignorant I have been even to imagine that the statue could be anything other than Burgundian.

I note from one of Laurence's catalogues that in January 2011 she handled the sale of a heavily bearded Apostle carved from walnut around 1420 to 1430, which she had identified as being from a grand altarpiece believed to have stood in the Cistercian Abbey at Theuley in Haute-Saône. This had been dismantled and broken up, presumably around the time of the French Revolution. Seventeen other statues from the same altarpiece had been identified over the past hundred years or so, and every so often a new one emerged into the marketplace.

The walnut wood sculpture of an Apostle from the Theuley altarpiece, sold by Piasa in January 2011

Laurence's Apostle at 49.5 cms was much smaller in height than The Saint, and I don't think him nearly as beautiful. In fact he looks very much like my late Uncle Jack, whom many would have called handsome, but none, I think, beautiful. But the Apostle had the advantage that he had preserved through six hundred years his decoration of polychrome enamels and gold leaf, whereas my statue has been stripped down to bare wood and wax-polished to a glowing but inauthentic patina. In her catalogue notes, Laurence compared the carving of the Apostle to that of the Mourners, which were known to be by Claus de Werve, and concluded that although he was clearly from the same period and in the same style, it would be stylistically risky to attribute him to the chisel of Claus. Nonetheless, the statue went on to sell at the 2011 auction for a spectacular price. Could it be that perhaps my Saint is the nineteenth Theuley statue?

Next question: who am I going to be dealing with? One piece of real progress during these nervous days is that I become convinced from my reading of Laurence's auction catalogues, together with information about her which I find online, that she is someone with an appropriate level of expertise to authenticate and advise on my statue. Her website biography is impressive, and she comes across as full of integrity and fiercely independent, with a quiver-full of successful attributions and publications under her belt. Her distinctions include appointments to two French national honours: *Chevalier dans l'Ordre National du Mérite* and *Chevalier dans l'Ordre des Arts et Lettres*. She's a big cheese, a *grand fromage*.

And she is also by far the most interested and enthusiastic expert that I have contacted. I decide provisionally that I'm going to stick with her. But that of course means that I have to get the statue to her in Paris and make sure that everything to do with the export, authentication and either sale or return of the statue is safe, secure, legal and affordable. I realise that my immediate future relationship with The Saint has potential to become exceedingly complex. I need to do some fast learning.

For starters, if Laurence is indeed independent, then how does she relate to an auctioneer? I discover that the French auction industry is Byzantine in its complexity, hedged about by legislation, regulation and bureaucracy. I set myself the task of getting to understand how it works. By the end of Day 37 I could easily write a whole chapter on this topic (which, much later, is precisely what I do: see Chapter 11). However, in order to preserve such scant narrative flow as this book might possess, I'll only provide a short summary at this stage.

It appears that unlike UK auctioneers, firms in France are required to procure expert advice from approved external practitioners. Laurence Fligny is one of these independent self-employed consultants, specialising in haute époque antiques. As such, she has agency relationships as an expert adviser with a number of auction houses. She is engaged by them to liaise with the seller of an object; to appraise, authenticate and attribute it and provide an estimated sale value; to prepare the catalogue entry; to assist with marketing and publicity; and finally to be in attendance at the auction itself to present the object to the bidding audience.

The main auction house for which Laurence acts as agent is called Piasa. Piasa is the eighth biggest auction house operating in France. The firm is privately owned by a group of connoisseur/collector/investors which reads like a who's who of France's financial and commercial great and good. Its founders include Laurent Fabius, the current Foreign Minister and a former Prime Minister of France. So from my point of view as a punter, they are kosher.

Piasa is part of a consortium of auction houses called Drouot, which provides accommodation, marketing, accounting and support services for its member firms*. Drouot is a long-established French institution, having had a virtual stranglehold on the Paris auction market until fairly recent years when the global brands Sotheby's and Christie's were permitted to open their own salerooms and rapidly became the market leaders. I'll have much more to say about Drouot later on.

Looming above the entire French auction structure is the *Conseil des Ventes Volontaires de Meubles aux Enchères Publiques*, a government regulatory authority which has extensive powers to whip the industry into order. Auctions of fine art, antiques, wines, racehorses, classic cars and other categories of luxury goods produce almost infinite temptation and opportunity for corruption, fraud, theft and assorted crimes. After a raft of public scandals, the powers of the *Conseil des Ventes* were strengthened in 2011.

Days 38–43 (3rd–8th December). Now that I've started to get my head around the French system of auctions, it's necessary to find out if I'm allowed to send The Saint to Paris. I've heard of things called Export Licences which can prevent valuable works of art from being taken out of the UK. More investigations required. I discover from the Arts Council England website that

---

*   Since 2013 Piasa have held their auction sales not at the Hôtel Drouot but at their own salerooms in rue du faubourg Saint-Honoré

"Certain cultural objects more than 50 years of age and valued above specified financial thresholds will require an individual licence for export out of the United Kingdom whether on a permanent or temporary basis". Here's another official minefield to be negotiated. I get an approximation of an answer from a splendid forty-page manual of procedures, which becomes slightly less baffling after only the third or fourth reading[43]. It seems that there is a generic open licence which bestows automatic permission for any "cultural object" to be sent overseas *unless* it fits into a set of very specific categories. Actually, two sets of categories, because the rules for exporting between one European Union country and another are different from the rules for exporting to a country outside the EU. It is only necessary to apply for an individual export licence in respect of the object if it is valued at or above a specified financial threshold.

I look at the thresholds. There are two tables, one for exports within the EU and one for exports outside. Each table has a number of different categories of object, each category with a different value above which an application for an individual licence is required. The categories are almost entirely dissimilar between the two tables. My statue most probably falls into a very specific section under the rules for export outside the EU, described as: "Elements forming an integral part of artistic, historical or religious monuments which have been dismembered, of an age exceeding 100 years". For these items, the financial threshold is zero. In other words, if you want to send *any* such object outside the EU, you must apply first for an individual export licence. But for export from one EU country to another, this category doesn't exist, and The Saint seems to fall into the general category of "Any item over 50 years of age", for which the threshold is £65,000 before you need an individual export licence.

And then, supposing that it's determined that I do indeed need to apply for an individual licence for my Saint, how is the decision made to grant the licence and who makes it? Answer: there's an Arts Council committee whose job is to make the decision, using judgment and testimony from expert witnesses. Their decision is based on whether the object satisfies any of the three "Waverley Criteria", which are as follows:

- is it so closely connected with our history and national life that its departure would be a misfortune?
- is it of outstanding aesthetic importance?
- is it of outstanding significance for the study of some particular branch of art, learning or history?

If The Saint meets one or more of the Waverley Criteria, I won't get an export licence for him. Hmmm... Well, it's easy to see that he's almost entirely unconnected with our history and national life, so there's no way that he'll meet the first criterion. But in my humble opinion, assuming that he turns out to be the real McCoy, he is of outstanding aesthetic importance. And since I can't find a record of another example of Burgundian statuary of anything like equal quality in any UK public collection, it might be arguable that The Saint is outstandingly important to retain here for study.

So it seems to me that there's a chance that if I am required to make application for an export licence, it won't be granted. Tricky. And worrying.

But what if (as it appears) no-one within the UK has sufficient expert knowledge about Burgundian sculpture to judge if my statue is authentic, and genuinely more than fifty or one hundred years old, or to provide an authoritative attribution or a reliable valuation? What if the object must of necessity be exported before its authenticity can be established or its value is known? And what if the object is first exported within the EU (threshold £65k) and is then, still in my ownership, sold on to a buyer in an overseas country (threshold £zero)?

I'm confused. I phone the Arts Council and they are confused too. Too many hypotheticals for them to give an answer on the spot. Before they can give a ruling I would need to submit a formal application for a licence. This needs to include an appraisal and valuation. But of course I can't provide this without sending the statue to be examined by an expert in France. Which I might not be allowed to do because I haven't got an export licence. It must be valued before it leaves the country, but it can't be valued unless it leaves the country. A perfect Catch-22. I make a note to investigate further.

Next I start worrying about how I am going to get the thing to Paris. It seems at first that the best option is to take him. I get a large suitcase out of the attic to see if he'll fit in it. It's a bit of a squeeze, but he does. But what do I say if the suitcase is x-rayed at the security barrier? How do I explain a suitcase with a mediaeval statue in it? Do I need some sort of export paperwork? What if Customs want to cut him open to see if drugs are stored inside? What if he's subjected to a controlled explosion?

At this point I'm nervous about The Saint's potential value, confused about export licensing, panicky about transportation, and, in the background, as related in Chapter 2, still apprehensive about whether I have good title to ownership of him, or whether he might be stolen or looted property. Whoever said that buying and selling antiques is a piece of cake?

Day 44 (9th December). I email Laurence, apologising for not being in contact sooner and thanking her for sending the auction catalogues. I mention my discoveries about the Theuley altarpiece and ask if she thinks The Saint comes from there. I indicate that it is highly likely that I will select her to appraise and possibly to sell the statue, and mention that issues about the export licence and the transportation to Paris are causing me perplexity and might take some time to resolve.

Day 52 (17th December). A reply from Laurence:

"Dear Roger,
Your Saint John is indeed similar to the statuary of the altar piece of Theuley but it does not however belong to this group of sculptures. Personally, I have another idea which could be interesting but I need to have the statue for a few days in order to confirm this theory.

British law requires an exit permit for works whose value is equal to over £65,000. We have estimated the work at €30,000 to €50,000 [Huh? *Pardon?*]. It is therefore possible for you to send your Saint John without breaking British law so that we can carry out the necessary research and expertise which is only possible with the object in our view.

We therefore suggest, in order to avoid all risk, that you contact a specialised transporter who will confirm the formalities to be carried out or that he can carry out himself. In this respect the auction house Piasa is extremely happy with the service provided by [name and address supplied].

This person will provide you with all the information necessary for the statue to arrive legally on French territory. You could incur serious risks by bringing the object into France yourself if the statue were to go through French customs again. On the other hand, with the international road transport contract all re-exportation procedures will be legal."

I understand from this expert advice that the Export Licence issue can be safely set to one side. That's one worry out of the way (although, as will be seen, it recurs).

I also take the hint that if I try to take The Saint into France and it turns out not be problematic, it could yet be difficult for me to bring him home again if, after Laurence's appraisal, I decide not to sell him. The statue will need to be professionally transported and documented. The suitcase goes back into the attic.

Day 53 (18th December). I email the firm of specialist removal contractors recommended by Laurence. They are based in Central London and don't have any arrangements to collect goods from outside the metropolis. It is clear from my brief correspondence with them that whereas they will cheerfully and efficiently take a delicate and priceless work of art from London to, say, New York or Hong Kong, the notion of first collecting it from anywhere as remote and primitive as the capital city of Scotland is utterly beyond their comprehension or competence. Either I'll have to get the suitcase back out of the attic and take The Saint to them in London by train, or I'll just have to find a specialist remover who operates from Scotland. Surprisingly the London firm know of another firm, Constantine, who have a Scottish depot. I phone Constantine and speak to a very helpful lady called Cathie. They can pack the statue and deliver him to Laurence in their next consignment to Paris in a secure and high-tech air-conditioned temperature-controlled lorry, complete with all the necessary export documentation, and if required they can bring him back again. There are only two problems. First, they have absolutely no idea when their next Paris run is likely to take place; it might be weeks or months away. Second, the quoted price of £625 is over 50% more than I paid for the statue in the auction, and that's only for one-way travel.

Here's another headache to add to my growing tally of anxieties: financial risk. When I paid £1,000 for The Jug, I was pretty confident that if I decided to sell it I could get my money back. When I paid £400 for The Saint, I didn't know anything of the sort, but it was a much smaller amount and I couldn't care less if there was no profit to be made because I'd happily and proudly keep him if he turned out to be valueless. But paying out a large extra sum to get him to the expert for appraisal, a sum which would double in the event that he was worthless and had to be returned to me – well, that was a different matter altogether. An easy risk to take if The Saint is judged to be genuine, but a horrendous financial double whammy if otherwise. To justify the risk, I need to place a great deal of faith in Laurence's provisional opinion of The Saint, an assessment she has formed solely from my photographs.

I agonise. Then I think – what the hell, I must find out, Laurence is the only person who can tell me, I'll take the risk, I'll go for it. If it's nearly two grand down the swanny, well, I'll just have to put it down to experience and sell more stuff to make up for the loss. I decide against personally taking the statue to London. Instead I'll entrust him to Constantine and wait patiently until their next Paris shipment. Two factors help in my final choice of remover: I read on the Constantine website that they move the Queen's artworks around the world when lent for exhibitions; if they are good enough for her, they should be good enough for me. And I learn from Frances that she knows and approves of them: she has used Constantine at Edinburgh University Library to move priceless rare books from place to place.

Day 54 (19th December). I email Laurence to let her know about my proposed arrangements with Constantine. Does she wish the statue to be sent to her home address or to the auctioneer? What will be her arrangements for security while the statue is with her for appraisal? What are the auction house's small-print terms and conditions for sellers? If I consign The Saint for sale, what commission and charges are payable? Is there a date yet for the next Haute Époque sale?

Day 55 (20th December). A prompt and full reply from Laurence, enclosing the Piasa auction house's terms and conditions ("The small print should not, I hope, give you any sleepless nights!"). The statue is to be delivered to Laurence's address accompanied by an international waybill provided by the transporter. It will be put in a safe at Piasa's offices and insured for €30,000 until the sale. Piasa offer a reasonable-sounding all-in seller's commission fee of 15% of the hammer price, including cataloguing, photography, Laurence's fees and TTC (*Toutes Taxes Comprises*).

"There is no more to pay other than this cost. If the object is not sold (there is little risk!) there will be nothing to pay as there will be no sales fees.

The next Haute Époque sale will be fixed for end May / beginning June and it would be preferable for the statue to arrive in Paris before the end of January to have time to carry out an advertising campaign early enough for the promotion of the object to be done correctly.

I am very happy to be able to sell your sculpture and for the confidence you show in my work."

Days 59–61 (24th–26th December). The Saint, wreathed with a halo of tinsel, presides over our downstairs hall during the festive period. Our household for the holiday comprises a lapsed Episcopalian, a lapsed Jew, two non-religious daughters, their husbands, and three unbaptised grandchildren. Nonetheless we celebrate as always a secular but otherwise thoroughly traditional Christmas, the mystical presence of a holy and ancient icon of the Catholic church notwithstanding. On Christmas Eve we hold our annual get-together for Frances's family, some twenty-seven visitors in all. Any slight worries about offending our devout Baptist sister-in-law are unfounded. Passing through the crush in the hall between the front door and the kitchen, she doesn't notice The Saint, being fully intent on ensuring the intact survival of the giant banoffee pie which she has brought to contribute to the feast.

Day 72 (6th January 2013). I send an email update to Laurence confirming that I intend to consign The Saint to her for appraisal and sale through Piasa. I'm still having trouble with transportation, not having heard back from Cathie at Constantine whether or when they will have a Paris-bound load. Laurence replies encouragingly.

Day 82 (16th January). Cathie finally gets back to me and I confirm to Laurence that the statue will be on his way to her the week after next.

Day 87 (21st January). I drop The Saint off at Constantine's depot. On my return to the car, I discover the excited email from Christie's who are keen to sell him. It's too late, but Christie's enthusiastic if tardy response spawns a new anxiety – have I just gone to a huge amount of bother by arranging to send the statue to France when maybe Christie's could have come to the same result while generating a mere fraction of the angst? No, I remain happy with my selection of Laurence and Piasa. As it turns out later, I have good reason to be content.

The Revelation of Saint John

The Saint somewhat miraculously arrives in Paris by the date requested. On 30th January I receive an email from Benoît on behalf of Laurence. Presumably in order to save time they haven't used the services of their usual fairly accurate translator. Benoît's attempt to write in English is about as good as (ok, better than) any attempt that I might make to write in French. I quote it here in full for its charm, without any changes, corrections or editing:

"Dear Roger,
Your statue of Saint John is arrived on this morning and all is ok. It's very beautiful sculpture, I like it very mutch. I could become my researched and found more informations around the circle of Bourgogne's sculptors. I think we could have a good surprise in sale if that I fell is confirmed

You are going to received the paper about the depot and befor the sale, Piasa will send a contract of sale with the conditions of 15% TTC of charges (including assurance, storage, photography)

Thanks for your trust and see you for the result of my researches. (and sorry of my english…)

Best regards.
Benoît BERTRAND pour Laurence FLIGNY"

I reply with thanks. Then on 8th February, this from Laurence:

"My initial investigations with The Saint John statue have confirmed my hypothesis and I know with certainty which church this beautiful sculpture belonged to. This is very important as we will now be able to start an advertising campaign aimed at arousing the interest of French and foreign museums in this major discovery; they can thus prepare the purchase dossier.

In order to start this process, continue my research and organise advertising, all of which involves significant costs, I will need to have your agreement to sell the statue… A contract is on its way to you by post, I would be most grateful if you could return it to me duly signed as soon as possible, please."

Clearly Laurence is being coy about the precise nature of her discoveries about The Saint until she has a signed contract in her hands with my irrevocable commitment appointing her and Piasa to sell the object on my behalf. I don't blame her, and would behave in precisely the same way if I were in her position. She's obviously an astute business-woman as well as a world-class expert on the Haute Époque. A winning combination as far as I'm concerned.

The Piasa contract duly arrives. From what I can understand of it, it seems straightforward, and it's clearly a standard-issue take-it-or-leave-it kind of contract which wouldn't be amenable to change even if I were to object to any of its terms. Anyhow, I'm so excited that I don't pay much attention to the wording. I sign it and send it back by return. Frances and I are getting highly agitated and emotional. The tension mounts. 20th February – the Revelation of Saint John:

"Dear Roger,
Thank you for the signed contract that you returned to me.

I have been able to make some progress with my research of your sculpture. I have made an interesting discovery about The Saint John, I have found its 'twin' that is to say, the Vierge de Calvaire which was on the other side of the cross in the original arrangement. It is a Virgin that is still kept in the church of Saint-Genest de Flavigny-sur-Ozerain (Côte d'or).

A week ago, despite the bad weather I took The Saint John to Flavigny to compare it with the Vierge de Calvaire and confirm my theory. As you will see from the attached photos, I was not wrong. Despite the fact that the Virgin has kept its original colouring whereas the colours of your Saint John have been stripped off, the style and craftsmanship are identical. The sizes of the sculptures correspond precisely and the profile of the terraces [i.e. the chamfered bases of the statues] is identical which indicates they are by the same hand.

It remains for me to place it within the work of Claus de Werve or his workshop. It is a major discovery which is creating much excitement in French museums! In a few weeks I will send out a press release informing the market of the upcoming sale of this sculpture which will be of interest for both French and foreign museums and certain major collectors. I thus hope it results in a nice surprise for you!

In order to have as much information as possible, I would ask you to send me everything you know about this Saint John, date and place where you bought it, as well as where it came from prior to that sale (region and name of the previous owner). This would help me to understand and track its history."

Although you, readers, have known about the Virgin of Flavigny since near the beginning of this book, this was the first that Frances and I knew of

152

the Flavigny connection. Seeing Laurence's photo of the brief reunion of Saint John and The Virgin was well-nigh overwhelming **(See Illustrations, *Picture 12*)**. In comparison with the wonder and excitement of learning about Laurence's incredible discovery, any consideration of the monetary value of my statue was insignificant. In Chapter 12 I'll be saying a lot about what it means to be a collector and what it means to be a dealer, and why I decided to sell The Saint and The Jug – the two most remarkable objects I have ever owned. But for now, please believe me when I say that reading Laurence's email and seeing her pictures gave me the most exciting moment and the most intense Buzz of my long collecting (and dealing) career. Yes, it was even better than sitting wide-eyed and slack-jawed in the Paris saleroom a few months later watching the value of bids for The Saint steadily increase until the hammer finally fell.

Preparing for the sale

Between February and the date of the sale, which had been set for Friday 7th June 2013, I didn't hear very much from Laurence. She runs two big auctions per year at the Piasa auction house, and understandably she was too busy cataloguing and dealing with other clients to spend much time reporting progress back to me. I had signed the contract consigning The Saint for sale, and now it was her job to maximise the hammer price.

As related in Chapter 2, I found out from Malcolm Andrews of Johnson & Andrews auctioneers about the provenance of my statue. I emailed Laurence in early March to tell her that it had been in the private ownership of a descendant of the family of MacGregor's, an old-established Edinburgh furniture manufacturer, church furnisher and antique dealer, which had ceased trading in 2004. This information, which should satisfy bidders that the provenance was good and that The Saint wasn't stolen or looted property, found its way in simplified and very slightly garbled form into the auction catalogue.

Then in April, not having heard anything further, I did some internet searching to see if any of the promised pre-publicity for the sale had yet appeared. And it had. In a catalogue for a forthcoming sale, Piasa published a full-page announcement of their June 2013 haute époque auction, featuring a lovely big photo of my statue, estimated price €70,000 – €100,000 (Huh? *Pardon?*).

Around 16th April Piasa issued a short press release which was picked up and published by the online magazine *Connaissance des Arts*, headed *"Un chef d'œuvre de la sculpture bourguignonne vendu par Piasa"*. It was quickly reprinted in a number of other publications and several blogs. It gave a brief description of The Saint, which came from a *"collection privée d'Edinbourg (Écosse)"*. A few comments began to appear on Twitter and Facebook hoping that the statue would return to France, or better still, that it could be permanently reunited with the Virgin of Flavigny. Drouot, the consortium which provides accommodation and marketing for Piasa and many other auction houses, joined in the publicity efforts. They published articles in their weekly French-language magazine and a full-page feature in their monthly English language publication *La Gazette Drouot International* for May 2013:

> "Here is a discovery that ought to delight mediaevalists. The Virgin of Flavigny-sur-Ozerain (France), forsaken for many a year, has found her St John again – on paper, at least. John himself, after a sojourn in the private collection of an old family of Edinburgh antique dealers, is to be sold on 7th June in Paris by Piasa."[44]

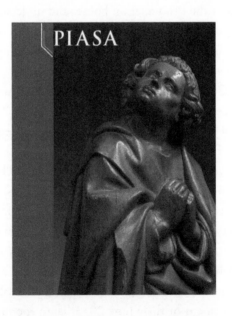

The front page of the twelve-page brochure issued by
Piasa to advertise the forthcoming sale of The Saint

154

Then Piasa issued a glossy twelve-page brochure about The Saint, containing a scholarly and extensively-referenced essay written by Laurence, printed in both French and English. It was superbly illustrated with photographs of my statue from several angles, with pictures for comparison of the Flavigny Virgin and a number of similar Burgundian sculptures known to be from the workshop of Claus de Werve. A handsome and authoritative publication, it gave me yet more confidence in my choice of Laurence to handle the sale.

And then, just a few days beforehand, I received my copy of the printed catalogue for the 7th June auction. It ran to 108 pages and was big, glossy, colourful and expensively designed and produced. There were to be 317 lots offered for sale, dating from the fifth to the eighteenth centuries, and including metalwork, furniture, bronzes, textiles, manuscripts, a few paintings, and lots of carvings and sculpture in stone and wood. Most pages contained descriptions and photographs of several lots. A few important and especially valuable or interesting lots had a full page to themselves. Estimated prices ranged from €50-€80 for Lot 77, a fifteenth century carved oak panel, to €8,000-€12,000 for Lot 98, a rare sixteenth century iron casket decorated in silver and gold. It was easy to find The Saint. He was Lot 70 and had ten, yes, ten whole pages of the catalogue all to himself, including fifteen photographs, a bibliography listing ten reference works, and, of course, that alarming estimated price range of €70,000–€100,000.

Although I didn't know about it at the time, preparations for the sale were going on not only in Paris and Edinburgh but also in the Burgundy village of Flavigny-sur-Ozerain. A modest campaign had been launched to bring The Saint back to his home village. M. Philippe Levantal was an elderly Parisian artist and journalist who owned a house in Flavigny. A seasoned conservationist and campaigner, he was prominent in 1971 in the popular but ultimately unsuccessful opposition to the demolition of the main Paris market at Les Halles. He was alerted to the publicity surrounding the sale of The Saint by a former colleague, the art historian Bertrand Jestaz, and, without much time or support, decided to raise funds to buy the statue and reunite it permanently with the Virgin.

Clearly a well-connected chap, M. Levantal rapidly contacted curators at the Dijon museums and the Louvre, the Mayor of Flavigny, a Deputy of the Côte d'Or Département, the Regional Director of Cultural Affairs, an Inspector of Historic Monuments, and the Lord knows who else. Somehow in the short time before the sale, a fighting fund of €77,000 was assembled to bid at the auction.

There is a French law which provides, where an item is of national historic importance, for the State to step in and seize the piece. The process, known as the right of pre-emption, allows the government to buy the object by matching the winning auction bid. It is then usually allocated to a particular museum or public collection for perpetual safe-keeping and display. The hope was that the promises of funding obtained by M. Levantal during his short campaign would be sufficient to allow The Saint to be pre-empted at the auction and returned to Flavigny.

Meanwhile, in the days leading up to the sale, what was going on in The House of Anxiety in Edinburgh? I had managed to calm myself down on a number of fronts. I had made my choice of Laurence as the expert responsible for taking the sale of my statue forward, and I was happy with that choice. Tick. The statue had been safely and securely (if expensively) transported to France. Tick. It had been authenticated as genuine and not a copy or fake. Tick. I had a satisfactory account of provenance which took theft and looting out of the story. Tick. Laurence had achieved what I was convinced no-one else could have achieved by researching and identifying The Saint with such expertise and passion. Big tick. The auction house was doing an excellent job of publicity. Tick. There was a high level of confidence it would sell at the auction and wouldn't have to be returned to me. Tick – not, of course, that I wouldn't have welcomed him back, but if he did have to come back I knew my anxiety levels would rise once more to dangerous levels.

But there was still plenty to worry about. Four things were keeping me awake at night.

Four Last Worries

First worry. Having been convinced on Day 52 by a soothing email from Laurence that there was no need for concern about the possible need for an Export Licence, I became worried again. You will recall her advice:

> "British law requires an exit permit for works whose value is equal to over £65,000. We have estimated the work at €30,000 to €50,000. It is therefore possible for you to send your Saint John without breaking British law…"

But now the estimated value was between €70,000 to €100,000, a range which, at the prevailing sterling/euro exchange rate, straddled the £65,000 threshold above which a UK Export Licence would be required. Did the much higher valuation negate the advice given previously? I wrote to Laurence in a panic and received the following advice:

"As far as British law about exports of works of art is concerned, you should not worry because your statue was sent to France for a value of 30,000 euros, i.e. much less than the English threshold of 65,000 pounds, and you have signed a mandate to Piasa for the aforesaid value. Moreover, the shipment from Scotland was perfectly legal thanks to the international consignment note. In other words, your good faith cannot be discussed.

As to a possible export from the French territory to a country that does not belong to the EC, Piasa shall ask in such case for an export licence bringing as an evidence that British law has been complied with when the statue was sent to France. The value in the catalogue, higher than in the mandate, reflects the research made after the statue arrived in France and the discovery of its provenance when I was able to confront your Saint John with the Virgin of Flavigny-sur-Ozerain; so, everybody should admit that such physical comparison was impossible when the statue was in the UK.

In summary, you have breaken no law and neither the customs, nor the competent English administration in charge of cultural works, can blame you."

That was good enough for me. I could score that worry off. Tick.

Second worry. I began to fret about Value Added Tax. You might recall from Chapter 8 that I had discovered that my small-time antique dealing activities were classified as trading by Her Majesty's Revenue and Customs. Therefore I had categorised myself as a self-employed dealer and for a couple of years had been declaring my very modest income to HMRC on my annual tax return. As a result I had uncomplainingly paid a titchy amount of income tax on my very small profits. A business must register for VAT when its turnover hits £77,000, but naturally, with the turnover of my micro-business barely reaching £3,000 up to now, the need for VAT registration hadn't crossed my mind. Now, however, with The Saint's new and vastly-increased estimated sale value, the unthinkable had suddenly become thinkable. Taking into account my sales in the current tax year, which included selling the Ashworth-Hepplewhite-Gray miner's safety lamp, a hammer price for The Saint of around €90,000 would send me hurtling through the VAT threshold. This new worry hit me with a loud thud.

Now, the great thing about VAT is that you only pay it on added value. If you're registered for VAT, you add the prescribed tax percentage to the price of the item you are selling, and you deduct whatever VAT you paid when you bought the item in the first place. Then you send the difference to HMRC. Leaving aside the millions of pages of small print, the principle is simple and elegant.

But what do you do if, as a registered trader but unregistered for VAT, you are selling an item at auction and you don't know if the price will be above or below the VAT threshold until the moment when the hammer falls? And what difference is there if you are trading in the UK but selling your item in France? If I were to register for VAT just in case, then I'd need to tell the auctioneer in advance so that the sale catalogue would include the information that the hammer price was subject to VAT. And who would I need to register with: HMRC or its French equivalent? I might go to all that trouble only to find that the hammer price was below the VAT threshold, or that The Saint didn't sell at all.

On the other hand, what would happen if I didn't register for VAT and The Saint then sold for a price above the registration threshold without VAT being re-charged to the buyer? In this eventuality, it seemed that I would have no "input tax" from which to pay what was owed to HMRC. But I would be liable to pay just the same, which meant that 20% of the sale price would be payable on top of any income tax which might be due. Horrors! More loss of sleep!

I contacted my accountant and tried to explain. "I bought this old wooden statue for £400 and now it might sell at auction in France for more than £77,000, so what should I do about VAT?" I sensed incredulity and barely-suppressed scorn at the other end of the phone. My accountant said he'd think about it and then called back to say that the problem was outside his firm's expertise, and would I like speak to a tax expert who worked for another firm and should be able to give me more specialist advice? I phoned the expert. I sensed more incredulity and barely-suppressed scorn at the other end of the phone. He said he'd get back to me, and when he did, he asked me to get information from the auctioneer about their VAT-charging arrangements. So I wrote to Laurence asking her to explain to me about the French VAT position in relation to the auction.

This flurry of activity took place around 21st May, when there was still (but only barely) enough time for a note to be printed in the catalogue saying that the sale of The Saint was subject to VAT. But by the time Laurence replied on 30th May, saying "I forwarded your email to Piasa auction because your request is out of my knowledge, dear Roger", the catalogue for the 7th June auction was already printed and issued. Any opportunity I might have had to charge VAT to The Saint's buyer had already disappeared. Oh, help!

There is a very long tail to this part of my story. A detailed account of my lengthy and complex post-sale struggles with HMRC over the VAT position could fill several more chapters of this book. But that took place after the auction so is not relevant here. I leave readers in temporary suspense (or terror) as to how much detail (if any) of the VAT denouement you're going to get.

Third worry. Was it OK for me to be selling The Saint at all? Yes, I know it was OK technically and legally, but was it really OK morally or ethically? It was complicated. So complicated that near the end of this book there's a whole chapter about this very subject. I won't go into it here, except to say that, yes, it was an issue (or a multiplicity of related issues) that was giving me considerable concern in the weeks and days before the sale.

Fourth worry. I fear that this worry will seem silly and immature, but in the days leading up to the Paris auction it loomed ever larger in my mind. What if the auction bidders spurned my beautiful Saint? What if he didn't attract any bids? What if he sold for a lower price than had been paid a couple of years ago for the smaller apostle statue from the Cistercian abbey at Theuley? True, the Apostle had retained its original polychromy and gilding, but it still bore that unmistakeable and slightly unfortunate resemblance to my late Uncle Jack. How upset would I be if French museums and collectors disrespected and rejected my pride and joy? By the day of the auction, only one thing really mattered to me – *Beat the Apostle!*

10

THE NORM

Am I Normal?

Before moving on to describe the day of the Paris sale and what came after, I wish to continue the investigation begun in Chapter 8. There, I tried to deal with the subject of whether I am a dealer or a collector, and arrived at the conclusion that I am a bit of both. I also concluded that being a bit of both is OK, and that many other of my fellow auction enthusiasts are likely also to be a bit of both.

The second stage of investigation is to find out if my behaviour is normal. Am I in line with The Norm in respect of my collecting and/or dealing? It's important to get clarity on this, because throughout this book I have been trying to set out my stall as an everyman when it comes to auction attendance and success. But it might instead be that I'm not an Ordinary Joe after all, but an Obsessive Johann – an alchemist, perhaps, like Johann Friedrich Böttger, who was incarcerated in Konigstein Castle by Augustus the Strong, Elector of Saxony, under strict orders to fill the Elector's empty coffers with gold – or else. During years of compulsive experimentation he failed to produce a single speck of gold, but in his efforts to develop a crucible able to withstand the intense heat required for the transmutation process, he found that he had transmuted stoneware into porcelain. Böttger's discovery of a recipe closely guarded by the Chinese for hundreds of years led to the development of Meissen porcelain, but sadly he died in 1719 aged just thirty-seven, poisoned by chemicals from his experiments, a victim of his obsession.

Now, I know that despite my apparent ability to turn unlikely antiques into hard cash, I'm no alchemist. But if it turns out that I conduct myself in a manner that is obsessive, weird, peculiar, eccentric or (potentially or actually) mentally ill, then readers who may be looking to my auction experiences to derive advice or wisdom or inspiration or (God forbid!) a role model, might feel short-changed.

In order to ascertain if I'm normal, and if I am, just how normal, I'm going to have to get a tad theoretical and a touch statistical. It'll be a four-stage process:

- *First*, I identify two specific classes of human behaviour for scrutiny;
- *Second*, I propose a simple methodology for measuring the range and extent of these behaviour classes;
- *Third*, I examine some examples of extreme behaviour at the ends of the ranges;
- *Fourth*, I attempt to calibrate my own behaviour to see if I'm normal. I hope that readers will join in this part of the exercise too. Are you normal?

Step 1: Classes of Behaviour

The two classes of behaviour which I'm choosing to examine are ***hoarding*** and ***collecting***. In Chapter 8 I quoted the psychoanalyst Peter Subkowski on collecting, and decided that I'm an "integrated, mature" kind of collector, with a hobby that "does not necessarily lead to addiction". On hoarding, I quoted the Diagnostic and Statistical Manual of Mental Disorders, and concluded that because my habit of accumulating antiques and art objects doesn't cause impairment to myself or to other people, I wouldn't be clinically diagnosable as a hoarder.

What I wish to do now is to check those conclusions in a practical way by measuring my behaviour against that of other people.

Step 2: Methodology

If you consider the behaviour of any group of people in relation to a particular topic – anything you can think of – you'll invariably find that whatever it is, some people do none of it or hardly any, some people do lots and lots of it, but the vast majority of people do something in between.

Here's an everyday example of what I mean: let us imagine that you have given a questionnaire to a representative cross-section of 100 British adults to find out how many cups of tea and/or coffee they drink in a day. You discover that it's common to have a cup or two with breakfast, a cup mid-morning and mid-afternoon, and maybe one or two at another time – with or after main meals or at bedtime. Thus your analysis of the questionnaire has told you that most hot-beverage drinkers drink between three and seven cups (or, as it may be, mugs) per day, with the most common quantity taken by Mr or Ms Average being five.

You also find that there are quite a few people who either don't drink much (say two to four cups) or who drink quite a lot (say six to eight cups). But although they consume less or more than average, you don't think there's anything particularly funny about them. Thus you have discovered a normal range which stretches quite a long way on either side of the average or mean in the centre, and which accounts for most of the people who have filled in your questionnaire.

There is a small number left at either end of the scale who behave very abnormally. Some of these drink no tea or coffee or hardly any, and some drink lots and lots and lots of cups. Statisticians call these few the *outliers*.

You might be tempted to think that anyone who's an outlier in any particular type of behaviour that you happen to be measuring is likely to be a little odd, a bit peculiar. But not necessarily. We'll look at some possible causes of outlier-ish-ness a little later. But for the time being I wish to move on to Step 3: setting the limits at the extreme ends of the ranges of hoarding and collecting behaviour.

Step 3: Extremes

For this part of the exercise, I've invented two scales.

The first scale is intended to measure hoarding, and runs from the outlier at the low end who says, *"I am entirely uninterested in material possessions and own only those which are essential for my life"* to the outlier at the top end who says *"the main focus and purpose of my life is to acquire and accumulate material possessions"*. Mr or Ms Average is placed precisely in the middle between the two extremes. I will call this scale *the Reacher-Collyer Hoarding Scale*.

The second scale is intended to measure collecting, and runs from the outlier at the bottom who says, *"I am interested in art and antiques for their value only and for no other reason"* to the outlier at the top who says, *"I am interested in art and antiques as objects or sets of objects only and for no other reason"*. Again, the average person is in the middle. I will call this scale the *Goldbrick-PennyRed Collecting Scale*.

Note by the way that I haven't done any formal research to establish the validity of my behaviour scales. Not for the first time in the annals of science, the findings presented here are entirely the product of guesswork, imagination and intuition. I hope nonetheless that readers will find them both truthful and useful.

The Reacher-Collyer Hoarding Scale: *Reacher*

Jack Reacher is a fictional tough guy and hero created by the British-born writer Lee Child in a series of trashy, formulaic, but highly unputdownable page-turner novels. I confess to being somewhat addicted, and a number of otherwise respectable, well-educated, intellectual, book-group-attending persons of my acquaintance might also be pressed to admit to the reading of Reacher novels as a secret vice.

Reacher is a former Major in the United States Army who has seen much action and has been awarded a chestful of medals. Since leaving the Army, he has been a drifter, wandering throughout the US usually by hitchhiking or bus. Somehow he always seems to get involved in episodes of major crime and conspiracy, which he tends to solve single-handedly and with extreme violence, invariably after showing up the authorities (police, army, FBI, etc) as ineffectual, corrupt and generally namby-pamby. The only possessions he carries or owns are cash money, a bank debit card, an expired passport and a foldable toothbrush. He wears his clothes for two or three days, then buys new clothes cheaply from chain stores and throws the dirty ones in the nearest dumpster. He has no home and no fixed address, usually staying in basic motels and eating in cheap restaurants and diners. Out of his own lifestyle choice, he owns practically nothing, and he takes deliberate and careful steps to avoid becoming encumbered with possessions.

Jack Reacher is the outlier at the bottom end of the Reacher-Collyer Hoarding Scale.

The Reacher-Collyer Hoarding Scale: *Collyer*

Homer and Langley Collyer lived in a junk-stuffed brownstone mansion in then fashionable Harlem in New York. They were the first celebrity hoarders, and their story dominated the US media in the late 1940s.

The Collyer brothers had inherited the house from their parents and did not have to work to earn money. But their funds ran out and the mansion's gas, telephone, electricity and water were turned off for failure to pay bills. Their reclusiveness and eccentric behaviour fuelled rumours about treasures hidden within the house and this, in turn, led to a series of break-ins. In response, the brothers boarded up the windows with metal shutters and began to set booby-traps.

Homer went blind in 1934, after which he did not leave the house. Langley would venture out at night in relentless pursuit of junk, dressed in threadbare Victorian clothing and dragging a cardboard box on a rope to haul his treasures home.

*In March 1947, responding to an anonymous call, New York City police broke into the mansion (*See Illustrations, *Picture 13). After several hours of pulling out junk and throwing it into the street below, the body of Homer Collyer was found in a chair. Langley's body was found several days later just a few feet from Homer's. He had been caught in a collapsing mountain of newspapers, one of his own booby-traps. Homer, blind and paralysed, had died of starvation some time previously.*

Over 150 tons of junk were removed from the house, including 30,000 books, a horse's jaw, a human skeleton, an early X-Ray machine, innumerable newspapers, prams, bicycles, guns, bowling balls, sawhorses, plaster busts, eight cats, a Model T Ford, and many musical instruments including fourteen pianos.

Homer and Langley are the outliers at the top end of the Reacher-Collyer Hoarding Scale.

The Goldbrick-PennyRed Collecting Scale: *Goldbrick*

In 2012 Barclays Bank issued a report entitled Profit or Pleasure? Exploring the Motivations Behind Treasure Trends[45]*, which looks in detail at the reasons why people invest in "treasure". The report is fascinating throughout and includes the results of an in-depth survey of investors, which has the benefit of being a real-life survey and not one invented by a lazy author. One finding stood out for me:*

"Enjoyment is by far the most important motivation for owning treasure. Almost two-thirds [62%] of the treasure owned by respondents is held because of the pleasure that it brings them".

Fair enough, but that means that 38% of treasure is held for other reasons. Respondents cited a number of other motivations, including 18% of treasure held *"purely as an investment".* The report's definition of treasure is a little different from one that includes only antiques and fine art. It also includes gold held as bullion, and it's easy to see how the results could be skewed by some investors whose only interest in treasure is to have a few gold bricks kept under lock and key for them in someone else's vault.

But there do exist some investors who don't buy gold bullion but instead buy art and antiques entirely for investment, with zero interest in the objects themselves. Why do they bother when they could just as easily go for gold, or equities, or bonds, or currency, or derivatives, or property, or any other asset class which they might indeed have some interest in? The answer is simply that from a financial point of view, art can be as good an asset as the others. Highly respected indexes exist to track the performance of the most investable artists in terms of the auction prices achieved by their works, and there is a number of investment advisory firms who specialise in art as an asset. One of them was Beautiful Assets Advisors LLC, which operated the Mei Moses Fine Art Index until its takeover by Sotheby's in late 2016. The following is part of their take on the investment potential of art. I'm quoting it at length because of its magnificently mechanistic description of outlying life at the bottom end of the Collecting Scale:

"The beauty and uniqueness of art as an asset class is that it gives individuals the opportunity of gaining pleasure and excitement from its ownership in three distinct ways. The first beauty of art is the obvious one of emotional appeal obtained from the visual image of the object. The second beauty of art is the enjoyment most individuals obtain from the process of its acquisition. This includes, but is not limited to, knowledge acquisition, socialization with like-minded collectors and experts, excitement of the chase, meeting its maker, etc.

"The third beauty of art is its longevity and financial performance. Over the last three millennia there has never been a time when art was not important and appreciated. In general arts [sic] relative performance is based on the historical time period under consideration... art has

low correlation with other assets and thus may play a role in portfolio diversification.

"We have created Beautiful Assets Advisors LLC to concentrate on arts [sic] third beauty. We ignore the first two not since we feel that they are unimportant but that there are others more qualified to address these issues than ourselves. On this website we will address… the financial characteristics of the art asset class relative to other assets.

"We thus base all our findings on a proprietary database of objects that have sold more than once on a world-wide basis at public auction. This database now comprises… seven individual collecting categories: old master and 19th century, impressionist and modern, American before 1950, post war and contemporary, Latin American, British painting after 1950 and traditional Chinese works of art."[46]

It does seem that a proportion of those who spend their money on art and antiques lack any motivation at all other than potential profit, and are affected by no emotional, historical or aesthetic considerations. In practice you don't even need to take the trouble to view the work that you're investing in. Some art investment trusts let you buy units in a fund comprising works of art selected solely on the basis of investment performance and held in a secure environment where investors never see them. Some other marginally less soulless funds have their pictures selected by fund managers and advisers, but the high-rolling investors are allowed, under strictly controlled conditions, to take the pictures home in rotation to put on their walls to impress their friends.

At the type of auction that I frequent, it is very unlikely that I would come across one of these canny investors, but look! There's one, that sleek-looking chap sitting in the back row reading the Financial Times. Let us call him Mr Goldbrick. It could of course be Ms Goldbrick but it's statistically more likely to be a mister. He is the outlier at the bottom end of the Goldbrick-PennyRed Collecting Scale.

The Goldbrick-PennyRed Collecting Scale: *PennyRed*

The outliers at the other extremity of this behaviour class are much more likely to be auction attenders, but usually at the most esoteric and specialist sales. They come in many varieties, but among them I single out Mr PennyRed (in this case almost certainly a mister) for special attention.

Between their introduction in 1841 and the last issue in 1879, following which both the design and the printer were changed, nearly 21 billion Penny Red stamps were printed by the firm of Perkins, Bacon and Petch (after 1852, Perkins, Bacon and Co.).

No, that is the wrong way to start this section. 21 billion isn't nearly accurate enough. The actual number of stamps printed was 20,699,858,040[47]. Using the same basic design, three important variations of the stamp were produced over the thirty-eight-year period of production, using a total of 429 metal printing plates (See Illustrations, *Picture 14*). Each individual plate had different characteristics throughout its lifetime, producing sharply-printed stamps early on, and then losing definition and acquiring wear and scratches and other flaws towards the end of its useful life. Until 1854, the sheets were imperforated so you had to cut individual stamps off with scissors; thereafter the paper was perforated, but there were variations in the numbers of perforation holes. In addition, the stamps were printed in different shades of red ink on different shades of paper with different water marks. Then you have to think about the postmarks used to cancel the stamps, with some types and designs and postal locations and colours of marks being more interesting and desirable than others. Then there are the first and last dates of cancellation for each printing plate. And so on. And on. Since each plate was engraved with images of 240 stamps to be printed on a single sheet, and since each stamp on a sheet was overprinted with an individual letter code indicating its position on the sheet, you can easily see that no two Penny Reds out of the (nearly) 21 billion are identical.

A number of highly informative expert websites are dedicated to early stamps, and to give a flavour of collecting from a collector's viewpoint, I quote here from one of them:

> "The 1d red appears in many different shades. Correct identification of these shades is helpful when plating them as there are links between some shades and the plate they were printed from and also important as some shades are scarcer than others with a corresponding variance in price. The 1d Stars are particularly complex during the "Transitional" period issues of 1856-1857 when the paper used changed from blue to yellow/cream/ toned to white and many ink shades exist and the differences between them can be very hard to distinguish. As no definitive colour chart or measuring system exists at this time all that can be done is to view as many stamps as possible of the different shades and compare them with expertised items so that you become more knowledgeable about the items that you are buying and collecting. Ideally, a reference collection can be built up and constantly checked by reference to expertised items. It is very pleasing to have a range

of shades to show all the different colours which the 1d red appears in and my personal view ..."[48], etc, etc, etc.

If you get hooked on collecting Penny Reds, you naturally want to have in your collection, regardless of price paid, the best possible example of every variety from every plate.

Mr PennyRed is hooked. He is the outlier at the top end of the Goldbrick-PennyRed Collecting Scale.

Step 4: Measurement of Behaviour

We have looked at the outliers at each end of the range in our two classes of behaviour. We also know that Mr or Ms Average, aka the Man or Woman In The Street or possibly On The Clapham Omnibus, is bang-smack in the middle of each range. Now all we have to do is to calibrate ourselves on each of the ranges. One simple way to do this is graphically – by placing ourselves on a chart. For this part of the exercise, I'm using a variation on a well-tried technique called Quadrant Analysis.

As you can see in the diagram opposite, I have placed the two behaviour scales at right angles to each other, Reacher-Collyer side to side, and Goldbrick-PennyRed up and down. The outliers lurk at the at the very border of the chart: the Collecting scale with Mr PennyRed at the top and Mr Goldbrick at the bottom; the Hoarding scale with Jack Reacher at the left and the Collyer Brothers at the right.

Mr or Ms Average sits where the two scales cross; he or she is perfectly adjusted, with no need to worry about his or her degree of normality. But as we have seen with the example of tea- and coffee-drinking, the concept of normality stretches a long way to either side of the average. The closer you are to the centre of the chart, the more normal you are, but do bear in mind that it's possible to deviate well away from the central position of Mr or Ms Average while still behaving normally.

Quadrant Analysis is a useful method because, as the name suggests, it creates four quadrants between the scales which represent an individual's behaviour on both scales at the same time.

I have shaded these quadrants and have made an attempt at labelling each one with a generic type of behaviour which might be applicable to it. So:

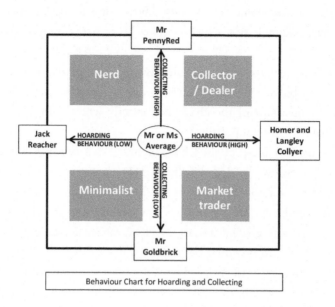

Behaviour Chart for Hoarding and Collecting

- if your hoarding and your collecting tendencies are both below average (lower left quadrant), I'm suggesting that you exhibit minimalist behaviour, with little interest in objects but high interest in wealth.

- if you are low on the hoarding scale but high on the collecting scale (upper left), you might be rather on the nerdy side, preoccupied with collecting but without much time for other material things, or, perhaps for other people.

- if you're high on hoarding but low on collecting (lower right), then you might, for example, be someone who indiscriminately amasses quantities of fairly random stuff in the confident expectation of turning a big profit – perhaps a market trader or car-boot sale regular might fit this definition.

- and finally, there are the folk who are high on the hoarding scale and high on the collecting scale (upper right quadrant), which – provided that they don't approach too close to the edge – is the place where you'll find "mature, integrated" collectors and professional expert dealers, who can happily combine their strong interest in antiques and art with normal functioning in the other departments of their lives.

I hope you get the general idea. It should be possible for each person to mark on the chart a suitable spot which matches his or her combined position on the two scales.

Now, let me have a shot at finding my own place. It isn't easy. It's important to be very honest. I have no doubt that I belong firmly in the upper right quadrant of the chart. But exactly where? How far from the central perfectly normal position?

After considerable thought I have included two versions of me. In my personal chart below, the circle labelled **Me(1)** represents my own assessment of where I fit in – rather above average on both scales, but not markedly so. But **Me(2)** represents my impression of where my dear wife Frances would place me if asked to give me a score – well above average on both scales, but higher in relation to hoarding behaviour. While noting that Frances might think me a little less normal than I consider myself, I find that both of these placings keep me within the normal range and comfortably away from the margins of the chart inhabited by the outliers.

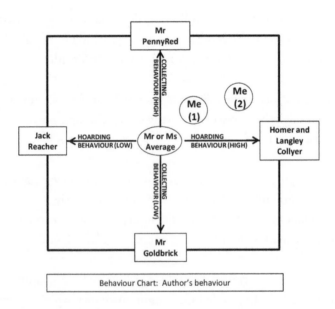

Behaviour Chart: Author's behaviour

It goes almost without saying that these attempts both to self-score my own behaviour and to second-guess Frances's opinion thereof are entirely subjective. Indeed it occurs to me that this whole exercise might merely have been an over-elaborate self-justification, an attempt, vain in both senses, to prove to my own satisfaction (if to no-one else's) that I'm normal, in the face of worrying indications *passim* that the opposite is true.

At the same time, while freely acknowledging the wholly spurious and unscientific nature of this theoretical model, I'd like to think that it might provide some food for thought, and perhaps even furnish a useful framework for measuring the behaviours that it purports to measure.

So now, readers, it's your turn. Here's a blank chart. Consider your own behaviour in relation to *stuff* as a collector (or not) and/or as a hoarder (or not), and mark where you fit into the chart. In which quadrant do you place yourself? How near are you to the centre or how near to the outer margin? Having found your position, are you comfortable there?

Are *you* as normal as *me*?

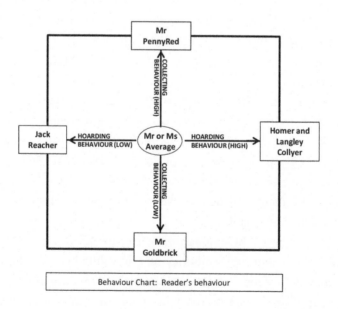

Behaviour Chart: Reader's behaviour

The Edge

Now that we have all marked our positions on the behaviour chart, there are three important further issues to consider, namely:

- *is it better to be normal than to be an outlier?*
- *are all outliers necessarily crazy?*
- *where's the best place on the chart to find random treasure?*

Starting with the first question, it has already been suggested that the author of this book might be trying a little too hard to be normal, and worrying a little too much in case he's abnormal. He seems to attribute enormous merit and advantage to being Mr Average, placed dead-centre in the chart, and he seems afraid, very afraid, of being an outlier. But what's so great about being average anyway?

It's safe. There's no risk attached. It's comfortable. It's cosy. You're well-adjusted, with no neuroses and no psychoses. You have problem-free relationships with family and community. As far as your possessions are concerned, you have what you need and you have what you want, no unhealthy cravings, no covetousness, you can take it or leave it. It's pleasant. It's beige. Perhaps it's a little boring. But it means that among your collection of lovely things you have a nice comfy sofa to sit on.

It isn't like that for the outliers. They lead tortured lives sacrificing their place in society in pursuit of acquisition or divestment. Look at *their* sofas: Jack Reacher has no furniture at all because he's hardly ever at home; Mr Goldbrick sits protectively on a pile of gold bricks; Mr PennyRed, having sold his sofa to buy stamps, sits on a hard chair at a plain table, plating; and the Collyer Brothers lost sight of their sofa many decades ago. It's lonely, uncomfortable, unpleasant.

But it isn't beige. By comparison with The Norm, the outlier's life is one of adventure and high emotion, veering wildly between the heights of fulfilment and the depths of disappointment. You're ready to pay a very high price to get what you want. You take risks, you experience discomfort or danger, you don't care what others think, you live close to the edge, you get excited.

Are all Outliers Crazy?

In the last section I asked what's so great about being average. In this section: what's so bad about being an outlier? There's an assumption in my theoretical model that if you're an outlier, you must necessarily be weird, obsessive, geeky. But of course it's an assumption not backed up by evidence. Measuring behaviour using my chart – or indeed in any way – is useful as far as it goes, but it doesn't tell you anything about causality or motivation or the mental status of your research subjects.

Here's what I mean. Let us for a moment go back to the tea and coffee example given earlier in this chapter. At the bottom of the scale you know from your research that a small number of people in a hundred don't drink *any* of either beverage. But you don't know *why* because you haven't asked the question. It's possible, however, to envisage a number of answers. Maybe they just don't like either drink. Maybe they avoid caffeine on medical advice. Maybe they are adherents to a religious sect which bans stimulants of all kinds. Maybe they think that tea and coffee have been laced by aliens with a mind control drug. Who knows?

Similarly a few outliers at the top of the scale have told you that they drink huge amounts of tea and coffee. Is it because they are hopeless, helpless caffeine addicts? Do they work in a hot, low-humidity environment and is this their preferred way to maximise fluid intake? Are they members of a privileged class of workless or retired people who spend their days flitting from café to café meeting their cronies (this being one particular box which Frances and I might tick)?

We don't know. All we know about the outliers is firstly that they behave in a distinctly abnormal way compared to those within what we have decided is our normal range. And secondly that they might be doing so for all kinds of reasons, which may on the one hand be perfectly understandable after explanation, or may on the other hand be indicative of addiction, obsession or other illness.

Thus, although there will always be a small number of people who operate at each extreme end of any behavioural scale, it doesn't inevitably mean that they are nut-jobs. Being an outlier doesn't have to mean that you are irrational.

Let's see how that last observation applies to my scales measuring hoarding and collecting. First, the Reacher-Collyer Hoarding Scale. Clearly both Jack Reacher and the Collyer brothers function far outside the normal range of behaviour. But does that mean they are madmen, sociopaths or psychopaths? Not necessarily. In fact, in each case the way they choose to live is a rational lifestyle choice. They don't commit crime or cause harm to others except incidentally as a result of (a) the exceptionally high body-count of villains who deserve all they get in the Reacher novels and (b) the vermin and unpleasant odours which doubtless affected the Collyers' neighbours. They do not attract special attention from the health authorities. They don't even harm themselves unduly. Reacher inevitably picks up a few light bruises and grazes while exterminating baddies and evil-doers wholesale, but that's an occupational hazard from which a hero will rapidly recover. And the eventual grisly demise of the Collyers after several decades of reclusive living might not be due to their hoarding way of life at all. It may be due to unrelated causes associated with ageing and lack of care: malnutrition, disease or dementia.

Now, the Goldbrick-PennyRed Collecting Scale. Here, those outliers with the very lowest scores might simply not be turned on by art or antiques. Difficult as it may be for me and other collectors to understand, it appears that some people just aren't all that interested in antiques. Their real passions might lie elsewhere: maybe in travel, or golf, or exercise, or cinema, or cooking, or poetry, or theatre, or fishing, or football, or hill-walking, or martial arts, or politics, or knitting, or work. This lack of interest in our sorts of objects might make them outliers at the lower end of the Goldbrick-PennyRed scale, but in many other aspects of the way they lead their lives they may be squarely in the middle of the scale as perfectly responsible well-adjusted citizens.

As for the highest scorers, the avid collectors, well, for sure, some Mr PennyReds will undoubtedly fall into Dr Subkowski's "non-integrated" category, suffering from a "secondary addiction or neurotic compulsion". The collector in this category will happily pay anything from a few pence to many thousands of pounds for new items for his collection, if necessary incurring debts. He will be obsessed with his collection, which will dominate his life and take up most of his waking hours. He will find normal functioning in society difficult, and may borrow or even steal funds to buy the next stamp or Star Wars figure or whatever it might be. But that description needn't apply to all Messrs PennyRed.

Frances and I once attended one of the auctions organised every few weeks by Robert Murray, the principal Edinburgh stamp dealer. We were there not to buy stamps, and not even to conduct observational research to support my hypothetical Goldbrick-PennyRed scale. We attended in order to bid for a collection of undistinguished silver crowns, as part of an ongoing project to accumulate five small hoards of bullion-grade silver coins to give to our five grandchildren. The declared plan is that while the children are small, the coins (which have been placed into small brown leather drawstring purses) will be available to them as playthings, particularly useful props when playing at pirates; and then, when they get older, the silver can readily be turned into cash as required for extra pocket money. The sub-text is a hope that possessing a few old coins will help to inspire them to become collectors just like their Grandpa did when given a purse of his own grandfather's coins around sixty years ago.

Attending the stamp auction gave us the opportunity to observe in the crowded and almost entirely male-populated saleroom a number of archetypal and unmistakable Mr PennyReds. But it was equally clear there was a much larger number of keen – extremely keen – stamp collectors who, while scoring as outliers at the high end of the Goldbrick-PennyRed scale, doubtless carried on useful middle-class middle-aged lives with normal relationships, families, and miscellaneous non-philatelic interests.

Finding Random Treasure

So there we are: if you're average, it's safe but it might just be a little boring, a little too comfy. If you're an outlier, it's difficult and edgy, but it could be exciting, and being an outlier doesn't necessarily mean you have to lose contact with the world.

Next question: where on the chart are you likeliest to be if you have an insatiable yearning, as I have, to sail your pirate ship in search of random treasure, or if you long to be the alchemist in his low vault or high tower who transmutes base junk into valuable antiques? Is it better to be average, in the calm dead centre of the chart, or to be an outlier inhabiting the dangerous, choppy waters at the outer margins?

In some ways, this is a non-issue. Because the chart on Page 169, showing Mr or Ms Average at the very centre of the Hoarding and Collecting scales, only looks that way when it represents a cross-section of the population at large. If you take, say, a sample of *any* 100 Edinburgh adults at random, and place a dot on the chart representing the collecting and hoarding behaviours of each of them, you should find that the dots are scattered pretty equally between the four quadrants, with the majority in each quadrant clustered towards the centre. By contrast, if you take a sample of 100 people in attendance at Johnson & Andrews or any of the other general auction houses in Edinburgh, and plot their answers on the chart, then you are likely to find a very different pattern of dots.

My prediction would be that there would be very few dots in the lower left (minimalist) quadrant, and a great many in the upper right (collector/dealer) quadrant. Mr or Ms Average wouldn't be placed in the centre of the chart, but probably fairly near to the Me(1) position that I marked for myself. In other words, the average auction-goer is likely to be significantly higher on both the hoarding and collecting scales than is the average random member of the public. People who belong in the other quadrants are much less likely to want to pass their valuable time hanging around at auctions.

So, in comparison with the population at large, it might be that all of us auction-goers experience a slight gravitational pull towards the outlier zone. Could it be that we *all* have that same potential to be discoverers of random treasure?

I suspect also that most readers of this book will give themselves a personal score in the upper half of both the Reacher-Collyer Hoarding Scale and the Goldbrick-PennyRed Collecting Scale. If you didn't, you probably wouldn't have picked up the book in the first place, and you almost certainly wouldn't have read as far as this chapter.

An Irony

To round off my rather doubtful venture into the realm of behavioural analysis, here is delightful piece of irony. When doing my research for this chapter, I discovered a 2012 press release reporting that a new world record price of £550,000 had been achieved for a Penny Red stamp (printed from Plate 77), sold by the dealers Stanley Gibbons. You might think, mightn't you, that the likeliest purchaser of the stamp was Mr PennyRed, thus achieving regardless of cost the ultimate acquisition of his obsessive collecting life? But no. The report quoted the buyer as saying:

"I am a strong believer in asset diversification and consider collectibles to be a part of a truly diversified portfolio. I am confident this iconic stamp, as history has shown, will prove non-correlative to other asset classes and will be a valuable portfolio contributor for myself and my children"[49].

The buyer wished to remain anonymous, but we know, don't we, that he wasn't Mr PennyRed at all. He was Mr Goldbrick.

Where am I?

To recapitulate. In Chapter 8, I looked at what it means to be a collector or a dealer and attempted to define and categorise my own behaviour. In a nutshell I decided that I was a bit of both, just like many of the other people I encounter in my regular saleroom haunts.

In Chapter 10, this chapter, I have been looking at the concept of what's normal. The Reacher-Collyer Hoarding Scale distinguishes between extreme minimalists and extreme hoarders, and I placed myself above average but well within the normal range. The Goldbrick-PennyRed Collecting Scale distinguishes between those with no interest in the art and antiques that they acquire and those with an all-consuming interest in acquiring particular items, and again I graded myself high but normal.

I haven't yet finished my analysis. I wish to address two more issues. In what way and to what extent do I respond to art objects and antiques aesthetically? And how do I arrive at the crucial decision as to what to keep and what to sell?

I'll come to these matters in Chapter 12, but in the meantime, I'm conscious of having left readers hanging on waiting to hear about the sale of The Saint. It's time to leave for Paris.

11

SELLING THE SAINT, 2013

Hôtel Drouot

It is Thursday 6th June 2013, late morning. Frances and I arrive at Paris Charles de Gaulle airport, then find our way to the Roissy-bus stop which takes us through the congested outskirts of the city and into the centre, dropping us off at the terminus beside the Opéra Garnier. With the help of a map, we eventually reach our small hotel in Rue la Bruyère. It's a ten-minute walk but takes around half an hour, our joint map-reading skills and sense of direction not being notable for sharpness or accuracy. Not a problem. We are in no hurry: it is a warm sunny day and Paris is looking beautiful. We check in, find a cafe, have a spot of lunch, then make our way to the Hôtel Drouot, a pleasant stroll through narrow streets and across busy boulevards.

The Saint will be auctioned tomorrow. Today is viewing day. We want to see how he looks on display to viewers, how he stands up alongside the other objects in the sale. We want to do a little preparation for tomorrow's big adventure: to familiarise ourselves with the layout, to get an idea of how an auction is conducted in France, to discover if we can understand what's going on, to make ourselves look less like a pair of foreign bumpkins. And we'll see if Laurence Fligny, our expert, or her assistant Benoît Bertrand are there so that we can introduce ourselves.

Drouot is an extraordinary institution, emerging from the *Chambre des Commissaires-Priseurs de Paris* which was founded in 1801 at a time when most activities in Napoleonic France were being codified and regulated by the state. In 1852, having outgrown their former accommodation, they opened their vast new premises in Rue Drouot, from which the organisation derived its present name. From this base, Drouot operated as a consortium or cartel of *commissaires-priseurs* or professionally-qualified licensed public auctioneers, to establish a near-monopoly in the Paris auction market. This cartel was only broken in 2002 when, against fierce opposition, a law was enacted to open up the market to overseas operators, notably Christie's and Sotheby's.

Alongside Drouot's secretive, arcane, self-serving and monopolistic organizational structure, there grew a separate but not dissimilar organization called *l'Union des commissionnaires de l'hôtel des ventes* (UCHV). This trade union of Drouot porters and removers came over time to operate like a cross between a secret society and an organised crime syndicate. The UCHV club was limited to 110 members, and behaved as an ultimate closed-shop, ensuring that portering jobs were not only highly paid but also hereditary, being passed on from father to son over multiple generations. UCHV members were known as *cols rouges* for the red collars on their smart black uniforms. Most of them hailed from villages in the mountainous Savoie and Haute-Savoie *départements*, and premiums of up to 300 times the annual basic salary might change hands for the privilege of obtaining one of these most desirable of sinecures. What made them so desirable was, unsurprisingly, the manifold opportunities for fraud, corruption and theft which came with the job.

A Courbet fell off the back of a lorry; a Picasso was found in a porter's home; stories circulated about porters driving Audis and Porsches. Questions were asked. An investigation was conducted. 6,000 objects were discovered in Drouot's store rooms which could not be traced to vendors; evidence was found of theft of consigned items and collusion between *cols-rouges* and certain individual *commissaires-priseurs*. After nearly 150 years of opacity and abuse, a major scandal broke in 2009, a second major blow to Drouot's reputation just a few years after the loss of its monopolistic position in the Paris market.

Forty-three *cols rouges* and six auctioneers were prosecuted. Thirty-eight were convicted and sentenced to prison terms of up to three years and fines of up to €60,000. The UCHV itself received a heavy fine and was dissolved by order of the court. The sentences weren't handed down until 2016, after seven years of court proceedings, but by the time Frances and I arrived wide-eyed within the hallowed portal in 2013, Drouot had already got its act together. It had reorganised its structure and strategic management in a much more transparent and democratic way, with a substantial nod to good practice in corporate governance. The UCHV had faded away and portering was contracted-out to private operators, with CCTV cameras discreetly placed throughout the august premises. Most of the dodgier small auctioneers had left or been thrown out of the consortium, and Drouot had almost recaptured its former reputation for integrity, its respectability and its importance as a focal point of the French fine art and antiques market.

While the two big international auctioneers have overtaken every individual French-owned house, Drouot as an aggregation of more than seventy firms of independent *commissaires-priseurs* still dominates the market in terms of the sheer volume and value of sales, with more than 2,000 public auctions per year, selling some 600,000 individual lots for a total hammer price of over €400 million. From the huge Rue Drouot headquarters known as Drouot-Richelieu, and also from several other outstations in metropolitan Paris, Drouot still considerably outsells Christie's and Sotheby's together.

As for my selected auction house Piasa, it's as respectable and reputable as you can get and in 2013, before moving to its new premises, was the third-biggest auctioneer offering sales through the Drouot organisation.

Having read about the history and background, we weren't expecting the Hôtel Drouot to be a hotel in the sense in which we understand the word. You can't stay there overnight, however much you might want to. In France the term Hôtel is still used in an archaic sense in the names of large, grand free-standing houses where people meet and business is conducted. So we expected the Hôtel Drouot to be an enormous ornate palatial nineteenth-century pile like so many other hôtels in the centre of Paris. Instead we found a sharp 1980s building, all concrete, polished travertine, plate glass and stainless steel, with a huge entrance lobby furnished with big marble registration and information desks, and guarded by security men who glance indifferently into your bags. A bit like a large office building or a small airport terminal, but with a big difference: the people. In other equally busy places, you might see a cross-section of the population, or just shoppers, or just smartly-dressed business-people or just tourists. At Drouot, you are likely to see mostly people who measure high on the Reacher-Collyer Hoarding Scale and the Goldbrick-PennyRed Collecting Scale. And they look different from the general population. Not standardised or homogeneous, just different.

They also, of course, look different from the equivalent group seen at a British auction house, because there's a distinct Parisian overlay. For the women, it's something to do with the deployment of hair, shoes, handbags and the draping and tying of scarves. For men, it's hair (silver), unstructured jackets and designer spectacles. Not that this is a fashion show, because the crowd includes a number who look as if they might have spent the previous night or the previous six months sleeping under the bridges of Paris. But because it's Paris, dowdiness and ordinariness are in short supply. Unlike at Johnson & Andrews in Edinburgh, you don't see many trainers, jogging bottoms or football shirts.

Drouot hosts an incredibly wide range of sales, which include items at the very top and very bottom of the antique and fine art markets. Some very specialist sales appeal especially to the outliers, attracting bidders from among those remotest from normal functioning within society. For example one auction on view today is dedicated to the dispersal of a collection of several hundred sculpted portrait busts, some marble, some plaster, some old, some modern-ish, some estimated at a few thousand euros, some with low values, a few very beautiful, most very ugly. Evidence provided by the nature of the collection itself suggests that its deceased collector may have been something of an eccentric; and similarly you might expect to see among the crowd of buyers a few who are scarcely on speaking terms with any version of normality.

But at the same time, many of the individual busts in the sale might appeal to a fashionable homeowner who wants a conversation piece on display in her living room, or to an interior decorator with a commission to fit out a retro-styled boutique. So you might also expect to find among the bidders some ordinary sort of folk from the centre of one or other of my hypothetical behaviour scales. And maybe even a few from the very opposite end of the scale – for example a dealer focussed on getting something which looks right in a particular design concept but which is of no intrinsic interest to him- or herself and doesn't engage any emotions except as a piece of merchandise with profit potential.

Yes, they are all here in the lobby at Drouot. On the one hand an incredibly heterogeneous mix of people, but on the other hand, all with a specific common motivation: to attend auctions and to buy antique and collectable objects. Thus, we find ourselves amongst a crowd of very diverse but very like-minded people, clearly ranging from the weirdest of obsessive collectors and hoarders at one end, to the smoothest and most elegantly-turned-out of obsessive investors and dealers at the other end. Plus a majority of ordinary, normal auction punters in the middle. People like us, in fact. But mostly French.

Except that on this one occasion, it is Frances and I who are the farthest outliers. We're not punters, not buyers, but sellers, and not ordinary sellers, but the people selling the stellar item of the Piasa sale, of the Drouot week, of the French auction day. It's a strange feeling. We feel like we should be the stars of the show, but at the same time we are delighted to be entirely unknown and anonymous. We feel conspicuous in our foreignness but at the same time insignificant and invisible. We have a complete understanding in principle of what is about to happen but virtually no comprehension of what anyone is saying. Frances understands more than me, but catching the drift of casual conversation at Drouot is very different from listening to the President of France making a set-piece speech in perfect diction. Frances has few problems with the latter but many problems with the former. As for me, I can read French fairly fluently, but when it comes to understanding the spoken language – *rien!*

We know perfectly well that the show will go on regardless of whether we are present or not, because it isn't us but The Saint who is the centre of attention. Self-conscious, but well aware that no-one knows or cares who we are or why we are there, we go in search of the biggest-ticket item in the whole sprawling edifice. The building has 16 large salerooms arranged over three floors. There will be about half a dozen auctions going on simultaneously tomorrow, which are all on public view today, and there are about half a dozen auctions going on right now. Signage is poor. The escalators are out of action and there's some construction work going on.

Confused and disoriented, we finally find our way to Room 7, the Piasa sale of *Haute Époque et Curiosités*. It's a big sale, well-displayed, with some jaw-droppingly beautiful objects if you happen to be the sort of person who can make an emotional and aesthetic connection with mediaeval religious artefacts. We move around the room slowly and methodically, delighted to see in the flesh all of the lots whose photos we have already seen in the printed and online catalogue. We can't see The Saint at first, but we don't whizz around the room looking only for him, thinking that we might look a bit naive and foolish if we merely rush up to him, gawp and then leave.

There he is. In a corner, shielded from the other lots by screens, individually spotlit, accompanied by a life-size board-mounted cut-out colour photo of the Virgin of Flavigny. Beautiful as he is, and obviously the show-stopper object, he seems to stand out from the other auction lots slightly less than he did when standing atop our hall chest in suburban Edinburgh, competing

182

for attention only with a grandfather clock and a Swedish modernist ceramic vase converted to a lamp. This shouldn't be surprising but it is. Delighted as I am to be in my statue's company again, I feel somehow slightly deflated. My anxieties redouble. What if after all he's not as special as Laurence has made him out to be? What if no-one wants to buy him? What if he fails to outsell the Uncle-Jack-lookalike Theuley apostle? I keep these thoughts to myself. Frances doesn't know about these irrational worries of mine. In fact she won't know about them until she reads this book.

At a desk in the corner of the room sit an elegant couple, talking earnestly to an equally elegant auction viewer. We recognise them from their website photographs to be Laurence and Benoît. When the potential bidder moves on, we go to introduce ourselves. Laurence is tall, slim, early forties, with studiedly unruly blonde hair, the essence of understated Parisian chic. Benoît is the besuited male equivalent. We greet them politely. They look a little blank for a moment until they understand who we are, then greet us back equally politely. There follow a few minutes of smiling but rather stilted conversation, with my almost non-existent spoken French closely matching Laurence's lamentable spoken English, and Benoît's halting English not quite matching up to Frances's rather more fluent French. There is a smattering of cross-translation, plenty of cross-purposes and substantial non-comprehension between all four parties. It's a brief, friendly meeting, but not effusive and not a meeting of minds. Understandably, it doesn't matter to them whether we are there or not. They have more important tasks at hand, mainly involving schmoozing potential buyers and doing whatever last-minute things that may be done to encourage and maximise bids for The Saint and for the other 316 lots in the sale. We're all considerably relieved when we part with cheery *au revoir* and a promise from Laurence to reserve us some seats at the sale tomorrow.

Then we go to look at the other sales on view in the building (which is how I know about the sale of the collection of busts) and at the sales in progress in other salons.

The French at Auction

In the UK, anyone can set themselves up as an auctioneer. There are no mandatory qualifications, no permissions to seek, no licences, no special regulations, no government regulator. An auction house is a commercial business like any other. If it's a small owner-operated saleroom like Johnson & Andrews in Edinburgh, you arrive on sale day to find the auctioneer (Malcolm), an assistant or porter or two, a clerk who sits next to the auctioneer to record winning bids, and a couple of office staff to issue invoices, take payment, and sometimes to convey bids on behalf of telephone bidders. During the sale, some auctioneers still employ the old-fashioned method of identifying each lot coming under the hammer by having a porter physically show it to the audience. But most these days have a big monitor behind the podium which shows a photograph. In many but by no means all salerooms, since the fairly recent advent of online bidding, there is some extra technology with an operator on hand to take real-time internet bids. If it's a big auctioneer like Bonham's or Lyon and Turnbull, both of which have posh salerooms in central Edinburgh, it's a similar set-up but there will be more staff and they will be better-dressed, and most probably called Poppy.

In France, it's different. Most things to do with auction sales and with those who conduct them are legislated, codified, regulated and prescribed; those which aren't are determined by convention and tradition. On our initial visit to Drouot, we popped our heads into each of the rooms where sales were going on. There was a jewellery sale, a general antique sale, a sale of paintings and illustrations, that collection of busts, and some others. As with so many aspects of our Drouot experience, Frances and I were fully aware of what was happening but at the same time totally mystified. Our confusion wasn't caused by merely being unable to understand what was being said, because we had lots of supporting information: in each room there was a monitor showing a photo of the lot under the hammer, with a short description and the estimated price. The screen even showed the amount of the current bid as bidding progressed, helpfully converted from Euros into sterling and US dollars.

No, it wasn't the principles of what was happening that confused us, and it wasn't the fact that the proceedings were conducted in high-velocity low-key demotic French. What we couldn't work out was the process of selling: why did it need so many officials and employees to conduct a sale, and what on earth were they all doing?

For starters, in several of the salerooms into which we peeped, it took some time to work out who was the auctioneer, the *commissaire-priseur*, the government-licensed official who must preside over every public auction. Although there was always one person seated on a slightly higher dais than the others, he or she often appeared to be fairly remote from the proceedings, totally lacking the charisma and audience engagement skills that characterise *all* British auctioneers, and clearly with little interest even in scanning the room to catch bidders' eyes. Every so often the auctioneer would summon up enough energy to pronounce "*adjugé*", with or without the use of a gavel, to signify that a lot was sold and to move on to the next one. But otherwise they seemed scarcely to participate at all.

On one side of the more or less somnolent auctioneer sat at least two clerks, whose role appeared to be to take the official record. One of these was responsible for working the computer system to show the progress of bidding for each lot, and for calling out any live internet bids received. The clerks appeared also to be holding commission bids on behalf of absentee bidders, and would throw such bids into the proceedings from time to time.

On the other side of the auctioneer, at a lower level, sat the independent expert, whose job, like Laurence's, had been to catalogue the lots in the sale and to produce estimated prices. The role of the expert on the day of the sale was to read out the catalogue description to the audience. In the sales which we spectated, some did this with energy and enthusiasm, others mumbled. Occasionally, during bidding, one of the experts might call out a bid, so we assumed that they too must be empowered to act on the instructions of absent bidders.

At the side of the room was a row of staff members armed with telephones, who were taking instructions from bidders as the sale proceeded. Their role was easy to understand, and they did their work as we would have expected it to be done in a British saleroom.

Then there were the porters, no longer Savoyards from the UCHV in black uniforms with *cols rouges*, but burly red-overalled workers from Drouot's current transportation contractors. It seemed that instead of relying on a picture on a monitor screen to identify the lot being offered for sale, it was an essential component of a French auction that the object should be physically displayed to the bidding audience. A simple enough task with an auction of easily-portable jewellery or antiquarian books, but not so easy if the lots include monumental items of antique furniture or stone sculpture which require to be located and either paraded across the front of the saleroom or pointed out very clearly at a rate of 100 lots per hour. To get it right, you need a large team of porters (present), a competent director or choreographer (quality seemed variable) and plenty of time for preparation and rehearsal (unlikely when trying to shift 600,000 lots through 2,000 sales every year). Our brief exposure to a single afternoon of Drouot sales suggested that the system works far from smoothly, but muddles along in a slightly chaotic fashion, involving frequent mis-identification of lots, much bumping-into-each-other by porters, gesticulation by the *crieur*, and significant levels of ill-feeling. In short, this aspect of Drouot's operations appeared much like every other busy workplace.

I have just mentioned the *crieur*, the final actor in the drama which unfolds before the bidding public – and, make no mistake, for all its mundanity the drama can get very intense indeed. The *crieur* is an official for whom there is absolutely no equivalent in the UK auction system. He – the ones that we witnessed in action were all men – is the single big personality in the saleroom, a combination of sergeant-major, choreographer, hustler, and market-stall barker. His job is to announce the next lot, to bully the porters into locating and displaying the item, to get the bidding going, to call out successive bids for the clerks to record, to throw in any commission bids that have come his way, and to indicate to the *commissaire-priseur* that bidding has stopped and the hammer price has been reached. After the sale, he's responsible for gathering payment and overseeing the issue of the *bulletin* which permits the buyer to claim the lot and remove it.

The job calls for charisma, chutzpah and a barrow-boy mentality, embodying all that appears to be lacking in the personality of the auctioneer. It's as if a British auctioneer has been carefully bisected along the line between professionalism and showmanship and separated out into two distinct roles. The *commissaire-priseur* is Dr Jekyll; the *crieur* is Mr Hyde. If Dickens had been a French novelist he would have had a closely-delineated *crieur* amongst his characters, and his illustrator Phiz would have chosen him as a subject for an engraving. Lacking Dickens and Phiz, we have some splendid illustrations of *crieurs* in action by the incomparable caricaturist Honoré Daumier **(See Illustrations, *Pictures 15 and 16*)**, and this description of the role in a French work of 1867 (my translation):

> "It would be a mistake to think that huge lungs and a loud voice are
> sufficient. To collect numerous bids when the bids don't exist requires
> a temperament of consummate deceitfulness. The trick is to warm up
> a cold audience who just don't want to buy, to communicate to them
> the sacred bidding flame."[50]

Whatever might have been their reputation and image in the nineteenth century, I'm not suggesting that there's anything dishonest about the Drouot *crieurs* of today. But during that enthralling Thursday afternoon at Drouot, watching several of them plying their trade, we came to the conclusion that if you were recruiting for a new *crieur*, your person specification would need to specify "jack-the-lad" high among the essential characteristics.

Returning to our hotel, Frances and I felt we had acquired at least a slight understanding of what we might expect to see and hear the next day. We were as ready as we were likely to get for tomorrow's big adventure: the sale of The Saint.

The Jug and The Saint and The Big Red Vase

I have been attempting to write at least a few lines of this book every day, partly trying as a first-time author to discipline myself, and partly trying not to lose the thread (such as it is) of my narrative. But it's hard to write a book and hard to find the time to do so. I'm retired and should have all the time in the world, but it doesn't work that way. Current events intervene to hamper my attempts to record historical events. I am writing this particular section in mid-July 2014. We are not long back from a holiday visiting delightful National Trust Tudor manor houses in Warwickshire. It's a warm summer, and the garden needs attention. Our daughter Sarah has been coming and going with her two small children to escape from her half-demolished house in its late stages of renovation. On Saturday they are moving in here for a week. As soon as they leave, we're off to Aberdeenshire for a few days to visit our younger daughter Hannah and family in their new house. We had a wedding to attend last week; Australian cousins visiting this week; meals out with two sets of friends tomorrow; the Edinburgh Festival starting in a couple of weeks' time; a weekend break in Copenhagen booked for next month following a big dinner for our fortieth wedding anniversary. It's a tough old life.

When I started this book, as noted in Chapter 6, I made an agreement with myself to use for my writing the hours (mostly early morning and late evening) which I would otherwise be using to list items for sale on eBay. I've kept to this pact and haven't sold a single item for more than six months. Because I only deal in antiques as a hobby (Saint and Jug excepting), the resulting loss of income is piffling. But note that when I contracted with myself, I only undertook to sacrifice my *selling* time to the writing endeavour, and not my *buying* time. In this way, my one-in-one-out collecting policy, which had been progressively weakening since adoption some two years ago, has been entirely thrown out of the window. Frances frequently threatens to dispose of some of the consequent clutter in the same way.

This week has been a particularly bad week. Or a good one depending upon which way you look at it. A new auction business started up in Leith – competition for Johnson & Andrews – and last Friday I had to go to their first sale to support the auctioneer, whom we know. I returned having bought eleven lots, some more sensible than others. I'm not about to enumerate them all, merely to let you know about a single session with an unusually extreme eleven-in-none-out result.

Then on Monday it got worse (or better). I did my regular rounds of the local charity shops and came back with two pots. One is a tiny lidded jam pot by a good Scottish potter, charming but unexciting. The other is a great big red vase (See Illustrations, *Picture 17*). I knew from my own experience and knowledge that it is a Chinese monochrome sang de boeuf vase, a type of object that I've admired for many a year but never expected to own. I wasn't expecting to get to own one any time soon. So, naturally, even before parting with my £6.99 in the charity shop I had a good Buzz going. I could tell that it wasn't brand new, because it's got a small worn paper label on the base with the number 22 written in ink faded to sepia in what seems to be a Victorian hand. It's in lovely condition with no obvious chips or cracks other than the crackle in the glaze which it's supposed to have. It's lovely quality and extraordinarily beautiful, and I've spent the whole week trying to research it. Here's what I know so far: if it's the real thing, it's a Langyao-glazed vase in a *guanyin zun* shape made in the imperial kilns at Jingdezhen during the reign of the Kangxi Emperor between 1661 and 1722, in the early part of the Qing Dynasty. If it isn't the real thing, it could be a copy made in China at any time between 1722 and last week. So I've sent pictures to some people who know how to tell an old one from a new one. Could this be the next Saint?

I'll keep you posted.

So, an exciting and enjoyable week, but little wonder that I have scarcely found a moment to continue my writing. I really must finally bring my story to its climactic point – the fall (*le coup*) of the hammer (*le marteau*) to confirm (*adjuger*) the auction sale (*la vente aux enchères*) of The Saint (*Le Saint Jean de Calvaire de l'Église de Saint Genest de Flavigny-sur-Ozerain*). I find I have a quiet moment. Let us proceed to a crowded auction room in Paris.

The Sale Begins

When Frances and I took our reserved seats in a middle row of Drouot Saleroom 7, we were fairly comfortable that we would be able to follow what was happening. But that was the only thing that we were comfortable about. We felt excited, nervous, edgy, foreign, exposed, anonymous. Did anyone other than Laurence and Benoît know who we were? Would The Saint attract any bids at all? Would he reach his estimated price? Would he beat the Theuley apostle?

The sale duly started at 2.30pm, and we soon found that we had the gist of what was going on. Progress was a little slower than the average rate of 100 lots per hour, because generally there was enthusiastic and competitive bidding, and many lots were comfortably exceeding their highest estimated prices. Clearly this was a popular sale attended by interested buyers with well-lined pockets. Encouraging so far. As the sale proceeded, we became aware that the room was becoming more and more crowded. Turning in our seats, we could see a crush at the back of the hall with the standing audience spilling out the doors. Spectators were gathering in force to witness Drouot's major event of the week: the sale of lot 70.

The moment arrived. The auctioneer mumbled. Laurence read out a brief description of the lot. The long bank of telephone operators to the left of the room poised themselves over their phones. A porter displayed The Saint to the audience and placed him temporarily on a stand at the front of the room. The *crieur* paced about in front of the podium seeking out bids from the audience and the telephone operators. Bidding was opened at €50,000. Although I hadn't set a reserve price with Laurence, she wouldn't have agreed to a sale at a lower price. A first bid was received and recorded on the monitor. Haltingly, in thousand-euro steps, bidding from the audience and telephone bidders climbed to €70,000, then faltered. The price had reached the low estimate. So far so good. The room held its breath.

The Hammer Falls

After a short, anxious pause in the bidding, other bidders started to come on board. The price continued to climb, soon exceeding the €77,000 budget gathered by the Flavigny-sur-Ozerain community for their pre-emption attempt. I wish I could describe the next two minutes in detail, but to tell the truth, it's all a bit of a haze. All I know is that it seemed to be both an instant and an eternity. In order to give a detailed account I would need to make up incidents which I can't actually remember, and since this book is strictly non-fiction, I can't do that. I can't say if the bidders were present in the room, or on the telephone, or on the internet, or had left advance bids with the *crieur* or the experts or the clerks. I can't say if there were multiple bidders, or at what point the bidding changed to a tussle between just two competitors. I can't say if or at what stage a hush fell upon the room in excited anticipation of the point at which the hammer would fall. I can't say whether Frances or I took a single breath as bids for The Saint crept up to Laurence's upper estimate of €100,000 and then carried on. I suspect not.

But I can say that the bidding continued beyond the upper auction estimate. And continued, slowly, inexorably. Then it halted. The combined efforts of the *crieur*, the *commissaire-priseur*, the clerks and the telephone and internet bidding operators failed to squeeze any more bids out of any more bidders. A dramatic pause, and the hammer fell at €200,000. Huh? *Pardon? Oui, deux cent mille euros.* Two hundred thousand euros.

Stunned, we remained in our seats while the next few lots were sold. Then we quietly left the saleroom and the Hôtel Drouot. We walked a few hundred metres until we found a Haagen-Dazs café in Boulevard Haussmann, where we sat at an outside table and calmed ourselves with large ice creams while responding to congratulatory texts from friends and relations who had been following the sale online. As I recall, we were strangely subdued. But I do remember one comment. As we sat, we saw a shiny black Maserati passing by. To make conversation, I said to Frances: "We could afford that".

When auctioneers publish their results, the convention is that they show the amount actually paid for the item by the buyer. This includes the hammer price plus the auctioneer's commission plus tax payable on that commission. So the Drouot and Piasa records show that the actual price paid for The Saint was not €200,000 but €248,380. At the sterling/euro exchange rate on the day of the sale, that was about £210,000.

Here are some statistics:

• Out of some 600,000 auction lots sold at Drouot in calendar year 2013, my statue was one of just 153 which sold for more than €150,000.
• He came in fourth in Drouot's 2013 league table of Classical Sculpture.

- He was equal ninth in the list of Piasa's top sales in 2013.
- He set a world record for works attributed to Claus de Werve and his workshop.
- He sold for 612.86 times the amount that I paid for him at Johnson & Andrews. This multiple was not my Personal Best: in fact The Saint came third in my all-time league table of relative re-sale profitability. I'll tell you about the second-placed item in Chapter 13 and the overall winner in Chapter 14.

Result!!!

But not unalloyed good news. Remember the Theuley Apostle? With a final price of €250,857 paid for him in January 2011, he beat The Saint by a whisker. However, I wasn't quite as upset by this outcome as I had expected to be.

12

THE AESTHETE

What's in this Chapter

I'm not quite at the end of the story of The Saint, but I'll be relating what happened after the sale a little later. On re-reading what I wrote in the chapter just ended, I note with mild dismay that while it had a strong emotional content, the heightened states in which I portrayed myself in Paris were mostly of the basest kind, including fear, paranoia, greed, triumph, gloating, and the rest. This chapter also has an emotional slant, but in it I'll try to adopt a rather loftier tone.

Away back in Chapter 8 I looked at a range of definitions available for those who study, acquire and dispose of fine art and antique objects. I tried to find a suitable term to define myself, and concluded that I can be described as a collector and part-time dealer, just like many of the peers who I meet in the saleroom most Saturday mornings.

Then in Chapter 10 I set out to discover how normal I am with reference to my collecting and dealing activities. I enlisted the aid of two imaginary behaviour scales and satisfied myself (if no-one else) that my behaviour is well within the normal range.

In this chapter, two further issues are addressed. Firstly, how I respond to art objects and antiques aesthetically, in the hope that by extension, my findings might also resonate with people who are like me, assuming of course that there are any others like me. Secondly, how I decide what to keep and what to sell, again hoping that there will be resonances amongst my readership.

Neither of these issues lends itself to use of the pseudo-academic approach attempted in Chapter 8 or to the pseudo-statistical approach attempted in Chapter 10. I'll try to explore them in other ways.

Philistine versus Aesthete

I define the aesthetic response as the extent to which your attachment to an object is determined not by its value, not by its rarity, not by the urge to own it, not by the fact that a celebrity owns a similar one, not by someone else telling you how excellent it is, but by something much less tangible: by your personal and subjective perception of a particular quality or set of qualities present in the object which incite in you a strong emotional attraction. Although I'm calling it the aesthetic response, it doesn't mean that in order to experience it you have to be someone who is conventionally regarded an aesthete. As for the particular quality which ignites your aesthetic response, you could label it as beauty, but that doesn't mean it has to be beautiful in any conventional or widely accepted sense.

In this section I intend to be quite reticent and to skirt some dangerous waters. The main difficulty is to talk about aesthetics without getting drawn into matters of quality or taste. I don't intend to say much about either, because opinions about quality and taste uttered by critics, curators, connoisseurs and more generally by members of the chattering classes, tend invariably to mask aesthetics with a thick and impenetrable overlay of irrelevant issues: intellectualism, elitism, money, markets, politics, snobbery, fashion, race, class, gender and more. There are critics who state as a fact that the pinnacle of human artistic achievement was reached in the Italian Renaissance. Bernard Leach insisted that "the qualities of the pottery of the T'ang and Sung dynasties [reach] the height of ceramic beauty"[51]; others say the same about pots made at Iznik or Urbino or Meissen or Sevres or Worcester. Yet others say that you can only properly appreciate art if you are a Gentleman.

Some critics say old is good and new is bad; others say the reverse. In paintings, some say that only representational art is real art; others favour abstraction. Some expend huge amounts of energy distinguishing between art and craft; or between "real" art made by named artists, and "folk" art made by unnamed craftspeople and artisans, often dismissed as inferior. Critics don't merely know what is art and what isn't, and whether it's good or bad, but they also presume to tell everyone else.

I am not engaging here in a polemic against all art criticism. I am no more qualified to do that than I am to tell anyone whether a piece of art is good or bad. Moreover, I'm happy to read and listen to a certain amount of art criticism in order to learn, to inform myself of others' opinions, and (hopefully) to enhance my own aesthetic enjoyment of art. As I have argued earlier in this book, I don't consider The Eye for art as being entirely innate, but as a faculty whose development can be refined and enhanced by learning and experience built upon a basic foundation of aptitude. I think similarly about the aesthetic response.

As for my own opinion about taste, I tend to go along with the potter and commentator Grayson Perry's view that taste is not a thing in itself but merely an evanescent construct of class and culture:

> "Professional aesthetes in deconstructed suits and statement spectacles would love it if there were strict overarching rules of good taste. I fear they search in vain. I started my research with a full set of prejudices about the "inferior" taste of the working class I had left behind. I now find myself agreeing with the cultural critic Stephen Bayley that good taste is that which does not alienate your peers. Shared taste helps bind the tribe. It signals to fellow adherents of a particular subculture that you understand the rules. Within the group of, say, modified hatchback drivers, there is good and bad taste in loud cars in much the same way as there is good and bad taste in installations within the art world. Outsiders may find it baffling or irritating, but that is of less importance to insiders than impressing one's peers."[52]

What I would like to be able to do is to leave all matters of quality and taste aside and talk about the aesthetic response in isolation. But, of course, it's impossible to fully isolate aesthetics from the hugely complex web of social, political and psychological stimuli with which it is interconnected.

However I do believe that it is possible to distinguish between people in terms of the *intensity* of their aesthetic response to beautiful objects. This in itself is a dangerous statement because it could lead into interminable discussion about what I mean by the term aesthetic response. For example, what's the difference (if any) between the way one might respond emotionally to, say, a blue sky with light fluffy clouds in it, and a *painting* of a blue sky with light fluffy clouds in it? If there is indeed a difference, I wouldn't know how to describe it, and I am certainly not competent to comment on it. So yet again I'll sidestep an important issue and avoid being drawn into this particular controversy.

To recapture my easily-lost thread, I believe that some people will have a stronger response than others, to a real or a painted blue sky, or to anything else which might, however loosely, be labelled with the epithet beautiful. Let's call those with the weakest response Philistines, and those with the strongest response Aesthetes.

You can't scientifically measure it because everyone's aesthetic response to every object is unique and personal to him- or herself. Thus, everyone is abnormal, and thus, everyone is normal, and thus, attempts at calibrating any individual on a quadrant analysis chart would be pointless and meaningless. Mr Goldbrick is interested in art and antiques for their value only and for no other reason, so you might expect him to be a Philistine. But if you take him to a garage and stand him in front of a 1956 Mercedes-Benz 300SL Gullwing, he might be struck dumb in contemplating its sculptural lines. On the other hand Mr PennyRed is obsessed with collecting every possible variant of his stamp, and you might expect him to have the qualities of an aesthete. But it might never have occurred to him that the Penny Red is an object of beauty; and he mightn't know what you are talking about if you point this out to him. Jack Reacher seems an archetypal Philistine, but perhaps when passing through Chicago to evade the authorities and eliminate a few villains he might stop off at the Art Institute and spend ten minutes in rapt contemplation of Edward Hopper's *Nighthawks*, admiring the painting's quietness, mystery and alienation. History doesn't record whether Homer and Langley Collyer experienced an aesthetic connection with any of the thousands of objects which they hoarded in their home, but Homer was an accomplished musician so we can assume he felt an aesthetic response with his ear even if not with his eye.

As for me, when it comes to fine art and antiques, I'm nearer to being an aesthete than a philistine. I have objective proof of this.

Around twenty years ago, I had a middle management job in the National Health Service. I was busy all the time with work, caring for my children, studying in the evening for an MBA degree, paying off the mortgage, helping to care for my ailing mother-in-law who lived with us. Collecting was banished to the background, with no money for buying or time for selling. Saturday mornings were spent not at the auction but cheering on the school hockey team.

My boss was called Ken. He developed an interest in psychometric testing, and decided that in order to help with our professional development, all the managers who reported to him should be subjected to a battery of tests. I duly spent a full day filling in questionnaires, and the next day Ken met with me to discuss my results. Compared to my peer group (male, 40s, UK-based, graduate, management grade) I turned out to be not all that much different from the average, albeit a little more liberal-minded and quite a lot more neurotic. But in one out of the thirty personality facets measured it turned out that I'm an outlier. The odd one out? Artistic interests, described in the report's narrative section thus:

> *"High scorers on this scale love beauty, both in art and in nature. They become easily involved and absorbed in artistic and natural events. They are not necessarily artistically trained nor talented, although many will be. The defining features of this scale are interest in, and appreciation of natural and artificial beauty. Low scorers lack aesthetic sensitivity and interest in the arts."*

On this measure, my score was near the maximum.

I don't recall hearing any more about the psychometric testing episode at the time. Nothing came of the exercise. Shortly afterwards Ken resigned from general management in the NHS and re-trained as a clinical psychologist.

Out of curiosity, I have just re-taken a simplified version of the same battery of psychometric tests, which is now in the public domain and available online[53]. The result two decades on: just the same. My highest score out of the thirty personality traits remains artistic interests. The ninetieth percentile. What a surprise!

Not-the-Jug

To demonstrate, I am going to try to tell you in detail about my aesthetic response to a specific object.

The object is a jug (**See Illustrations, *Picture 18***). It is not The Jug which figures so prominently elsewhere in this book, so I shall refer to it as Not-the-Jug. Here are the facts. Not-the-Jug is a large-ish salt-glazed stoneware jug, made in the 1950s at Winchcombe Pottery by the potter Ray Finch (1914-2012). It is squat, brown, plain and undecorated. I bought it about two years ago for £2 at the Johnson & Andrews weekly outdoor junk sale. At some time in the past it has been shattered into many pieces and inexpertly repaired. Even if it were in perfect condition it wouldn't be worth more than a few tens of pounds because Ray Finch's work isn't much collected and is not rare. So there isn't much to recommend Not-The-Jug in terms of market value, collectability, or critical acclaim. Studio pottery in general is not currently fashionable, except for work by a few potters who have somehow broken into the mainstream market and become celebrities. But Ray Finch was no Edmund de Waal or Grayson Perry. He was a quiet, self-effacing man who avoided publicity and contented himself with making beautiful understated pots, running his pottery, and passing on his skills to new generations of potters. As a result he's probably less well known and his work is less desirable than that of many of the younger generation of potters who learned their craft (art?) from him.

The long-established Winchcombe Pottery was revived from a moribund state in 1926 by Michael Cardew after he parted company with Bernard Leach in St Ives. Early on, he employed the retired potter Elijah Comfort and the boy potter Sidney Tustin to help him run the pottery. Ray Finch came along in 1935. Unlike the local artisans Comfort and the two Tustins, Sid having been joined by his brother Charlie, Finch was a middle-class lad with an education and a well-formed philosophy of life, and he soon became Cardew's second-in-command and then a full partner. Eventually he bought the business from Cardew and for the next sixty years and more he was the owner, principal potter, teacher and mentor to new talent at Winchcombe. The pottery started by making slip-glazed earthenware but then progressed to stoneware in the early 1950s. I think that Not-the-Jug is from the early period of stoneware production.

Not-the-Jug is 20 cms tall and 17 cms in diameter across its belly. It holds about two litres of – not water; shall we say cider or porter? The shape is a shape that hasn't changed much in thousands of years. You can see mediaeval jugs using the same forms in pretty well any local museum in Britain and throughout much of Europe. The body is globular, narrowing to a flat base with no footrim. The neck is wide and flaring, the top rim flattened to a slight concavity. The spout is beautifully formed: because of its serious damage I wouldn't risk filling Not-the-Jug with liquid to see how it pours, but I have

197

not a scintilla of doubt that you could pour a pint of a traditional brew from it to form a perfect head of foam in your pewter tankard without a single drip or dribble. Faultless pouring is of course a rare quality in a jug, as witnessed by the annoyingly irremovable discoloured rings found on the flat surfaces of most antique tables and sideboards.

There is no decoration other than indented bands below the neck and above the base. Below and above these, the clay has been left with visible throwing rings, while in the wide band around the belly the clay has been smoothed. Evenly spaced around the widest part of the pot are six low-relief tabs, formed in the wet clay by the potter's thumb – a minimal style feature seen in thousand-year-old Chinese and Korean pottery. The handle is in perfect proportion to the body, simple in shape and attached without adornment or fuss, its only decoration a thumb-tab at the top to match those on The Jug's shoulders. Again, it's rare to find a big jug with a comfortable handle elegantly fashioned. At the base of the handle is Ray Finch's personal seal, the WP monogram for Winchcombe Pottery with a small dot to indicate that the pot was thrown by Finch himself.

The salt-glaze is a delicate, glossy caramel colour, like that seen on Bellarmine-type jugs from northern Europe. The salts thrown into the kiln during firing have given the surface a very slightly pitted orange-peel look and feel. The inside of Not-the-Jug is glazed too, with a greenish-grey ash glaze. Not all jugs are glazed inside and out. As a result, some jugs leak.

I have sixty or seventy jugs of one kind or another in my house, and many – perhaps a substantial majority – wouldn't pass any test of full functionality: too heavy to lift, dribbly pouring, leaky, too big, too small, awkward and uncomfortable handle. Not-the-Jug is fully fit for its purpose of containing and dispensing liquids. As an artefact and a functional vessel, Not-the-Jug is entirely satisfactory. It ticks every box.

Aesthetically too, Not-the-Jug satisfies. Unlike the Grecian Urn contemplated in Keats's Ode, it has no figurative decoration, but it nonetheless has a story to tell to anyone who takes the trouble to hear. It's a story about simple modest understated country craftsmanship, but at the same time it's complex and sophisticated – not a rustic pot created by an unschooled n^{th} generation village artisan repeating the style of his or her ancestors. No, this pot, while simple and minimalist, is a fully self-conscious artistic production by a potter heavily influenced by the Arts-and-Crafts aesthetic as espoused by Finch's master Cardew, underpinned with unmistakeable echoes of far eastern pottery as Anglicised and promulgated by Cardew's master Bernard Leach.

Of course you don't need to know all that stuff in order to experience deep aesthetic communication with Not-the-Jug. You only have to look at it (correction: I only have to look at it) to feel that it is an artwork of simple, quiet, sensual beauty, all in superb proportion, full of warmth from the colour and richness of the glaze, inviting and wonderfully tactile. For me, it embodies the very nearest you can get to full satisfaction from contemplating a ceramic object. For many of my readers, as I freely acknowledge, it's an old out-of-date dull worthless broken brown jug made by someone you've never heard of.

Well, that's the aesthetic response for you. Even if you could measure its intensity on a scale, you couldn't define its nature. When it comes to likes and dislikes, we're all as mad or as not-mad as each other. As someone once said, there's no accounting for tastes. No statistics either.

Keep or Sell?

Here's a paradox. I have done my best to demonstrate that I can get highly emotional about the objects in my collection, that I form very strong attachments to them, and that I derive huge satisfaction not only from contemplating them but also from owning them. I have also said elsewhere in this book that Frances and I find ourselves in retirement in reasonably comfortable financial circumstances and not in desperate need of extra money. Why, then, did I choose to sell to the highest bidders The Saint and The Jug, the two best and most extraordinary objects that I have ever possessed?

This is my next matter for investigation. Will a more thorough analysis of the Reacher-Collyer Scale and/or the Goldbrick-PennyRed Scale, or a correlation of my relative positions thereon, explain why or how I choose which objects to keep and which to sell? Or is it something to do with the intensity or lack of intensity of my aesthetic and emotional attachment to an object? Or any combination or permutation of the above?

In seeking an answer to these questions, I get little or no help from my two hypothetical behaviour scales or from the self-analysis of my relationship with Not-The-Jug. It seems clear that, except for the very furthest outliers, most non-materialists will over time accrete at least some possessions, and most hoarders will divest some; that some pure investors become attached to their purchases, and some avid collectors will on occasion sell an item even if only to buy a better or rarer one. But unfortunately I haven't thus far discovered any pointers as to how or why the choices are made; how owners make decisions that some objects must stay and others must go.

The conclusions that I will reach in this part of my investigation will, I hope, be a truthful account of my personal behaviour (otherwise I have been wasting my time doing all the self-examination required to write this book), but my hunch is that no two collector-dealers use identical criteria for making their selections. When in Chapter 10 I was discussing hoarding and collecting behaviour ranges I was attempting to draw some general conclusions. But when it comes to this matter of keep-or-sell, I can only try to explain my own individual choices and actions. And I'm not even certain that I will be able to provide a convincing account of how I make those.

Note incidentally that I start this argument from the default position that objects are for retention and that the decision to be made is about disposal. Perhaps that is the mark of a collector. Perhaps the non-collector (who is only likely to be included in my behaviour survey as an outlier, and who is unlikely to be reading this book) starts out from the opposite viewpoint: that disposal is the default and there needs to be a reason to keep an object. It's difficult for me to get my head round that thought, but I present it for completeness.

If you are a collector, here are some reasons that you might give when asked why you have decided to sell something from your collection:

Collector's reasons:
- To improve the collection by buying a better specimen.
- You already have another better specimen so have no need for this one.
- It's chipped/worn/creased/scratched and you must have a perfect one.

Financial reasons:
- You need the money.
- It is too valuable to afford the insurance.
- It wasn't worth anything when you bought it but now it's worth a bundle.

Commercial reasons:
- You're a dealer and selling is what you do.
- You bought it specifically to re-sell for a profit.

Aesthetic reasons:
- It's horrible – you were mad to buy it in the first place.
- It's junk – get rid of it. It doesn't match the other objects in the collection.
- It's the wrong colour.

Practical reasons:
- To make space.
- You are downsizing your collection.
- You bought it by accident or as part of a larger lot.
- It's too big or too small to display.

Emotional reasons:
- You don't like the object or can't make a connection with it.

Fashion reasons:
- It used to be fashionable but now it's kitsch.
- Nobody collects this sort of thing any more.

Taste reasons:
- Your taste has moved on to other things and this object has become an anomaly.
- You are embarrassed to have it in your house.

Security reasons:
- It can't be kept safely in the house because of the grandchildren, the dog, the damp.
- It is a museum piece and this house isn't a museum.

Philanthropic or altruistic reasons:
- Another collector wants it more than you do.
- It's too good or too important to be stuck in a private collection in a suburban semi – it needs to be properly documented, researched and preserved.

When disposing of an object (by selling or on rare occasions by giving it away), I have at one time or another cited all of the above reasons and no doubt many more. But are these decisions to keep or to sell always rational ones? I doubt it. If my collecting and disposal behaviour was entirely rational, my house wouldn't be so full of junk as it is.

Sometimes people ask me why I spend my days shuffling around charity shops and auction rooms, instead of sitting with my feet up, or playing golf, or fishing, or gardening, or doing other things that my peer group of retired professionals do. My standard explanation goes something like this: "It's a hobby. I buy an object that I like the look of. Then I bring it home to examine it and learn about it. Then I decide on one of three possible outcomes: to keep it in my collection; to sell it; or to give it away. It's an enjoyable pastime, and what's more it's self-financing, doesn't cost me a penny, and doesn't do any harm".

It's a neat and simple story, and mostly I believe myself when I'm telling it. But it is incomplete because it doesn't explain how I make the decision, and sometimes I feel disingenuous because it isn't completely true. My standard answer masks two bald facts to which I have to confess. Firstly, I think that I probably do have some kind of fairly mild, currently non-pathological, compulsion to buy objects, and in many cases I find it quite upsetting to dispose of them, although I acknowledge the necessity do so in order to keep a grip on my family and social functioning and on my mental wellbeing. Secondly, I sometimes buy for the sole purpose of re-selling at a profit, and I take a mild satisfaction in keeping a tally of my success rate using aggregate income from sales and relative profitability compared to purchase price. Thus, my stock explanation, with its implications that I buy objects in order to examine and study them with a view to admitting them to my Collector's Cabinet of Curiosities, is in fact mere self-aggrandisement. I use it to imbue myself with superior qualities of connoisseurship and/or dilettantism which I have shown in a previous chapter that I don't actually possess. My actual motivations are more complex and less high-falutin' than I pretend.

Similarly, I'll always be able to select a reason from the long list given above to explain why I have decided to sell a specific object, but that might not always be completely true either. It might be something else altogether. It's time to stop the avoidance tactics and own up to the real reason why I sold The Jug and The Saint. It's difficult and embarrassing, but I'm going to come out with it.

I didn't feel worthy to keep them. There. I've said it.

Intimidated by The Jug

It's an odd thing, having an object of major cultural significance in the house. To start with, it's an enormous responsibility. The Jug came home from Johnson & Andrews and was with us for less than two weeks before I took it in to Bonham's for dispatch to London and eventual sale. It was pottery, and pottery can easily shatter. At the time, in 2007, we had no grandchildren yet, but we had a large, overweight and extremely friendly Golden Retriever called Phoebe who could happily sweep an entire collection of ceramics onto a tiled floor with one cheerful wag of her tail. She never did so, but only because of constant vigilance by Frances and me. The Jug was a bit grubby when it came home and needed a wash, awkward and risky in our unforgiving ceramic kitchen sink. Then it had to be photographed, requiring it to be posed and balanced in a number of unnatural and potentially dangerous positions in order to get shots of its identifying marks and other features.

In The Jug's short period with us it moved from shelf to shelf, mantelpiece to bookcase to hall chest, seeking a position where it didn't look like what it was – an outlier. As I've said before, it wasn't a conventionally beautiful object. It was heavy, confusingly decorated and very very brown. At the same time it had enormous presence and a certain magnificence. You couldn't walk past it without stopping, looking and saying "what on earth is that extraordinary jug?" But it just didn't seem comfortable in our house.

And I just didn't feel comfortable about having it there, and not because of how much money I had paid for it. True, £1,000 was a lot for an old pot, but I had occasionally paid that amount or more for an object before, such as the odd picture or piece of furniture or an item of jewellery for Frances. Anyway it's not unexpected for a household to contain a few items of similar or greater value – the sofas in the living room, the flat-screen TV, the computer, an engagement ring, not to mention the car and the house itself.

Neither was it the potential re-sale value of The Jug that made me decide to sell it. When I bought it I was confident that I could get my money back if I re-sold it, but did not expect much more. Even when I was told by the Bonham's expert that it might sell for £3,000–£4,000, it wasn't a foregone conclusion that I would consign it for sale. The money would be a great help at a time when things were rather tight, but I didn't need money so much that re-sale was an absolute imperative. I could have kept it as a prized object amongst my assorted collection of antiques and art works. Of course when the hammer eventually fell at £12,000 The Jug was already long gone from my hands, but even if I had known in advance that the price would be so high, I could still have decided to keep it. But instead I chose to sell it.

Another thought. I have said much earlier in this book that at the time when I bought The Jug, I had never seriously studied or collected ceramics, and possessed only a very unfocussed and random assemblage of pottery and porcelain objects. It was the purchase and re-sale of The Jug that set me off on collecting studio pottery. Whereas before I scarcely owned any examples of this particular category of ceramics, I now have a house-full, including some spectacular pieces by some very notable potters, although none with anywhere near the re-sale value of The Jug. What if I had found my Jug *after* instead of *before* forming my studio pottery collection? Now in 2016 instead of then in 2007, now, when my financial position is a little more comfortable, would I wish to keep The Jug as the star and centrepiece of my collection? Or would it still make me feel uncomfortable and intimidated? Would I still feel that someone else – be it a connoisseur, a museum, a private collection, an investment fund – would be more suitable and more worthy to own it than me? Would I re-sell it? I think so.

Bouleversed by The Saint

Unlike The Jug, The Saint fitted into our house beautifully. Standing on the hall-chest at the bottom of the stairs, he presided for the eighty-seven days that he was with us. Frances would often catch me standing looking at him, sometimes talking to him. On occasion I would catch Frances giving him a friendly hello as she passed. She doesn't get as attached to and anthropomorphic about inanimate objects as I do, but she does have her moments.

The Saint didn't cost much to buy, and for the first few weeks after buying him I had no real notion about his age or origin. Until the day he was sold, I didn't have a clear idea of his value. He was aesthetically stunning; he wasn't fragile; he looked fabulous on display in the house; he didn't represent a major investment; I had no financial imperative to profit from him; I didn't find anything unconscionable about his religious and iconographic significance.

But although he was by a huge margin the most extraordinary and beautiful object I had ever owned, I knew from the moment he came into my possession that he wasn't for keeping. Why not?

Humility is not something I am noted for. But being in the intimate presence of The Saint made me feel humble: almost overcome by his beauty, his age, his spirituality, his history and the astounding fact of his survival. I have no problems about forming an emotional relationship with an object of this kind – I'll happily do it in a transitory way in a museum or a gallery. However, being the owner of such an object; being responsible for its safe passage between now and perpetuity; giving it the attention and diligence that it requires as a tiny but significant beacon in the world's cultural history – no, sorry, but it's just too much for me. And then there is the moral and ethical dimension to ownership and disposal of such an important object, but I'll try to approach that thorny issue in Chapter 14.

This has been a difficult chapter to write. I tried to talk about aesthetics, an academic and intellectual task for which I am entirely unqualified; and I tried to talk about my own individual aesthetic response, a task for which I should be qualified but for which I don't have confidence in my ability. And then I tried to analyse how and why I choose to keep some objects and dispose of others. And then I owned up to feeling unworthy to keep the best ones. Do I feel better for having got it all off my chest? Up to a point, yes. But I might feel better still, readers, if I had been absolutely and completely up-front and open with you and told the whole story.

There's a bit more, which confounds and contradicts much of what I have written in the last several pages. Because sitting on a shelf immediately behind the desk at which I am typing this book is another item which I own, quite as rare and historically important as The Saint or The Jug if not as valuable. It's beautiful and it's captivating and it's desperately fragile and it belongs in a place where it can be better cared for and protected and studied than is possible in my house with me as its owner. It intimidates me and humbles me. If my house was burning down it would be the one thing that I would rescue from my entire collection. Like The Saint and The Jug it was bought in recent years at Johnson & Andrews saleroom in Edinburgh. But unlike with them, I couldn't bear to part with it for worlds. It is a little book, and I'll be writing more about it in the next chapter.

13

VALUE

What's it Worth?

What makes a buyer pay as much as £14,400 for an old brown pottery jug? As much as €248,380 for an old wooden statue? Why not more? Why not less? The Jug is made of a couple of kilograms of Cornish clay, intrinsic value precisely nothing. The Saint is made out of a seven-kilogram log of walnut wood, also with no intrinsic value. I could go into a charity shop today and buy a brown pottery jug for a pound or two, and that's what it would be worth. I know because I have bought dozens of them, including Not-The-Jug which, despite its (to me) hypnotic beauty, wouldn't have much market value even if it were in perfect condition instead of shattered and repaired. Statues of saints aren't quite so common, but you can find hundreds of them listed on eBay from just a few pounds upwards.

As we have seen, The Jug is not like other jugs, and The Saint is not like other statues. They are both very special. They are extraordinarily rare examples of their respective genres, made by exceptionally celebrated artist/ craftsmen. They are of international significance culturally and academically, and excite enormous interest from museums and collectors. Both objects are at the summit of importance in relation to the classes of artefact to which they belong.

So it might be equally interesting to ask what makes a buyer pay as *little* as £14,400 for The Jug and as *little* as €248,380 for The Saint?

Bernard Leach and Michael Cardew were both seminal figures in the development of modern studio pottery, jointly and severally exercising a huge influence on virtually everything that came after them in their field throughout the world and up to the present day. Their three-year collaboration at St Ives from 1923 to 1926 produced a large amount of innovative and important finished work, but only one object is known which they signed jointly: The Jug. Viewed in this light, £14,400 seems cheap.

Here's another world-class collaboration: that of Vincent van Gogh and Paul Gauguin, in Arles in the summer of 1888. What would be the price if a spectacular picture painted jointly by them and signed by them both came onto the market? £100 million? Easily! OK, I know that Bernard and Michael aren't quite as famous as Vincent and Paul, and I know that studio pottery isn't quite such a mainstream taste among connoisseurs and collectors as post-impressionist painting, but it's a huge price difference, isn't it?

Claus de Werve was the Duke of Burgundy's official sculptor, and second only to his more famous uncle Claus Sluter as the most important and influential sculptor in the "International Gothic" style of the late mediaeval period. Sluter's innovative naturalistic portrayal of religious subjects was further developed by Werve and his successors, and together they had lasting influence on the development of Renaissance sculpture in Northern Europe, and even on the sculptors of the Italian Renaissance from Donatello onwards. Sluter's style also influenced painters, and foremost among these in the Burgundian empire was Jan van Eyck, an almost exact contemporary of Werve. Van Eyck was busy painting in his studio in Bruges at much the same time as Werve was at work in Dijon carving the Flavigny Calvary group. Both were in the service of Duke Philip the Good, and if they didn't know each other personally, it is highly probable that they knew each other's work. Now, if a rediscovered painting by van Eyck came onto the market, what would it fetch at auction? Many tens of millions for sure. Again, a big difference between that sort of price and the mere quarter of a million euros paid for The Saint.

An economist might be able provide a theoretical model for determining the price of an artwork, but I can't. I studied a little economics forty years ago while working for my Chartered Secretary professional qualification, and then again later as part of my MBA degree. Never could make head or tail of it. I did however get a basic grasp of the principles of supply and demand, how the price of a commodity is determined by variations in market demand operating against variations in supply; the number of people wishing to purchase an object against the number of objects available to be purchased.

Forty years ago when Frances and I first set up home in Edinburgh, we spent all our savings buying medium-quality Georgian and Victorian furniture to furnish our flat. In those days it was more expensive to buy, say, an antique mahogany dining table – even a fairly medium-grade one – than buying new. There was plenty of supply, with lots of old tables available to buy in auctions and antique shops and in the articles for sale columns of the newspapers, and there was plenty of demand from among the young upwardly-mobile professional classes. They were expensive things, but we really wanted one, and we were ready to pay the going rate. As far as I recall, we paid £175 for ours in about 1976, representing perhaps a month's joint take-home salary. It's a decent, unspectacular late Georgian mahogany sectional dining table, and, no longer used for dining, it's standing across the room from me right now as I type, groaning under the weight of a mass of unsorted, unidentified and unsold studio pottery. And what's it worth today? If it had kept up with inflation, the price now would be £1,325.87[54]. But in fact it's still worth about £175, or maybe a little less. No-one wants brown furniture any more. It's all brand-new IKEA stuff, or, if you go for second-hand, you want mid-century retro teak or rosewood veneer, not Victorian and Georgian mahogany or oak. The supply is still there, but the demand has dropped like a stone for all except the very best quality pieces.

At the top end of the market, however, phenomenal prices are paid, with the most desirable objects being valued in multiples of tens of millions. For paintings, of course, from van Eyck to van Gogh to Bacon and Pollock. For big blingy diamond jewellery. For almost anything old and Chinese, following the upsurge of capitalist and commercial activity in China, which has spawned thousands of multi-millionaires, many eager to spend their money in the best salerooms buying up artefacts, principally porcelain and jade, to repatriate to China for their private collections. Since the wholesale destruction of art objects during the Cultural Revolution, much of the good stuff that survives is outside China, and the new wealthy classes want it back at virtually any price. Ditto for almost anything old and Russian. A selection of the next big things: collectable cars, street art, ethnic art, all already selling for millions in the more rarefied salerooms of the world.

Scarcity is usually an important determinant of price: classical economics says that the rarer and harder to get a thing is (gold, bread in a famine, heroin), the more people who want it will pay for it. But in the art and antiques world it doesn't always work in that intuitive way. If a thing is so rare that it hardly ever gets to the market, it might be that there is only a very small population of collectors who wish to buy it. Burgundian sculpture is incredibly rare; but collectors and buyers of Burgundian sculpture are rare too, at least at present. Supply and demand have met each other at a price point which seems astronomically high to us punters who frequent local salerooms, but which is only a small fraction of the prices paid for Impressionist paintings or for Italian Renaissance sculpture. Everyone wants a Picasso, and Picasso was exceptionally long-lived and prolific, so there are thousands and thousands of his works about, many of them, like his prints and ceramics, produced in multiple editions. His work comes to the market all the time, and the more that is available for sale, the higher the prices realised. In this case, it seems that the availability of supply stimulates demand rather than satisfying it, and prices keep on rising.

We have spoken about fashion, but fashion is only one driver of the way that the market moves. Another source of market influence – or, less politely, of manipulation or of downright exploitation – is the coterie of high-end dealers and gallerists, whose handsome livings are made from promoting and racking up prices for new and established artists and craftspeople. Their power is exerted over well-heeled clients with insufficient reliance on the quality of their own taste to choose for themselves art objects that they like and wish to own.

Taste and thus collectability and thus price are also affected by curators of public galleries and museums, and by critics, and by media coverage of celebrity collectors. The public knowledge that Brad Pitt and Angelina Jolie were enthusiastic (and incidentally knowledgeable) collectors of Arts and Crafts style antiques did wonders for the prices of objects designed and made by Archibald Knox for Liberty of London.

Finally, as we have seen earlier, the price of top-end art and antiques is racked up by Mr or Ms Goldbrick, who, in times when it's necessary to diversify the investment portfolio or to find a safe haven for surplus cash, treat this particular class of objects as commodities for trade and speculation.

I have tried to show in this book that my own collecting life hasn't been especially influenced by market forces such as those that I have just described. I buy to satisfy my own aesthetic needs as they develop over time. I buy opportunistically, according to my own fancies without seeking advice from dealers. I couldn't care less what the celebs are buying. I normally buy for pleasure and not for profit, but will happily take a profit if the opportunity arises. I rarely go out looking for a particular object; I simply go and see what's there. And I buy within a very low price band, usually paying just a few pounds, occasionally a few hundred, very rarely a thousand pounds (The Jug), but never thousands and thousands.

This behaviour has three consequences. First, that my house is full of objects that most fashion-followers would not find to their own taste. Second, that as with the brown mahogany furniture, a proportion of my stuff is worth much less now than its price when originally purchased. Third, that other than the stories of The Saint and The Jug, which you already know, you mightn't expect me to have much more to add to this chapter from my personal buying and selling experience which would throw light onto my arguments about how objects acquire or fail to acquire value.

However, I do indeed have two tales to tell. The first is about a little glass vase. The second is about a little book. First, the vase.

Gallé, Smith and the Martin Brothers

You might recall that in Chapter 7 I mentioned a tiny purple glass vase which I bought in the early 1970s in a jumble sale and gave to Frances (See Illustrations, *Picture 10*).

Browsing in the public library in those far-off pre-Internet days, I discovered that the vase was made by the celebrated French art nouveau glass maker Emile Gallé, and that it was valuable as well as beautiful. Tiny and delicate, it lived for a few years on Frances's dressing table, but somehow it never seemed comfortable, barely noticeable amongst our other, rather chunkier possessions. With no high shelf or glass-fronted vitrine for protection or adequate display, it risked being swept off its surface and smashed. But it was too lovely to simply put away in a cupboard. The vase was an outlier amongst our stuff. Pretty as it was, it was impractical to keep in our house and deserved to be owned by a specialist collector who could protect it and fully enjoy it and show it off alongside other objects of its period or by the same maker.

So we decided it was a seller, not a keeper. I identified Sotheby's Belgravia as the best auctioneer for art nouveau at the time, and they put it in their Decorative Arts sale on 10th November 1976. The little vase, lot number 39, sold for £80, a multiple of 800 times the purchase price. We were delighted.

Frances and I decided to invest the money in a pair of abstract oil-on-board paintings by a well-established Scottish painter by the name of Robert T. H. Smith (See Illustrations, *Picture 19*). At the time, Bob was a work colleague of mine, his income from painting being insufficient to allow him to live without a day-job. I bought direct from the artist and he gave me a small discount on the gallery price of the pictures. We still have them hanging in our living room and they have given us immense pleasure over the years, much more than we would have derived from the little vase.

Now, it might be of some slight interest to note the varying relative values of these objects over the intervening thirty-seven years between then and now. The clever inflation calculator which I used above to tell me the current value of my dining table tells me that the hammer price of £80 from selling the Gallé vase in 1976 would be equivalent to £606.11 today. Gallé glass remains hugely popular and collectable, but for smaller and less colourful pieces such as my vase, its value hasn't quite kept up with inflation over the period. From looking at prices currently paid for similar objects I estimate that if the same vase were to re-appear at Sotheby's today it might sell for a hammer price of just £300 – £400.

And how have the Bob Smith paintings done over the same timespan? When I bought my third painting by him just a couple of years ago (at Johnson & Andrews), I paid a mere £120 for it, and it's a much larger picture than either of the ones that I bought in 1976. So the value of Bob's work has scarcely increased even in cash terms over four decades. I don't care about this in the least, but these are fabulous pictures by a good modern abstract artist, and as such they illustrate how quality items can fail to acquire value in the art and antiques world over long periods of time.

I wonder what it is – or isn't – about the paintings of R. T. H. Smith that has caused them to fail commercially? I can think of a dozen or more of his Scottish contemporaries, none of them a jot more talented than him, whose works are now selling for thousands of pounds a pop. And of course there are many others, mostly artists whose names I have never heard, who didn't even get the recognition accorded to Bob and who either threw out their paints and brushes altogether, or who make work only for their own pleasure. Bob had catalogued solo shows in well-known commercial galleries, his works were featured in the big-city annual exhibitions and reviewed in the press, and some were bought for public collections. But they didn't catch The Eye of the market. His pictures were slightly dark, slightly edgy, slightly modernist at a time when modernism was becoming old-fashioned. Modernism is back to being trendy again now, and these paintings would look superb in today's retro domestic settings. But it is too late for R. T. H. Smith's work to become the next big thing.

In our frequent conversations during coffee breaks at work during the 1970s and 1980s, Bob predicted to me that his work would never become popular during his lifetime, and I fear that he was right. His reasoning was that he simply took too long over each picture, as a result of which his output was very low. It took him several years to produce enough work for each solo exhibition. So he never produced enough art to come to the full notice of the Scottish art-buying public. It was the very scarcity of his work which depressed its prices. Another prediction that Bob made was that his work would acquire value after his death. Sadly, he died suddenly in 2016, and at a recent memorial exhibition mounted by his family, Bob's last pictures were sold for just a few hundred pounds each. I rather doubt whether they will ever be more valuable.

Due to an unfortunate inability to throw documents away, I've kept the catalogue from the Sotheby's sale in November 1976 where my Gallé vase was sold. Browsing through it, I've found a postscript to this story about value. Lot 596 had an estimated value of £150–£200, so I might have been able to buy it for about twice the amount I received for the vase or twice the amount I paid for the Bob Smith pictures. It was a stoneware lidded jar in the shape of a comical and grotesque bird, a very early example of a "wally bird" tobacco jar made in London in 1881 by the four highly eccentric Martin Brothers **(See Illustrations**, *Picture 20*). These birds have become fantastically popular, and if this particular specimen re-appeared at Sotheby's today, you would expect to see an estimated price of at least £20,000.

If I had had the extra money to spare in 1976, would I have bought the wally bird instead of the Bob Smith paintings? Unlikely.

A Tale of Two Psalters

My second value story is about two books, one of which was bought on 16th January 2010 by me at Johnson & Andrews in Edinburgh. The other was bought on 26th November 2013 by a Mr David Rubenstein at Sotheby's in New York. I have never met Mr Rubenstein, who lives in Bethesda, Maryland. I would very much enjoy meeting him so that we could swap stories about old books, but am not likely to meet him. He and I have some things in common: we're both Jewish men in our mid-sixties (he's ten months younger than me), we both love old things, and we each own a little seventeenth-century book of psalms published for use in the non-conformist Christian church.

I have already referred to my book: it's the object mentioned in Chapter 12 that I'd rescue if my house was burning down, an exceptionally rare item of cultural importance, an object which scares the wits out of me to own, but which I wouldn't sell for worlds. The other book in this story, the one which belongs to Mr Rubenstein, is known as the Bay Psalm Book.

The title page of my little book has the following words:

THE
whole Booke of
PSALMES
in Prose and Meeter:
Truelie conferred with the
HEBREW Text
Printed at Edinburgh, by Andro
Hart, Anno 1617

Mr Rubenstein's book's title page says:

THE
WHOLE
BOOKE OF PSALMES
Faithfully
TRANSLATED into ENGLISH
Metre.
Imprinted 1640

Not a lot of difference so far. Here's a more detailed comparison:

	Andro Hart Psalm Book	**Bay Psalm Book**
Date	1617	1640
Place of publication	Edinburgh, Scotland, UK	Cambridge, Massachusetts, USA
Book size	101 x 76 mm	174 x 107 mm
Binding	Original exceptionally rare Scottish binding from Andro Hart bindery, broken at the spine and in unrestored condition	Re-bound in black morocco leather in 1850
Condition	Text believed to be complete and undamaged. Minor soiling throughout and small chips to corners of some leaves. Damage to flyleaves.	Minor losses and restorations. Manuscript corrections throughout. Some browning throughout, occasional minor marginal chips or tears, a few tiny scattered ink-holes.
Provenance	Unknown	Boston Old South Church
Rarity	One other copy listed in ESTC (English Short Title Catalogue)	Ten other copies known

As you can see, on the face of it my book has the edge over Rubenstein's. Mine is one of only two known copies, the other being in the collection of the National Library of Scotland in Edinburgh. I have seen it there and have compared the two copies. Theirs is very similar to mine as far as the text goes, and is in a similar original Hart binding, but at some time in the past it has been restored according to an outdated taste for trying to restore old books to what they looked like when new. This has involved extensive repairs to the stamped leather binding, and cropping of the page edges which have been re-gauffered and re-gilded. It looks superb but these days book conservation is more about stabilising wear and damage and preventing further deterioration than about making a book look like new. So in my inexpert opinion, my unrestored copy is the better one of the two.

The Rubenstein Bay Psalm Book is one of the best of the eleven known surviving copies, but has been considerably repaired and altered over time. Errata have been corrected in manuscript; during re-binding one leaf was reversed; one or two pages have been reinforced with backing sheets; there are a couple of minor textual losses; and the undistinguished 1850 binding has suffered from wear and has had repairs.

Bluntly, it's undeniable that my 1617 copy of the Andro Hart Edinburgh psalter is earlier, more original, less interfered-with and considerably rarer than David Rubenstein's copy of the 1640 Bay Psalm Book.

And what are they worth? I paid just £24 for my psalter at Johnson & Andrews. That's a ridiculously low price for such a rare and important book. I haven't yet shown it to any experts, but I estimate that if it were put into a good antiquarian book auction here in Edinburgh, the price would probably be something more than £1,000 and something less than £2,000. So if I wanted to sell it (which I don't), I could expect to make a very substantial profit. As for David Rubenstein's book, he paid US$14,165,000 for it, making it the most expensive printed book ever sold in the world.

I have omitted to mention before now that David Rubenstein is listed at number 810 in the Forbes list of the world's billionaires[55], with a net worth of $2.4 billion derived from being the boss of the private equity investment firm Carlyle, of which he was a co-founder. That's why I'm unlikely ever to meet him. He has a particular interest in historical documents, and in addition to the Bay Psalm Book he owns original copies of the Magna Carta, the Declaration of Independence, and the Emancipation Proclamation. A major philanthropist, he buys them not to keep privately in his library, but in order to lend them for public exhibition in museums and libraries.

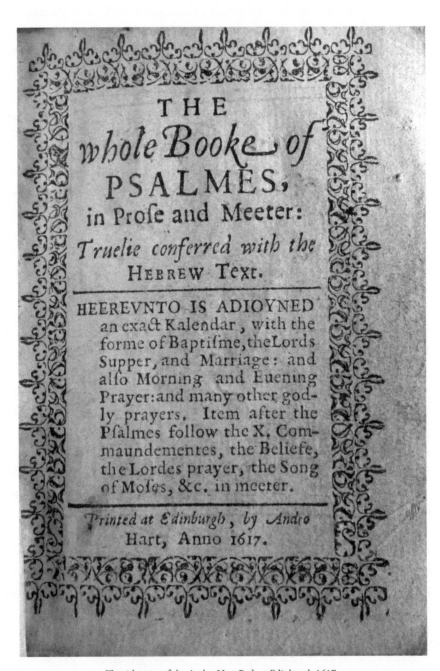

THE
whole Booke of
PSALMES,
in Profe and Meeter:
Truelie conferred with the
HEBREW Text.

HEEREVNTO IS ADIOYNED
an exact Kalendar, with the
forme of Baptifme, the Lords
Supper, and Marriage: and
alfo Morning and Euening
Prayer: and many other god-
ly prayers. Item after the
Pfalmes follow the X. Com-
maundementes, the Beliefe,
the Lordes prayer, the Song
of Mofes, &c. in meeter.

Printed at Edinburgh, by Andro
Hart, Anno 1617.

The title page of the Andro Hart Psalter, Edinburgh 1617.

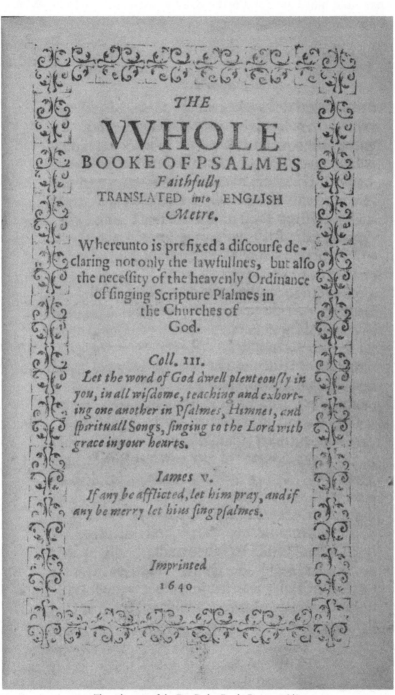

THE

VVHOLE

BOOKE OF PSALMES

Faithfully

TRANSLATED *into* ENGLISH

Metre.

Whereunto is prefixed a difcourfe declaring not only the lawfullnes, but alfo
the neceffity of the heavenly Ordinance
of finging Scripture Pfalmes in
the Churches of
God.

Coll. III.

*Let the word of God dwell plenteoufly in
you, in all wifdome, teaching and exhort-
ing one another in Pfalmes, Himnes, and
fpirituall Songs, finging to the Lord with
grace in your hearts.*

Iames v.

*If any be afflicted, let him pray, and if
any be merry let hims fing pfalmes.*

Imprinted
1 6 40

The title page of the Bay Psalm Book, Boston 1640.

So, why would he pay out 14 million bucks for an old psalter when I could have sold him a rarer and better one for just a teensy bit less? What's so special about the Bay Psalm Book? Well, admittedly there are a few significant differences between his book and my book. Mine contains the metrical translation of the Psalms made in the 1560s by Thomas Sternhold and Matthew Hopkins, which had been reprinted regularly since the late sixteenth century in many editions by several printers in England and by a few in Scotland. The Bay Psalm Book on the other hand contains a completely new translation of the Psalms, prepared by and for the Puritan population of Massachusetts and printed in this edition for the first time, a mere twenty years after the Pilgrim Fathers arrived in the ship *Mayflower* at Plymouth Rock. My book was one of several volumes of psalms printed over a number of years by Andro Hart in various sizes and formats; a few copies exist of each of the other editions but none is quite as rare as mine.

However the Bay Psalm Book has the distinct additional lustre of being *the very first book in English ever printed in America*. So it isn't merely a book, it's a totemic historical landmark. And it isn't just a landmark, it's a portable one, and one which can be bought and sold and exhibited with the philanthropist's name attached to it, and it's almost certainly the last one which will ever come up for sale, the others all residing in public collections or owned by venerable institutions.

Even so, this very exceptional piece of first-ness seems to add a most extraordinary premium to its value compared to my book. But curiously, the opinion of Sotheby's appears to be that the Bay Psalm Book derives the greater part of its auction price from its scarcity rather than from its historical significance. I know this from watching a brief video interview given to the New York Times immediately after the sale by David N Redden, the then Vice-Chairman of Sotheby's, who conducted the auction[56]. He seems very much more impressed by the book's extreme rarity than by its status as the first English book printed in America. He mentions the latter fact only in passing, while enthusiastically comparing the 11 known copies of the Bay Psalm Book with 48 copies of the Gutenberg Bible and 200 copies of the Shakespeare First Folio.

By this measure, and thus encouraged by the wise words of so august and authoritative a figure as the Vice-Chairman of Sotheby's, my psalter should be more valuable than David Rubenstein's. Perhaps I should be asking him for considerably more than $14 million for my book rather than considerably less. But I know he wouldn't be interested. Anyway, my book is not for sale.

14

QUALMS

Neurosis

You might have thought, mightn't you, that a pastime as innocuous as buying and selling antiques would give rise to scarcely any moral or ethical issues, or uncertainties or ambiguities or dilemmas or anxieties? I daresay that for many of my fellow bidders at Johnson & Andrews, their collecting and dealing lives are carefree, sunny and untrammelled by doubt or confusion. But not mine.

I wrote in Chapter 12 about recently re-taking an online psychometric test which I originally underwent some twenty years ago to find out if I'm still as much of an aesthetic outlier now as I was then. I am. My next highest score in the test was in the section dealing with neuroticism:

> "Your score on Neuroticism is high, indicating that you are easily upset, even by what most people consider the normal demands of living. People consider you to be sensitive and emotional... People high in neuroticism... respond emotionally to events that would not affect most people, and their reactions tend to be more intense than normal. They are more likely to interpret ordinary situations as threatening, and minor frustrations as hopelessly difficult."

I have insufficient self-awareness to agree or disagree strongly with this commentary. As to whether it's down to nature or nurture, or a combination of the two or something else entirely, I really couldn't say.

I could, I suppose, attribute this neurotic and anxious streak to my close genetic (but probably not familial) relationship with Woody Allen and Larry David, with Bob Dylan and Leonard Cohen, and even with David Rubenstein, who wonders aloud whether his philanthropy is "because of guilt or gratitude"[57].

Or I could put it down to being separated at birth from my mother who became ill from complications arising from a caesarean section. I wasn't reunited with her for three months, and in the interim I was passed around, a small and unwelcome parcel, alternately neglected and smothered by a succession of incompetent nannies and pernickety Jewish aunties; the former serially unable to satisfy in point of efficiency and cleanliness the obsessive demands of the latter, and the latter unable to withstand for more than a few days at a time the incessant mewling and puking of the monkey-like new nephew, simian son of Simeon. My one surviving aunt, now aged ninety-nine, invariably reproaches me for the occasion, sixty-eight years ago, when I vomited over her dress.

Or do my neuroses stem from other traumas? Was it from spending my adolescent years in a West End pub surrounded by an unusually diverse array of adult behaviour and life choices? Or from my parents' decision, when I was at the sensitive age of sixteen, to take the family into exile in a house in a Berkshire field, far from my beloved Central London and from the beneficial effects of street lights and teenage school friends?

Or perhaps it was a combination of the above, or none. But whatever the origin of my neuroses and anxieties, I find that my collecting and dealing behaviour inevitably engenders in my breast a welter of moral and ethical doubts, uncertainties and questions. Sometimes I can solve them more or less to my own satisfaction and move on; more often I leave them hanging unresolved, an annoying and unscratched itch.

This chapter contains a selection of some of the itchiest ones.

Caveant Emptor et Vendor

As an auction buyer, I revel in a bargain. The Buzz of discovery is greatly enhanced by the self-satisfaction gained from winning for almost no money a rare, interesting, beautiful, valuable object that is appreciated for its true worth and interest by none of the other parties involved, not the seller, not the auctioneer, not the other bidders, just by me, the expert, the connoisseur, the top dog of the moment. I scorn the auctioneer for his or her ignorance and lack of professionalism, I deride the vendor for lacking the common sense to identify the object and to make an effort to sell it through an appropriate outlet. Most of this childish and immature exultation and self-congratulation takes place in the privacy of my home, because, as recounted much earlier in this book, I have no wish to be known by auctioneers and regular fellow bidders as either an insufferable smart-ass know-all or as the person who made a bundle from that old Jug or that old Saint.

By contrast, when I'm selling an object rather than buying, I usually know precisely what I'm selling, and I work hard to find out the best way to sell it. So as far as I'm aware, I have never put myself in a position where a buyer might be able to exult at my expense. But I have on occasion found myself outraged on behalf of another seller when objects have been sold much too cheaply. So there I am, locked in the dilemma of simultaneously gloating over a bargain and agonising that an object has been sold too cheaply.

I don't think I have introduced the reader to my long-time friend Bill. Many years ago he was a colleague of Frances's at the University Library, but then he moved on to a more senior post in another Scottish city, where he has settled in retirement. I got to know him well because Bill, like me, is an amateur collector and dealer, and a regular at his local saleroom which, like his home town, will remain nameless in this account. Two or three times per year when we find ourselves in the same city we meet to swap auction stories over a meal. Bill is knowledgeable about many different branches of collecting but he is mainly interested in buying and selling pictures. Here is a story that he told me over a long lunch:

"A few months ago I was much later than usual arriving at the saleroom for my weekly Tuesday afternoon viewing. I hadn't had time to look at the online catalogue, and had only about twenty minutes to find out what was on offer before they closed at 5.00pm. But I wasn't too concerned because the next day's auction was one of their quarterly silver and jewellery sales, which are usually just the standard selection of silver and EPNS tableware and second-rate Victorian rings and brooches. I was there for form's sake, out of habit, just in case, but I had no hope or expectation of anything catching my eye.

"But I was wrong! In the sale were about twenty lots of coins. I know a bit about coins and I was gobsmacked! It was the best collection that I had ever seen

for sale. Boxes full of proof sets. Stiff-covered albums of long date runs of high-grade half-crowns, florins and shillings. Boxes and tins of interesting miscellanea. A few single gold coins including an amazing Scottish hammered gold coin of King Malcolm III. Two large coin cabinets, each being sold as a single lot, each with multiple drawers, each drawer containing thirty coins, mostly silver, mostly in lovely condition, mostly scarce, and with more than a few fabulous rarities. At a quick glance I noticed an 1847 Gothic Crown coin in uncirculated condition, worth at least £3,000 by itself, and a 1658 half-crown with the head of Oliver Cromwell, worth maybe £1,000 to £1,500.

"To decide on what to bid for and how much, I would have needed at least an hour of viewing and several hours of hard googling. But I only had a few minutes to view on that afternoon, and a busy evening, and another appointment on the Wednesday morning, so scarcely a moment to do any research before the sale started. Not that I expected to win anything, partly because I'd been buying a load of other stuff in the recent past and was pretty skint, and secondly because a sale like this should attract a lot of dealers and big-time collectors willing to pay high prices.

"But my regular auctioneer only publishes her catalogue a couple of days before the sale, and she doesn't use any of the online platforms for internet bidding. So the sale hadn't had enough time or publicity to attract dealers and high-rolling collectors. And there wasn't anyone on her staff who could answer technical numismatic enquiries from absentee bidders about varieties and condition. On the day, all the usual suspects attended the auction, but only one serious coin buyer, who's the local coin dealer. He must have thought that he'd died and gone to heaven.

"The auctioneer started off by saying that she hoped bidding for the lots would be high because the proceeds of the sale were to be used to help support the vendor, an old man, in a care home. I thought that was quite touching. But when it came to the bidding, the coin dealer had practically no competition. I was a bit naughty and deliberately bid up a few lots to a higher price, not expecting to win, but just to stop him getting some of the most spectacular lots too cheaply. But the sod was able to buy up a full year's stock of prize items for just a few thousand pounds, a tiny fraction of what that collection would have fetched in a specialist auction. I was absolutely furious on behalf of the old bloke in the care home."

Listening to Bill's story, I was furious too. Partly with whoever had failed to look after the old man's interests and had consigned the coins to a totally unsuitable auctioneer. But more so with the auctioneer, who, even as a local generalist, should have been able to recognise that such a collection was of major interest. From Bill's description it was obvious that those coins were shouting out to be expertly lotted, catalogued and photographed individually, and marketed in such a way as to draw the attention of the collecting community. It wasn't only the obvious thing to do for the benefit of the old man, but it would have been good business for the auctioneer who always stands to make much more profit from selling goods at the right prices.

I voiced my outrage loudly. But Bill hadn't finished. The story got worse.

"A couple of weeks later, I was talking in the pub to a chap I see there quite often, and he happened to mention that he was very busy sorting out the house and belongings of his next-door neighbour Douglas, an old, reclusive bachelor who couldn't cope at home and had moved into a care home. Douglas had been a lifelong collector of books, model trains and coins. The books had been offered as a gift to the local library, the trains were to be donated to a collectors' club, but at least the coins had fetched a good price. They had been consigned on the advice of Douglas's solicitor to a local auctioneer.

"I felt awful. I didn't have the heart to tell the chap how much old Douglas's coins were undervalued. He's a nice bloke, and he voluntarily took on a monumental job when he agreed to handle Douglas's affairs, but he knows nothing about coins. He should have been able to rely on the solicitor to find him the right auctioneer, and on the auctioneer to get the right price. So I don't blame him. He told me a few months afterwards that Douglas had recently died, so he didn't live long enough to be personally disadvantaged. But it's a sorry tale, isn't it?"

Yes, indeed, a sorry tale, and one which demonstrates the importance of selecting the most appropriate outlet for the sale of your antique and collectable objects.

But for me – what a dilemma! I feel vicariously angry and upset on behalf of poor old Douglas, who lost a fortune to a coin dealer due mainly to an auction failure. But at the same time I find that I can summon up scarcely a morsel of righteous indignation in relation to the previous owner of The Saint, who lost an even bigger fortune to me for precisely the same reason. The two cases are similar, but my reactions to them are utterly divergent, and I find it rather awkward to live with the paradox. But I also find that having profited from The Saint to the tune of a shedload of cash provides some degree of comfort.

223

And I take comfort from the knowledge that although similar the two cases aren't identical. In the case of the coins, the sellers (Bill's pub acquaintance and Douglas's solicitor on behalf of Douglas) might not have had any knowledge of the true value of the coins, but even the most general of general auctioneers should have been able to spot at first glance that the collection was very special. Bill's auctioneer was clearly negligent in failing to recognise the need to sell them properly.

In the case of The Saint, the seller, scion of the renowned MacGregor family of Edinburgh dealers and church furnishers, might have been expected to have an awareness that he was selling a valuable family treasure; and Malcolm Andrews, a general auctioneer, might be excused for not instantly recognising a sculpture by Claus de Werve. After all, the experts from Sotheby's didn't recognise it either.

And I'm also comfortable that in neither case was the buyer blameworthy: the coin dealer on his super-successful day, and I on mine, merely made legitimate winning bids in a public auction. But it still doesn't feel quite right. I don't suppose that coin dealer has lost much sleep over it, but I have.

Where does Charity Begin?

Another dilemma: what should one do if one gets The Buzz in a charity shop? If you make big money from something bought from a charity for almost nothing, are you robbing the charity and profiting from its loss? Should you refuse to buy the item but let the shop manager know that it's a valuable antique and encourage her to sell it appropriately? Should you insist on paying the shop there and then what you think the object is worth? Should you wait until after you have re-sold the item and donate the profit to the charity? All the profit or just part of it? And what if you wish to keep the item and not sell it? Should you donate the value to the charity from your own cash flow? In which case, what if you can't afford to do so?

Or should you tell yourself that the only reason that many people go into charity shops is to see if they can spot a bargain and make a profit, and it's the urban myths about major discoveries that keep the shops full of paying customers? In which case you can justify keeping the money from your discovery by convincing yourself that you are acting in the charity's interests.

Or you can simply buy stuff in charity shops and re-sell it for profit with equanimity and an untroubled conscience and without turning it into a major ethical drama. You can, but I can't.

It's happened to me several times. There was a time when I bought a whole collection of about twenty pieces of Irish Shanagarry pottery which was priced at £5. I had to insist before the shop assistant would accept that I didn't want change from a ten pound note. I re-sold it all on eBay for £200 and have felt awful about it ever since.

Some time later I bought from another charity shop nearby a lovely coffee set and a number of other pieces, all from the fabulous Leach-influenced Crowan Pottery. Many of the pieces were individually priced, but the chap behind the counter said that the price for the whole collection was £7.50. I protested and after some argument made him accept £50. I also made him write down my name and phone number, volunteering to look at any other odd pieces of brown pottery which might be donated to the shop, and either to advise him about pricing or to pay a fair price myself. Results? I sold the pottery for over £300, keeping only one small perfect celadon-glazed jug in my own collection. But I didn't get any calls from the shop asking for advice. The very next time I went back, I spotted a wonderful lidded jar in heavy white grogged porcelain, a late and superb work made by none other than Janet Leach, the widow of Bernard, worth £400–£500 but very obviously a keeper, not a seller. This time, my previous advice and offers of help having been spurned, I paid the £3 written on the price sticker and left without comment.

In another shop I bought for £16 a magnificent stoneware split-pod-form sculptural vase by the legendary studio potter Alan Wallwork (**See Illustrations, *Picture 21*)**. I had always wanted one but had never considered spending the £400–£500 needed to buy a properly priced example. I brought it home and put it on the window-sill in the dining room, where it still stands, but then I immediately found my enjoyment of it seriously impaired by feelings of guilt. There was I, with a lifetime of aesthetic pleasure ahead of me (it's positioned opposite my seat at the dining table and I enjoy it anew every day), and there was the charity shop in Stockbridge, Edinburgh, which could have made a day or more's takings from this one object.

But there was a problem. I wanted to keep the vase in my collection. Selling it was out of the question, so there were no proceeds to donate to or share with the charity. Should I therefore salve my conscience by giving the full value to the charity? No, because much as I liked it, I wouldn't have been prepared to pay its full market value at auction or in a gallery. If I was ready to spend that much money, other equally lovely stuff would inevitably have got in the way. After fretting overnight, I decided that the fair thing to do would be to donate to the shop the amount I would have been prepared to pay for the Wallwork vase in a general auction of the type that I frequent in Edinburgh. I concluded that I'd be ready to spend around £100 but not more.

The next day I went back to the shop, explained to the lady behind the counter that I had bought a vase yesterday much too cheaply, and handed her four £20 notes. She was surprised and pleased, but it was easy to see that she thought me totally and utterly barking mad. She may, of course, have been correct. I also offered my name and phone number in case any other weird brown pots came up which they needed help to identify and price. I did subsequently get one call from her, and went into the shop to find that she wanted me to pronounce judgment on a fine set of Minton's art nouveau tube-lined fireplace tiles. Not my speciality at all, but I suggested that they wouldn't get the best price by selling them in the shop, and thought that an eBay sale would be more appropriate. I even offered, if the charity didn't have its own eBay selling outlet, to sell the tiles on their behalf. The lady said she would have to ask her manager about that, and I haven't heard a word from them from that day to this. Presumably they had put me down as a madman or a crook. Or both.

I still occasionally go into that shop, but I rarely buy anything these days. Their prices for the few low-grade pieces of studio pottery on their bric-a-brac shelves are now ridiculously high. I can only assume that their pricing policy has been artificially inflated by the memory of that nutter who came in with the twenty pound notes. Bad move!

Another charity shop tale. In Chapter 11 I interrupted my story about the sale of The Saint in order to explain that current events had temporarily diverted my attention away from the writing of my narrative. I had bought a big red Chinese vase in a charity shop, and I promised to keep you posted about progress towards its identification and either retention or disposal (See Illustrations, *Picture 17*).

Here is the denouement. The Big Red Vase, whose initials I now capitalise, turned out indeed to be a rare and desirable find. Through trawling internet images of similar pots, I discovered a dealer and collector in Atlanta, Georgia, who owned three or four of the best examples of Langyao-type copper red vases. I emailed him with some photos and he replied enthusiastically saying that mine just could be the real thing. Then I sent pictures to Sotheby's and Christie's and they both replied asking to see The Vase with a view to including it, if they thought it authentic, in their next big London sales of Chinese porcelain. A similar vase, albeit slightly larger and with excellent provenance, had recently made the second-highest price in a high-profile international auction at Christie's. Exciting!

I eventually settled on Lyon & Turnbull as my auctioneer of choice. They are the most upmarket auctioneers based in Edinburgh, but on this occasion they were holding their twice-yearly Asian art sale at a venue near Cambridge. Their estimated price printed in the catalogue was £800-£1,200. Very satisfactory. In the event, however, The Vase sold for a whopping £13,750 including buyer's premium. Very much more satisfactory! At a multiple of 1,967 times what I had paid for it just a few months earlier, The Big Red Vase currently tops my relative profitability league table, beating the little Gallé glass vase into second place, and The Saint into third place.

So… how guilty did I feel about having got it from a charity shop for just £6.99? Very guilty. And what did I do about the guilt? What would you do, readers? I guess I could have invited anyone who reads this book to take part in an online poll, the results of which might have informed my decision. My predicted outcome would be:

> 25% of respondents would say, "You shouldn't profit at the expense of the charity. Give all the money to them".
> 25% would say, "What are you on about? You bought the vase fair and square. The money's all yours".
> 25% would say, "Hmmm. The fairest thing to do is to share the money with the charity".
> 25% would say, "Oh for God's sake. Get a life"!

And of course that wouldn't have helped at all. In the end, after several sleepless nights, I divided the proceeds (rather less than £9,000 after deduction of the auctioneer's commissions and VAT) into four roughly equal portions. A quarter was given as a donation to the charity; a quarter was split into two and given to my daughters; a quarter was put aside for payment of income tax and incidentals, and Frances and I kept a quarter for treats and to buy more stuff.

That seemed fair, but I don't really know for sure if it was the right thing to do.

Charities and Charities

As if my difficulties about giving the proceeds to charity weren't enough, I have a further layer of moral complexity to throw into the mix. What if you disapprove of the charity in whose shop you have discovered random treasure? Here is a situation which hasn't happened in real life but which could happen. For the avoidance of doubt let it be known that the following anecdote is entirely fictional and is not related to the charity from which I bought The Big Red Vase. I do however know of a charity which behaves in exactly the (to me) despicable way that I describe below, but, unlike the charity in this made-up story, it doesn't help the homeless and it doesn't operate any shops.

Such is the allure of charity shops to me that I rarely stop outside one to consider the name or purpose of the charity before entering, elbowing aside a small crowd of elderly shoppers, and plunging headlong towards the bric-a-brac shelves. One day, I went into a shop that I hadn't been into before (you see – I told you this was fiction!) and spotted a – a – let's make this anecdote really exciting and say I spotted a small, chipped, cracked Chinese tea bowl, painted in bright colours with a hen and a cockerel pecking at some corn. Buzzing wildly but feigning nonchalance, I paid the 99 pence written on the price sticker, asked for it to be wrapped in a bit of newspaper, left the shop and zoomed home to my computer at warp speed.

Before long I had confirmed my hunch that this was no ordinary Chinese tea bowl. Just over 10 centimetres wide, it was from the fifteenth century, Ming Dynasty, Chenghua period, a genuine Doucai Chicken Cup, an incredibly rare example of the most desirable item of Chinese pottery in the world. I photographed it, sent the pictures to Sotheby's, consigned it for their Asian sale, and a while later received a cheque for – let's make it a big dramatic story – £250,000. That was because of the chip and the crack: the last perfect example sold by Sotheby's fetched $36 million (See Illustrations, Picture 22).

Guilt-ridden at the thought of having profited so obscenely from a charity, I decided after much agonising to share my good fortune with them. I went back to the shop, but instead of entering, I read and memorised the charity's name from the sign above the door. It was an organisation I hadn't heard of before. Then I returned home and wrote out a cheque for half of my profit. I drafted a nice letter and looked up their website to get a correspondence address. Browsing the website I found out more about them.

The charity's stated purpose was to run an advisory service to help homeless people to find permanent places to live. There was a declared religious connection, but I don't have a problem with that, my feeling being that if people are motivated by religious beliefs to equate good work with God's work, then that's just as valid as doing good work for any other reason. The charity's website was very professional, its strategy and marketing were innovative, it had won a number of charity-of-the-year types of awards, and it had received resounding testimonials from clients housed through their auspices, plus ringing endorsements and patronage from assorted celebrities including minor royalty. Doing good work in a professional way. I approved.

Then I decided to find out about their financial position and governance: did they need my money and would they use my donation properly? This meant looking at their latest annual report, which I eventually found by drilling down through several strata of the website. And away down there buried in amongst the statistics where only the most assiduous enquirers were likely to spot it, I discovered a year-on-year table showing how many of its homeless clients the charity had succeeded in converting into followers of its own particular brand of religion. And I discovered that if you wish to use their advisory service in the hope of getting a home, the adviser allocated to you will come to the first meeting accompanied by a "befriender" whose job is to offer you friendship, to talk to you about God, and to pray with you. In the main body of the website it doesn't say anything at all about this aspect of your interaction with the charity. But it isn't voluntary: it's all part of the service.

Whoa there! A charity like that might be doing good work, and it might be doing God's work. Its approach might be attractive to many people, but it isn't to me. To my mind, charity is about giving help with no strings attached. It's not an exchange. It's not about thrusting religion into the faces of beneficiaries when they are at their weakest and most vulnerable. I'm not suggesting that the charity will refuse to help clients who reject the spiritual element of the package – the charity regulator wouldn't tolerate that – but I am suggesting that proselytising susceptible clients isn't an acceptable activity for any charity that I'm involved with. So am I going to support them by sending them my big cheque? No way!

Now I'm stuck with the money, with too much conscience to spend it on myself, and too much conscience to give it to the charity. I still feel I have deprived them of a fortune, but at the same time I heartily disapprove of the way they go about their business. What should I do? Do I give the money to some other charity of which I do approve (but why would I, and how would I choose?) or do I stop fretting and keep it?

I don't know what I would do. How thankful I am that this was a fictional situation!

Public or Private?

I have claimed several times throughout this book that The Jug and The Saint were both objects of major cultural significance. If that's true, maybe it was immoral to offer them for sale on the open market. What might happen to them if they got into the wrong hands? Perhaps they might be purchased by some studio-pottery or Gothic-sculpture equivalent of Mr PennyRed, who would keep them in a private museum or gallery for his or her personal contemplation, and never again expose them to public delight or academic study. Or perhaps purchased by a cold-blooded, cold-hearted dealer who might sell them on for further profit to just such a private collector. Or perhaps by Mr Goldbrick, who has been advised by his Art Investment Consultant that this category of Jug or that category of Saint, if kept in a secure vault for x years, will have a y percent chance of producing a z percent return on the original investment. Or perhaps even by Langley Collyer (not by his brother Homer, who was more hoarded than hoarder), to make two minor additions to the mountains of decaying detritus filling their ruinous Manhattan brownstone mansion, eventually to be bulldozed and taken to landfill.

Was I therefore morally bound to sell The Saint and The Jug only to public collections or museums which could guarantee to keep, conserve and display them in perpetuity, and to allow access to them by scholars and connoisseurs for study and appreciation? Easier said than done. First you have to select the appropriate museum. For The Jug, should it be a big museum with a world-class ceramics collection (example: the Victoria and Albert Museum in London); or a museum with a more local interest (example: the Royal Cornwall Museum in Truro or the Tate Gallery in St Ives); or a small specialist museum (example: the Leach Pottery Museum in St Ives); or maybe some other museum somewhere else which doesn't have outstanding studio pottery in its collection? For The Saint, should it be the Louvre in Paris or the Musée des Beaux-Arts in Dijon,

230

both with fabulous Burgundian sculpture collections? Or should I have sold him to the Commune of Flavigny-sur-Ozerain who had passed the hat round and collected €77,000 to bid at the Paris auction in the vain hope of re-uniting my Saint John with the Flavigny Virgin?

Then, once you have targeted your public collection, you have to get them interested in buying the object. To achieve this, you might need to find a dealer to intercede on your behalf, for a fee. Then you have to set a price – but how can you know the right price if you aren't selling on the open market? And then the museum has to be able to find the funds to pay you, which could be difficult in these days of austerity and cuts to acquisitions budgets.

And then, if your reason for wanting to sell to a museum is for a guarantee that they will keep, conserve and display the object in perpetuity, you have to get the museum to give you such a guarantee. Which is a non-starter. They don't commit themselves to keeping an object on permanent public display. The museum might want to re-organise their space. Or something more interesting or important or relevant to the collection might come along which needs to go into that display case. Or they might change their policy and decide to dispose of some objects in order to be able to buy others. I know that this happens because I've discovered that in 2003 the Museum of Art in Cleveland Ohio sold a big red vase rather like my Big Red Vase, with this note appearing beside its description in the Christie's catalogue: *"Property belonging to the Cleveland Museum of Art sold to benefit the acquisitions fund"*. If I were to sell them my Big Red Vase only to find out later that they had re-sold it, I'd be furious, but perhaps less so with that particular museum than with most others. I can forgive them just about anything, because they are fortunate enough to have one of the best collections of Burgundian sculpture outside France, including four alabaster Mourners from the Ducal tombs.

Or your carefully-chosen purchaser might turn out to be a totally unsuitable custodian of your precious object. The Church of Saint-Genest in Flavigny, beautiful and original as it may be, is so infested with damp and mould that I would be horrified to think of my statue lodged permanently there, the presence of his pendant Virgin notwithstanding.

No, selling privately to a public collection or museum might appear to have its attractions for a collector with a case of the moral and ethical heebie-jeebies, but when you take the idea apart, it doesn't make much sense. You could just as easily argue that the object should be sold to a private buyer: your object might well have a more secure future and be more greatly valued (for whatever reason) in a collector's air-conditioned cabinet of curiosities or in an investor's steel-lined vault, than on show in a public museum or gallery.

Philanthropy

For those of us with qualms about profiting from beautiful and important objects which have come to us cheaply or serendipitously, there is, of course, always the option of giving them away. Which brings me to the delightful subject of philanthropy.

How I would love to be a philanthropist! You give away money or valuable objects, you get the satisfaction of seeing them doing good in the world, you get your name engraved on plaques and printed in catalogues, you get interviewed and fussed over, you meet and are counted amongst The Great And The Good, you are invited to attend openings and receptions and to make speeches at them, you're remembered and memorialised after you're dead. And best of all, philanthropists can do all of that and still remain rich after giving millions away.

Inevitably, if you're going to be a half-decent sort of philanthropist you have to start off with much more money than you actually require to enable you to live your life in the way you want to live it. Sadly, very few of us are in that enviable position. If, like most of us, you need every penny you can lay your hands on, being a philanthropist is not an easy option. Giving away money that you don't need is an easy task; it is much harder to forgo a profit or a windfall when you have other higher priority non-philanthropic uses for the cash.

Frances and I are both in receipt of pensions from having contributed for decades to the superannuation schemes of our public sector employers. I have a modest additional private pension accumulated from my not-very-successful years as a small business owner. And we have our state pensions. We have paid off the mortgage on our house, run a second-hand car, take holidays when we feel like it and are in debt to no-one. A comfortable existence but not such that if a significant lump sum comes our way unexpectedly we can afford to give it away. We have daughters who are making their way in the world. We have grandchildren who we wish to be able to help. We have blocked drains and a leaking roof. We are less energetic in the garden than in former years and need paid help with cutting the lawn and the hedges. In later life we might find that we need to use our small financial reserves to pay for carers.

So if I'm fortunate enough to find an object which can be turned into a pile of money – as I was with The Saint and The Jug and The Big Red Vase – then deciding to give the object or the money away as a philanthropic gesture is a much bigger deal for me than it would be for, say, Bill Gates or David Rubenstein to give away an item worth a few million dollars or the cash equivalent. I'd have to think about it much harder than they would, because even a small gesture would have a much bigger impact on my financial future and that of my family than a big gesture would have for either of them.

Moreover, giving away my statue or my Jug to a public collection, however big a gesture it might seem to me, frankly wouldn't mean all that much to any of the major galleries or museums. Important as my items are, they have much more significance standing on the hall chest in my house than they would have as part of the collection in the V&A or the Louvre or the Metropolitan Museum or the Hermitage Museum, where they would be merely two more world-class objects amongst tens of thousands of others. If you really want to register on the radar of these institutions as a philanthropist, you'd have to come across with a Gutenberg Bible or a Van Eyck painting or a Bay Psalm Book.

If I turned up with The Jug under one arm and The Saint under the other (difficult but possible), saying, "Here, you can have these", I would probably get a nice thankyou letter from an assistant curator and that would be the last I'd hear of it. My precious objects would likely be put away in a storeroom until such time in the indeterminate future when resources allow for them to be catalogued and labelled and a decision made as to whether they might fit into a display, or should stay in storage, or should be discreetly deaccessioned and disposed of.

Because the whole philanthropic exercise would be so much more important to me than it would be to my chosen beneficiary institution, I fear that my self-sacrificing donation would almost certainly end in disappointment, disillusionment and bitterness. Who do these curators think they are to insult me by refusing to shove aside the Mona Lisa or the Declaration of Independence or Van Gogh's Sunflowers in order to make space for my pot and my statue?

I have evidence from two sources that this would most probably be the case. Before his retirement some years ago, my friend Bill was the person responsible for developing the greater part of the collection in a big university library, with a staggeringly large budget to spend on acquiring printed and digital materials. At our occasional long lunches, knowing that I love books and am interested in the workings of large public institutions, he likes to talk about his former work, and in particular about its many annoyances. Among the annoyingest was having to deal with a steady trickle of would-be benefactors wishing to donate a book or a box of books or a private library of books. "They are very important books". "I want them all shelved together". "I want them to be catalogued separately". "The complete collection must be kept, even if you already have duplicates on your shelves".

Often Bill would politely decline the donation altogether. Sometimes he would ask if he could just take some of the books, and then would inevitably get drawn into advising the donor about how to dispose of the rest. Frequently someone else in the university would have accepted the donation on the library's behalf and he would be lumbered. And free gift books aren't really free at all. From the moment they arrive they start to gather costs around themselves. The library must bear the costs of the staff time and other resources involved in transportation, conservation, storage, cataloguing, shelving, consultation and lending. All of which diverts time, money and attention from the library's core activities. It's little wonder that a librarian's or curator's face might fall and heart might sink when you arrive bearing your precious artefact for donation; precious to you, but routine to the library or museum – unless of course it happens to be a Shakespeare First Folio or a newly discovered Fabergé Easter Egg.

My second piece of evidence comes from an attempt of my own to become the world's least significant philanthropist.

In a charity shop in Edinburgh I bought for £4 a small framed single-sheet theatre poster or programme or handbill advertising an appearance on Wednesday 19th May by Mrs Warner in the part of Hermione in Shakespeare's The Winter's Tale. The performance was to include

THE STATUE SCENE
The most perfect ILLUSION Ever witnessed in this city

but unfortunately the poster didn't say which city the theatre was in, nor the name of the theatre, nor the year of the performance. However, it did include the ticket prices, which were shown as:

Boxes, 50 cts; Pit 25 cts; Gallery for Colored Persons 25 cts.

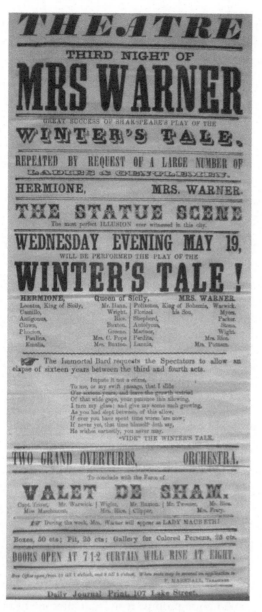

The playbill for Mrs Warner's perfomance in The Winter's Tale
at Rice's Theatre Chicago on Wednesday 19th May, 1852.

Unable to resist the challenge of such a perfect mystery, I sat for many hours at my computer trying to identify the city, theatre, year and actress. And blow me if Google and I didn't manage between us to solve the puzzle! The headlined star was easy to find: Mary Amelia Warner, an Irish-born actress whose career was spent mainly in London, where she became very well-known. Hermione was one of her most famous parts, and I found an image online of an engraving in the National Portrait Gallery in London which showed her playing that very rôle. The ticket prices shown in cents on the poster led me to begin by investigating theatres in the USA. I found out that Mrs Warner was documented as having toured the US in 1852 and again in 1853 shortly before her death, but I couldn't find any details of her itinerary. However, the segregation but not outright exclusion of Colored Persons to the gallery pointed to theatres in cities in the more northerly states. I finally arrived at the satisfactory conclusion that my poster was an advertisement for a performance at Rice's Theatre in Chicago on 19th May 1852, a Wednesday.

I also discovered that the Chicago Public Library has a collection of more than 2,000 Chicago Theatre programmes and playbills from 1848 to date. The eight earliest items in the entire collection are handbills for productions at Rice's Theatre, including seven from 1848 and one from 1855. Since there wasn't a copy of my handbill from 1852, I could assume that there was a fair chance that mine was the very last one in existence in the world. Flushed with success at recently having sold The Saint, I found myself overcome with philanthropic generosity and decided to donate this unique object to the Chicago Public Library.

I sent a chatty email and a photograph to a named librarian in the Library's Special Collections Department. No reply. Several weeks later I wrote again, still chattily. This time I got a reply saying that the Special Collections Librarian had passed my email on to the Librarian of the Theatre Collection, and giving me a contact email for the latter. I emailed her (chattily) and after some delay received a polite but not fulsome reply that the Library "would be pleased to accept your kind and generous donation". I carefully packed it and sent it expensively by Special Delivery, emailing to let her know it was on its way and asking for acknowledgement of safe receipt. No reply. Two months later I wrote again. This time I got a prompt reply, thanking me nicely: "The playbill is a beautiful part of Chicago's theater history, and we are excited to add it to our collection". I was gratified. She asked me to sign and return a Deed of Gift document which said:

> "The above-named donor hereby gives, transfers, assigns and delivers as an unrestricted gift to the Chicago Public Library all legal right, title and interest in and to the property described below... The

undersigned, being the legal owner or the authorised representative of the legal owner of said property, hereby attests to the legal transfer of said property to the Chicago Public Library. The title to said property shall henceforth remain in the Chicago Public Library without reservation."

I printed out the document, signed it, scanned it and returned it with yet another chatty email. No reply.

That was two years ago. While writing this paragraph, I've looked at the Library's website to see if my poster yet appears in the catalogue of their playbill collection. It doesn't.

I wasn't expecting the Chicago Public Library to fall at my feet in a swoon of obsequiousness, overcome by the wonder of being given a small poster which had cost me £4 in a charity shop. But on the other hand, it does strike me that you need to do something pretty spectacular in the way of philanthropy in order to get a measure of self-satisfaction and smugness commensurate with the degree of effort and self-sacrifice involved in your donation.

That isn't, of course, a reason not to make the donation. But if you're in a state of anxiety about whether morally and ethically the right thing to do is to donate your precious object to a public collection, then this sort of experience, plus Bill's testimony as an erstwhile representative of a beneficiary, might be enough to give you considerable pause.

Collective Ownership of an Egg

My final qualm in this chapter isn't even my qualm. It belongs to a journalist called Serena Kutchinsky, by whom, in the moral-and-ethical-doubts-and-questions department, I have been comprehensively trumped, out-classed and out-qualmed.

Ms Kutchinsky, with whom I have nothing in common except, again, a few million Ashkenasi Jewish genes, is the daughter of the late Paul Kutchinsky, a London jeweller who was commissioned in 1990 by an Australian diamond-mining company to manufacture the largest jewelled egg in the world as a showcase for their pink diamonds. Modelled on the legendary Easter eggs made for the Russian Tsars by the jeweller Peter Carl Fabergé, but much bigger, the egg was made from 15 kilograms of 18-carat gold and 24,000 diamonds, and contained a complex and delicate mechanism that peeled back its shell to reveal a miniature library and portrait gallery (**See Illustrations, *Picture 23***).

The magnificent egg was taken on a world tour and exhibited to enthusiastic crowds around the globe. But sadly no buyer came along who was was willing to pay the £7 million price-tag. Eventually it was sold to a Japanese businessman, and now stands in the entrance hall of his French Renaissance-style chateau in Tokyo.

The making and showing-off of the egg turned into an obsession for Mr Kutchinsky, and led indirectly to the ruin of his business and the break-up of his marriage. He died aged fifty in an accident a few years later.

And where do the qualms come in? Serena Kutchinsky must understandably feel that her life has been seriously affected by her late father's obsession with his Golden Egg. She feels outraged that the most precious thing in his life, a thing of record-breaking magnificence, beauty and value, should be locked away out of public view in a Tokyo businessman's downstairs hall.

Ms Kutchinsky's indignation has manifested itself in an unusual way. Her personal emotional attachment to the fate of a single valuable artefact has alchemically transmuted into a full-blown system which embraces the future of all valuable antiques and fine art throughout the world. She proposes that such objects should not be privately owned at all but should be compulsorily taken into collective ownership and put on permanent public display. In a radio talk[58] she suggested that:

> "Any... items which date back over 50 years or are over a certain value and emerge onto the market, would become the property of an international agency governed by the United Nations and modelled on UNESCO. It would be composed of a panel of experts from the world of museums, fine art and auction houses who admittedly would see a fall-off in business, so this would provide some handy re-employment."

I don't intend to provide a detailed critique of Ms Kutchinsky's proposal, which I consider has more political, economic, financial, commercial and aesthetic holes in it than her father's egg has diamonds. I'm merely relating the outlines of her story to illustrate how it's possible for a single individual's intense concern about the fate of a single valuable object to metamorphose into an entire system for dismantling capitalism and reforming the ownership of private property. But can any artefact be worth that much or be that important? I doubt it.

As for the object itself – well, I've looked at the pictures and regret that this particular egg is not to my taste. It's a great big overblown piece of 1990s bling, which to my Eye appears as a curiosity with intrinsic value but no artistic merit, and for whose permanent resting place I could think of nowhere better than the private foyer of a reproduction French chateau in Tokyo. To my Eye, there was much more aesthetic satisfaction to be found in the other Golden Egg that has featured in this book, the gleaming modern chrome and formica fast-food restaurant which I gazed upon from my bedroom window as a teenage boy living over a pub in Charing Cross Road, in 1960s swinging London.

15

AFTERWARDS

What to do

In early 2007 I sold The Jug and a few weeks later received a cheque from Bonham's for about £10,000, representing the hammer price less their seller's commission, other costs and VAT. Having spent £1,000 on buying The Jug, I was left with a profit of some £9,000. I paid the cheque into the bank.

Then I got word from my accountant that for various reasons to do with business losses there weren't any capital gains or other kinds of taxes to pay, so all I had to do then was to decide how to spend the money. It wasn't a difficult decision. I gave a cash present to each daughter, and simply put the rest into the current account to be used for the general living expenses of our household. If that seems boring, it was. Boring but very helpful because cash was in fairly short supply. Around that time I had let it be known that I intended to retire from my company on my sixtieth birthday in the following year and I was hoping that one or more enterprising and ambitious members of my staff team might come forward with a business plan to take the firm over from me and carry it on as a going concern. Sadly it didn't work out that way, because by the latter part of 2007 it was becoming clear that something was going badly wrong with the retail financial markets in which the company conducted most of its operations, and the firm began to slide into a slow downward spiral. No-one in their right mind would have paid me to take over the business, and – wisely, as I had thought – I had made very certain only to employ a team of people who were in their right minds. Sensibly, no-one came forward.

To keep the business going as long as possible and to prevent redundancies among the employees I cut my own salary in half, and even then I had to help to support cash flow from my own funds. So it was very helpful to have the profits from the sale of The Jug to help keep us afloat for a bit longer than might otherwise have been possible. My retirement date in October 2008 coincided almost exactly with the worst possible date in all of history to sell a financial services business. But at least I was able to close down in an orderly fashion and subside into retirement with my reputation intact, without incurring any debt, but unable to look forward to the wealthy retirement that I had confidently foreseen years earlier when I left the National Health Service to start up my own business.

By 2013 when I sold The Saint, my personal circumstances were very different. Frances and I were both retired from regular employment and our public sector pensions had clicked in. We weren't rich, but we are people of fairly simple and non-extravagant needs, and we had saved enough to anticipate a reasonably comfortable dotage. In these circumstances, suddenly receiving a cheque for £145,000 from the Paris auctioneers came as a shock and triggered off a whole new train of events. Two questions immediately arose:

Question 1: What to do with the money?
Question 2: What to do with the money?

Now, these two questions might look identical and sound identical (you wouldn't even vary their intonation or emphasis if you asked them out loud), but they are quite distinct. Question 1 is about ways to *keep* the money, or at least how to keep as much of it as possible. Only after having settled that issue could I focus on Question 2, which is about how to *spend* the money.

Question 1: What to do with the money?

It's not all that uncommon for people to find themselves in possession of a large chunk of money which has materialised more or less out of the blue. It might be an inheritance from a deceased parent or other relative; or a big win on the National Lottery; or a pension lump sum received on retirement; or a matured endowment policy. All of these cases have one important thing in common: once you get the money you can do what you like with it, all of it.

There are no tax implications. Your legacy will come to you net of inheritance tax; your pension lump sum, Lottery winnings and endowment maturity are not subject to tax. Or you might get a big pile of money from the proceeds of selling Auntie's Chinese teapot which has been in the family for years and years. In this case the vase will count as a chattel, and there may be some Capital Gains Tax due, but the calculation of how much to pay is relatively straightforward.

I have written in earlier chapters about my low-level post-retirement hobby of selling, mostly through eBay, a few antiques and pieces of studio pottery. Although I thought of myself as a collector and not as a dealer, I discovered in 2010 that the rules of Her Majesty's Revenue and Customs required me to register as a self-employed sole trader. Which I duly did, and for a couple of years I paid a teeny-tiny amount of income tax on my teeny-tiny turnover from my nano-business. And so, because HMRC were aware of my buying and selling activities, the transactions involving The Saint had to be counted as part of my antiques trading business.

This meant that my annual turnover rocketed at a single stroke from around £3,000 to nearly £150,000. When this was added to other earnings from my pension and from a part-time consultancy job I was doing at the same time, my income in the 2012/'13 tax year, five years after my retirement, was more than three times as much as in the very best year of my unspectacular professional career. My sole trader status meant that The Saint couldn't be counted as a chattel but as stock-in-trade, and my income from the sale would therefore be liable for income tax (maximum rate 45%) instead of capital gains tax (maximum rate 28%). To further complicate matters, my former turnover of £3,000 meant that I hadn't needed previously to bother with registering my titchy antiques business for Value Added Tax; but my revenues had now suddenly hurtled miles beyond the £77,000 threshold for registration.

Thus, very soon after the sale, the pure joy of selling The Saint and the pure delight of getting all that money were alloyed by uncertainty about how much I was going to have to give up to the tax-person, and an unpleasant anticipation of tedious and irksome negotiation and paperwork ahead.

I tried to deal with the VAT question first. You'll recall that on the advice of my regular accountants I had engaged before the sale a specialist firm of tax accountants to advise me on this impenetrable subject. They had failed to impress me with any helpful pre-sale advice, and had barely been able to suppress their disbelief and scorn at my suggestion that a £400 antique might cross the VAT threshold on resale. Over the next several months until I received a final ruling from HMRC they continued unfailingly to fail to impress me.

To my mild surprise, but perhaps not to anyone else's, it soon appeared that HMRC had no standard guidance or case law covering the purchase of a statue for four hundred pounds by a self-employed unincorporated non-VAT-registered antique dealer in Scotland, and its re-sale shortly afterwards in a Paris auction for almost a quarter of a million euros. The situation had to be taken as a special case with no easy precedents available. My unimpressive accountants first took advice from their French counterparts, who pronounced after some delay that I would not be required to register in France or pay VAT on the hammer price there. Then they wrote to HMRC and were eventually told that I should have registered for VAT in the UK and would be due to pay the tax. Then at my urging they appealed, and many weeks afterwards I received the happy news from HMRC that, for five pages of technical reasons which I partially understood at the time but then instantly forgot, there never had been any need for me to register for or pay VAT in the first place. This was advice which my accountants should have been able to give me at the outset, precedents or no precedents. They subsequently admitted this somewhat sheepishly when we had an edgy debriefing meeting to discuss my dissatisfaction at their poor performance in the light of their accompanying enormous invoice. In real life the process was a lot more complicated and worrisome than what I have just described. I would love to give you all the fine details, but perhaps it's best that on this rare occasion I should curb my natural tendency towards prolixity and spare you the annoyance and frustration that I had to suffer.

Yippee!! Having finally got the VAT question out of the way, I could focus on looking for ways in which I might be able to minimise my income tax liability. I had no intention to fiddle my taxes or to evade paying what was due, and I wasn't going to get involved with dubious trust schemes and offshore tax avoidance dodges. But there's no point in paying at the highest rates if it is possible to use HMRC's own rules in an open and honest way to pay less. Time to consult my independent financial adviser. Unfortunately my long term adviser Alan, who is a little older than me, had recently decided to withdraw from the financial advice racket, but he was able to introduce me to a young, enthusiastic and highly qualified successor who I shall call Cameron.

Cameron had a rather brash and patronising manner and we didn't always see eye to eye. But ultimately his advice enabled me to offset some of my tax liability by paying part of the cash from The Saint into my private pension tax-free. It was quite a complex arrangement which depended upon a few coincidental circumstances specific to my personal financial situation. It probably wouldn't work for most other people in a similar position (should there be anyone), so there's no need for me to try to explain it in detail (even supposing that I could). But I was comfortable that it was completely open and above-board and an entirely legitimate way to minimise my tax liability.

The VAT and income tax issues took more than a year to finalise after the sale of The Saint, and only then was I able to turn my mind to:

Question 2: What to do with the money?

This question is not about keeping the money but about spending it. By now I had rationalised my way out of most of the qualms, anxieties and ethical uncertainties anatomised in the last chapter, and I felt fairly relaxed about spending the proceeds of the sale of The Saint – or at any rate as relaxed as I can permit myself to feel about anything which requires a decision. So – how to spend it?

Buy a Maserati? Nope, happy with the Skoda. Cruise around the world? Nope, Frances gets seasick. Build an extension to the house? Nope, did that a few years ago with my NHS pension lump sum. Blow it on fine dining, booze and Havana cigars? Nope, get heartburn, don't drink, don't smoke. Buy a load more pottery for my collection? Sadly, nope, because the house is already overfull and Frances keeps a close watch over my tendency towards excessive and obsessive collecting behaviour. Drugs and dissolution? Nope. A floozy? No way!

How dull! Nope. Deciding on the two biggest items of expenditure was easy. Our daughter Sarah and her husband Iain and their two children had recently moved to a semi-detached house from their Edinburgh flat, and were planning a spectacular renovation and extension scheme. The Saint helped them to make it a bit more spectacular. Our daughter Hannah and her husband Niall and their two children had recently moved from Edinburgh to Aberdeenshire and were looking for a new house, but were stymied by soaring boom-town property prices. The Saint helped them towards a deposit on a detached house near an excellent primary school. Bang! That was more than half of the money gone, just like that! And I didn't find it dull or boring at all.

As for the remainder, it is sitting in my pension fund to be called on as we need it, to be used either to help boost our living expenses or for the occasional treat. And the first such treat? Almost inevitably, an extravagant purchase in the studio pottery department. Frances and I went to an exhibition of new pots by the fabulous Welsh potter Phil Rogers. We fell head-over-heels in love not just with one pot but with eighty of them: an installation of small Japanese-style stoneware guinomi or sake cups in a fitted display unit, each one subtly different from all the others, each cup and the whole assemblage hauntingly austere and beautiful. It was sold. We thought about it for a short while, remembering that our fortieth wedding anniversary was coming up in just a few weeks' time. What a beautiful idea! I could buy forty cups as my anniversary present to Frances and she could buy the other forty as her present to me. An unthinkable luxury in former times, but now – The Saint could pay! We went to the gallery owner and asked him to commission the potter to make us a new set, thus achieving total satisfaction and, to our minds, the best possible answer to Question 2 (see Illustrations, *Picture 24*).

What to Feel

I am concerned in case I have spent too much time in this book writing about the downsides of buying and selling first The Jug and then The Saint, and not enough time celebrating the upsides. Perhaps my accounts of the doubts, uncertainties, anxieties and neuroses that have afflicted me at different stages have given readers the wrong impression. Perhaps I have said too much about worries and problems, fretted too much about difficult processes and irksome people. Have I been looking my gift horses in the mouth? Have I denigrated the kindly goose that laid my golden eggs? Have I failed sufficiently to emphasise and celebrate the good luck or grace or skill or talent or alchemy or whatever-the-hell-it-was that led me to such important discoveries in very unlikely and unprepossessing circumstances? Have I perhaps come across to readers as Mr Miseryguts, or as one of my favourite fictional characters Eeyore the Old Grey Donkey? I hope not. If that's what you are thinking, I'm sorry to have misled you. It isn't like that at all.

Between the date that I bought The Jug, and the date that I'm putting the finishing touches to this final chapter, more than 3,000 days have passed. Let's imagine that on each one of those days you had asked me how I was feeling about having bought and then sold The Jug and later bought and then sold The Saint. Let's say you had asked me to score my feelings on a ten-point scale. A low score might signify negative feelings, such as indifference, boredom, annoyance, frustration, fear, intimidation, inadequacy, wish-I'd-never-bought-the-damn-things. A high score might signify positive feelings, such as delight, wonder, enjoyment, complacency, self-satisfaction, disbelief-that-such-an-amazing-thing-could-happen.

And let's say that you averaged out the 3,000 daily scores. Would the resulting average be a nice round five in the middle of the scale, suggesting that on the majority of days I was feeling quite equable and neither-here-nor-there about The Saint and The Jug, with an outlying number of days when I was depressed or annoyed out of all countenance, and a counterbalancing number of days when I was ecstatically, hysterically delighted?

No, of course the average score over the 3,000 days wouldn't be five! It would be at least nine and probably nearer ten. Because even on my worst days; even when floored by qualms about ethics and morals; even when fretting myself stupid about ownership, loot, export licences, safe transportation, VAT, income tax; even when having to deal with unhelpful, stupid, disbelieving, scornful people; every day I have been absolutely and utterly delighted about my two wonderful finds.

Without getting involved in an excess of Proustian introspection, I'd like to try to delve a little deeper into that feeling of delight, to see if it's possible to pinpoint just what it is that has kept me so buoyant every day about The Saint and The Jug. It is a complex emotion, a compound of feelings, some lofty and selfless, others base and ignoble.

Some of the loftier ingredients in the mix: the exceptional privilege of having been able to handle, examine and study two such amazing objects, not usually available to punters who go to museums to look at rare and beautiful things in controlled environments behind glass. The excitement of discovery, rescuing the objects from obscurity and risk, and the pleasures and surprises associated with identification and expert authentication. With The Saint more than with The Jug, the aesthetic satisfaction of a time (too short!) of closeness to an item of exceptional beauty. The contemplative satisfaction of having it beside me in the house and at my desk and being able to see further and further into it. The intellectual satisfaction of studying and reading about the objects and their materials, craftsmanship, style, influences, geographical and

246

historical context. The romance of tracing and imagining the stories of the objects' makers, history, owners, locations. The exciting detective work of investigating provenance and title.

And then the less noble ingredients: overweening pride, self-congratulation, vanity, intellectual superiority, smugness, competitiveness, greed, acquisitiveness, covetousness, avarice, contempt. And the intoxication, near to addiction, of The Buzz. Yes, they're all in there, all the nasty stuff mixed up with all the good stuff. Not a pretty picture overall, but my aim in this book has not been to paint a pretty picture. I have been trying to tell the truth.

What to say

If you have been fortunate enough to buy an antique object for a small amount and then to re-sell it for a very large amount, it's an interesting story which people want to hear. But, if you aren't a blabbermouth or a bore, you might not want to say too much about it for a whole raft of reasons:

- You don't want to get a reputation as either an expert or a lucky sod among the denizens of your regular saleroom. It will only encourage others to watch what you are watching and bid against you;
- You don't want to come across as too clever-clever, or, as my daughters would colourfully put it, too far up yourself;
- It's a long story and you don't want to risk people's eyes glazing over with boredom half-way through;
- It's a long story and you don't want to bore yourself to death by constant repetition;
- Although it's a true story, it might not sound credible: you might be disbelieved;
- You might be embarrassed if people think you should have given the money back to the innocent vendor, or given the object to a museum;
- You might think that even being able to risk £1,000 for an old jug and £400 for an old statue in the first place makes you sound a bit too showy-offy;
- Telling your story will encourage people to attempt to trump you with their own Antiques-Roadshow/Cash-in-the-Attic/Flog-It stories;

- Telling your story will encourage people to describe Granny's old teapot and ask you to tell them how much it's worth;
- Your audience probably only want to hear about how much profit you made and don't care much about the object itself and its story, which is the really interesting bit.

For all of the above reasons, I don't usually talk much about The Saint or The Jug. But sometimes I'm asked about them. It usually makes me feel rather awkward. I either become voluble and nerdish, launching into a detailed account which makes my hearers switch off after a few moments; or I'm evasive and monosyllabic, which makes them think me standoffish. I just can't get it right. Much happier writing about it than talking about it.

An example:

Frances and I have a couple of long-time friends from our university days, Rob and Jane. We meet them every so often to dine together and catch up with news. Rob and Jane live in a charming Georgian cottage in Fife, about twenty miles to the north of us. With plenty of money and excellent taste, they have adorned their house with some splendid antique furniture, porcelain and pictures. Rob is the main buyer, and he takes expert advice and usually purchases from high-end dealers; unlike me, he isn't a bottom-feeder guddling about in detritus and squalor in the murkiest depths of the marketplace. Rob and Jane were delighted to be introduced to The Saint when they visited our house for dinner around Christmas time in 2012, and they excitedly followed the story of his identification and sale as it unfolded. For the next year, they dined out on the story, with the result that many more of their friends and acquaintances know about The Saint than do Frances's and my friends and acquaintances. I can understand that. For them, it's a good dinner-table story to tell; for me, all ten of the reasons listed above inhibit me from talking much about it.

Rob and Jane are very close to each other in age, and a few months ago they marked their seventieth birthdays with a drinks party held at a hotel near their home. We were very much looking forward to celebrating with them, and to renewing acquaintances with various of their friends who we had met casually over several decades of regular visits to their house. But in the event, I didn't enjoy the evening very much at all. And why not? Because it seemed to me, albeit almost certainly to no-one else, that there were not two but three people in the room who were the centre of attention. Two of them, naturally, were the birthday couple, our hosts. And the third person of interest was that remote, non-small-talking, non-drinking, non-golfing, non-sporting, non-Munro-climbing, bookish friend of the host and hostess who had that amazing piece of luck with some old statue. During the evening I was accosted by at least half a dozen people, some who I hadn't seen for decades, most who I barely knew, all of them asking me to tell them the story.

It was embarrassing. In small-talk at a lively and convivial party, how much detail do I provide to enquirers? How long will they listen to the story that they have asked for, before regretting that they brought up the subject and edging off to chat with someone with whom they have more in common? It's painfully clear that they don't want to hear me rabbitting on about Claus de Werve and the Duke of Burgundy and Flavigny and the French Revolution and the difficulties of The Saint's identification and authentication and the excitement of the Paris auction. No, what they do want is for me to cut to the chase and get right down to the financial details – in full. But what should I say, how soon should I say it, how do I tell them the only bit of the story that they really want to know? Do I give them the figures and make myself sound mercenary and crass, or do I prevaricate and make myself sound evasive? In other circumstances – for instance if I were giving a talk about The Saint and/or The Jug – I might finally, diffidently, mention something about the money after a hour or so's history lesson accompanied by lantern slides; but here and now in this very particular social situation, I know that common politeness and social convention won't allow me more than two minutes of my interlocutor's attention.

When asked about my auction successes, I simply don't know what to say or how to say it. It's a problem to which I don't have an answer. All I know is that it makes me feel awkward and I'd probably just prefer it if people didn't know. Which raises another question: if that's the way I feel, why on earth have I written this book?

What to do Next

Completing this book nine years after The Jug, and four years after The Saint, how do I feel about these two adventures in the antiques trade? It might be natural to think that one could feel jaded or sated; that everything else would be an anti-climax; that there's no chance of ever making another discovery of nearly such importance and significance; that there's no point in even continuing to look.

What nonsense! Despite the fact that as my age advances many of my other recollections are disappearing at a worryingly fast rate, I find that memories of my statue and my Jug don't fade. I can remember very clearly and in great detail the train of events and the mix of emotions which I experienced with each of the objects. Setting out those events and experiences in this book has provided a level of enjoyment close to living them over again – from the sheer excitement of sitting in the auction room in Paris to the extreme tedium of sitting in the VAT accountants' office in Edinburgh. And I can still feel both The Buzz of The Jug and The Buzz of The Saint, and other Buzzes from other objects that I have discovered over the years and described in this book, and many more Buzzes from over half a century of buying and selling, none forgotten. If you ask me today to score how I feel on a ten-point scale, I'm still well up near ten.

So, am I likely to hang up my alchemist's pointy hat? No way! Can I still get The Buzz? You bet I can! The adventure continues. You've heard about the Big Red Vase, but there are other post-Jug and post-Saint stories too.

I'm still out two or three times a week looking for random treasure, roaming the charity shops, viewing auctions. I rarely come home without something-or-other – an item to display on our groaning shelves, or to sell in the hope of getting my money back, or to put back in the charity box. As ever, I do it for the sheer joy of handling and looking at the objects and the chance to learn something new. The possibility of profit is an incidental pleasure.

Two final examples to compare and contrast. Here's the first:

*One day recently I trawled the Leith charity shops and came home having spent £2 on a small ceramic vase (***See Illustrations**, *Picture 25). I knew that it was Japanese Satsuma ware, made for the export market and imported into Europe in colossal quantities in the late nineteenth and early twentieth centuries to satisfy the fin-de-siècle fashion for Japonisme. I also knew that although the very best and earliest Satsuma ware commands high prices, there's no market for everyday pieces made and sold to ornament the chimney-pieces of the Victorian and Edwardian lower middle classes.*

This particular vase is undamaged, more elegant and less over-decorated than some pieces, and bears a clear signature on the base in Japanese characters. I have seen tons of this stuff being sold in antique shops and auctions, but I have never owned a piece, nor taken the trouble to look at it closely, nor tried to understand about it. How to distinguish quality from rubbish, an individual piece by a good maker from a mass-produced bit of factory-made tat? Here, for just two quid, was an opportunity to immerse myself in Satsuma ware for a few hours and to learn the basics.

I won't give you a full rundown of everything I now know about Satsuma pottery. But the outcome is that I'm slightly more respectful of my little Japanese vase than I expected to be. I hadn't known that the real Satsuma ware is made out of thick crackle-glazed earthenware, and that the vast amounts of thinly-made Japanese porcelain which you see everywhere are a different kind of ware altogether. Gratifyingly, my bowl turns out to be the real thing, but its MADE IN JAPAN stamp means that it is a late production, probably made after the end of the Meiji period in 1912. To my surprise, I was able to identify the Japanese characters by comparing them with potters' signatures illustrated on the excellent Gotheborg website[59]. The mark means Nambe, but "it is not known whether the name denotes an artist or perhaps a factory/studio mark". And finally, by checking eBay past sales of similar items, I know that it would sell for practically nothing.

There's no place for the Satsuma vase in my collection, where it would be an anomaly. So, back to a charity shop it will go. But for my two pounds spent, I had an excellent evening of research and learning, and in any future encounter with a piece of Satsuma ware, I'll be better equipped to distinguish good from bad, quality from junk. A splendid investment.

And here's the second story:

After the remarkable success of The Big Red Vase, discovered in a charity shop for £6.99 and sold at auction for £13,750, I had a sudden and inexplicable fit of enthusiasm for Chinese porcelain. First action: to re-examine the very few other pieces of eastern pottery which had accumulated by happenstance in my collection over a great many years, just on the off-chance that something might be interesting or valuable. OK, it was a long shot, but if I was going to venture into what was for me new and unexplored ceramic territory, I might as well start in the comfort of home.

There followed a lengthy session of trawling internet images. Results: my Tang dynasty sancai-glazed rhyton or drinking cup – modern souvenir ware. A Jun-type baluster vase – a nineteenth century copy. A Qianlong period bowl made for export to Europe – not rare, not great quality, cracked. A large blue-and-white basin probably from the reign of the Yongzheng Emperor – charming but broken into two halves and riveted together, without significant value.

Finally, I took out of the dresser in the dining room a small green pottery bowl which I'd bought seven or eight years ago from Johnson & Andrews. I've lost the invoice but have a vague memory that I paid a piffling amount for it, perhaps £14, certainly less than £20. It was stacked haphazardly amidst a miscellany of unmatched crockery, ready to take its turn for serving crisps, peanuts, nibbles, whatever, when we had company (See Illustrations, Picture 26).

As with every artwork or antique that I buy, I had bought it because it sparked in me a strong response. But I knew nothing about it other than that it was from Asia, made of porcelain, and that the olive-green glaze which covered it was called celadon. The bowl had no maker's mark and I had thought it so anonymous and generic that discovering where or when it was made would be an impossibility. If you had asked me, I might have hazarded a guess that it was Korean, a modern reproduction. I liked it, had often spent some time admiring it, considered it beautiful but unidentifiable, and had thought little more about it.

But now I finally made an effort with it and found to my surprise that perhaps my little green bowl wasn't as ordinary as I had supposed. I learned from the internet that this particular variety of celadon ware was from China, not Korea, and that the intricate design carved into the clay under the glaze depicted the auspicious peony flower. If was the genuine article, my Peony Bowl wasn't modern at all, but was made at the Yaozhou kilns in the later years of the Northern Song Dynasty, at least nine hundred years ago. A number of very similar pieces had done well at auction, but condition was all-important. Mine was near perfect.

I wasn't convinced. The likelihood of finding a genuine fragile Song Yaozhou bowl in undamaged condition unrecognised at a local auction was surely even lower than that of finding a Leach-Cardew Jug or a Claus de Werve Saint. But just in case, on the strength of the information gleaned from the internet, I sent an email to Sotheby's Chinese Ceramics department in London. Their expert replied promptly and very positively, so I sent him the bowl itself, and – amazing! – he verified my tentative identification and – remarkable! – he provided a pre-sale estimated value in the range £4,000 – £6,000. Since we have many other nice bowls in which to serve crisps, I decided to sell the Peony Bowl, and in March 2015 Frances and I were present in the Mayfair saleroom to watch it sell for £16,250. I can't tell you what multiple that represents of the price that I paid for it, because I've forgotten the precise amount. But suffice to say that I consider it a good return on my original investment.

It would be a fitting and wholesome conclusion to my book to be able to report to readers that I derived greater enjoyment and fulfilment from the valueless Satsuma Vase than from the almost priceless Yaozhou Peony Bowl. But it wouldn't be true. The Peony bowl gave me enormously more satisfaction, firstly because it was so much more beautiful, and secondly because it was so much more rare and interesting. And thirdly, I confess, because of the money.

So, enthusiasm undimmed, I expect to continue searching for as long as there is old junk out there for me to sift through, or as long as I remain fit to do the sifting.

Romance

No doubt many readers of this book are also regular viewers of antiques programmes on daytime and early evening television. *The Antiques Roadshow* has been one of BBC TV's top ten factual shows every year for the last thirty-five years, and still pulls in an audience of over 4 million, week in, week out. The format has been exported all over the world, and the US version has been the number one show on the PBS system for almost every one of the last fifteen years.

> "Antiques Roadshow's appeal has little to do with antiques. Its millions of viewers might feign a passing interest in the pot or painting or Edwardian toy under the expert's magnifying glass, but that's not why they're watching. They're watching because Antiques Roadshow is about other people, and more importantly, other people's stuff. It's about the drama of one man's trash becoming another man's treasure. It's about our greed, our surprise, our credulity, our nosiness, our carelessness, and our past."[60]

I think that is a harsh and cynical view. Viewers' interest isn't all feigned. My experience is that alongside the greed, there's a huge amount of genuine fascination with the old and the antique. Alongside the envy, there's a genuine pleasure in seeing a valuable item being discovered, and genuine sympathy when a treasured family heirloom turns out to be a worthless piece of junk.

And, yes, of course, there's "I wish it would happen to me", but I'm not certain that everyone who says that – which includes, surely, everyone who watches the show – says it merely because they want the money, or merely because of the two minutes of fame on the TV. No, I believe that people want it to happen to them for the thrill, the excitement, the adventure, the sheer romance of it.

Much of the romance is to be found in the stories: stories embedded in each and every object which comes under the experts' scrutiny. Stories from the owner about where the object came from, who owned it before, family lore and legend; and stories from the experts about the maker, the materials, the techniques, the historical context. Who was there on that day in 1426 at the dedication ceremony for Claus de Werve's brilliant new Calvary Group? Did the Duke of Burgundy attend in person? What was the special quality in The Jug that made those two egotistical and irascible characters Bernard Leach and Michael Cardew agree for once to sign it jointly? Where and when and how in its 400-year life did the tiny, delicate, exquisite Andro Hart psalm book transmute by a reverse alchemical process from treasure to trash, from someone's prize possession to an unidentified lot in a Leith saleroom?

Who wouldn't want to play a bit part in a story like that? To be the alchemist who re-discovered at random a lost treasure, who restored it to recognition, saved it from obscurity and destruction, sent it on its way safely and securely into the future? Not everyone would give a damn. But I'm sure that almost everyone who has accompanied me through the last fifteen chapters would indeed give a damn. And I have no doubt that there's enough stuff out there still waiting to be discovered to enable everyone to have a fighting chance of doing the same for themselves. There's no special trick to finding a Doucai Chicken Cup or a Big Red Vase or a Jug or a Saint – or a unique Star Wars character, or the first Barbie Doll, or a Plate 77 Penny Red stamp. All that's needed is a little bit of aptitude, plus motivation, willingness to learn, a reasonable memory, a self-trained Eye and a lot – a lot – of time. Fast broadband helps too.

In the same way that it isn't a trick, it isn't a matter of pure luck either – unless you just happen to get lucky. For the rest of us upon whom Fortune doesn't smile, it's about putting in the work and the time. I can speak with authority about that. The Jug could have been pure luck. Or The Saint. Or any of the other finds whose stories I have related in this book. Or any of the ones that I hope to make in the future. But are all of my finds down to luck? No, nobody's that lucky.

EPILOGUE

Ars Longa, Vita Brevis

Between buying The Jug at one auction sale and selling it at another, I was its owner for less than eight weeks. Between buying and selling The Saint, I was his owner for less than eight months. Mere moments in the lives of two objects approaching 100 years and 600 years old respectively.

I have been able to discover and conjecture a considerable amount about the very long history of The Saint. Much less was discoverable about the shorter lifetime of The Jug. But at the moment when I bought each of them in the Johnson & Andrews Edinburgh saleroom, both were in an identical predicament. It is unarguable that each for a good proportion of its existence was someone's treasured possession, prized and admired, contemplated and displayed; equally unarguable that somehow, somewhere, sometime, each became separated from its own story, and severed from its identity. At the point where they entered the saleroom and were presented for viewing, they were unidentified items of low-grade second-hand junk.

We are not talking here about things which might have started out as ordinary or mass-produced and which then acquired value over time as fashions and collectors' interests have changed – a Clarice Cliff plate, for instance, or a miner's safety lamp. No, The Saint and The Jug were unique, special and important works of art (or craft) from the day they emerged from their makers' studios in 1426 and 1926, and must have been recognised as such by their first owners. But through the passage of time, the volatility of history, fashion, war, politics, economic change and human mortality, these two objects, one from Western Cornwall, one from Eastern France, came close to rock bottom in North Edinburgh.

Obviously it didn't have to be me who rescued them. I might have been away on one or both of those Saturdays. I might not have clocked them. I might have let myself be outbid. The mere fact that I had to bid very hard and, by my standards, very high, to win The Jug shows that at least one other bidder had recognised it for what it was. Doubtless any other buyer would have researched it and in some way or other would have restored it to its rightful place high in the studio-pottery firmament. As for The Saint, I'm not so sure that the underbidder nor indeed any other regular bidder at that particular auction would have had the tenacity, the tools and the sheer good fortune to be able to trace him back to the very church in Burgundy from where he was taken more than two centuries before. I could easily see him being kept unrecognised in another buyer's home, or traded around in the lower strata of the Scottish antiques market. But it's a fact that someone present at the sale was prepared to compete with me to pay more than £300 for him, so The Saint would surely have survived.

But it wasn't anyone else who bought them. It was me, and I'm proud of it. And I'd like to think that my short periods of ownership were not insignificant episodes in their passage through time. I rescued them from obscurity, facilitated their identification and authentication, made them available for brief public viewing and study, and sent them on their way to their next owners as prized and valued objects.

I have scant information about the two new owners. Ben Williams, the Bonham's expert, told me after the sale of The Jug that he thought the winning bidder was acting on behalf of a private collector. Benoît Bertrand, Laurence Fligny's assistant, reported that The Saint had also been bought by a private collector and would remain in France. That's all I know. Since each sale, I have periodically scanned the internet for traces of the two objects, but as far as I'm aware they haven't re-emerged onto the market or into a public exhibition. Did I, then, rescue them from obscurity only for them to disappear back into obscurity? Besides grabbing two exceptional opportunities for self-satisfaction and personal profit, what was the *point* of my intervention? What is it, exactly, that I'm proud of? Two things.

First, I was responsible for their *rehabilitation*. The world had forgotten about them before, but through the cataloguing and public auction sale process, there are now authoritative records in the public domain which describe them. A documentary trail leads from me through the auctioneers to the new owners. Even if The Saint and The Jug are locked away for good in private collections, it is known where they are. I gave them that very rare and fragile commodity which only really matters for the very best and rarest objects: provenance.

Second, I was responsible for their future *safety*. They were in danger before; they are safe now. Of course I can't be sure about this. I have no idea who the buyers were or what conditions the objects are being kept in. All I know is that two buyers each parted with a very large amount of money for an item with zero intrinsic value. So they must prize their purchases very highly and have enormous incentive to keep them safe.

But things which are remembered today can be forgotten again tomorrow. Things which are safe today can be destroyed tomorrow. Sir John Stirling-Maxwell, founder in 1931 of the National Trust for Scotland, a worthy organisation dear to my heart, described the Trust's purpose as "a cabinet into which [the nation] can put some of its valuable things, where they will be perfectly safe for all time …"[61]. Perfectly safe for all time? How magnificently, naively absurd!

You drop The Jug on your marble floor and it shatters to fragments. Undisturbed in your vault, woodworm eat The Saint. The elderly Japanese billionaire who paid $82 million for Van Gogh's portrait of Dr Gachet announces that the painting will accompany him to his cremation.

An earthquake strikes Assisi. The River Arno floods Florence. Islamic State dynamites Palmyra. Officially-sanctioned revolutionary vandals desecrate the church at Flavigny. Civilisations fall. Museums and galleries find themselves in war zones. In a crisis value disappears alongside safety. A famished collector exchanges a Michelangelo for a loaf of bread. You discover to your dismay that you can't eat your Golden Egg.

John Maynard Keynes, writing in 1923, said "In the long run we are all dead". Some time, soon or late, there will be nothing left of our precious, priceless antiques and works of art but ruins, dust, fibres and shards, and no-one left to contemplate them; a desert with the two severed legs of Ozymandias standing forlorn, but with no Shelley in attendance to sonnetize them.

It's easier to forget than to remember, and it's easier to neglect things than to keep them safe. There are no guarantees of permanence for The Saint and The Jug, or for any other work of human endeavour, however valuable, however beautiful. In 100 or 600 years' time, who knows where they will be or who will own them or indeed if they or our successors and descendants will continue to exist?

Sorry, not my department. I gave both objects a leg-up when they were at a low point. That's enough for me.

ACKNOWLEDGEMENTS

This book is all my own work and its faults are all mine. But I've had much help along the way to minimise them.

First, thanks to the readers who kindly read successive drafts and came back to me with comments both general and specific. Despite your suspicions, I took careful notice of everything that was said! In alphabetical order: Frances Abercromby, Bob Aitken, Romy Langeland, Emma MacDonald, Iain MacDougall, Sarah MacDougall, Mary Marshall, Kim McAllister, Niall Rowantree, Judith Semple, Catriona Semple, Ron Smith and Hannah Stewart. Thanks to the Edinburgh Facebook EGGs for their encouragement, and to Gwinny Gordon and Jason Tully for help with a tricky technical problem.

Next, thanks to the many people who don't know how much they have contributed – the auctioneers, dealers, curators, academics and experts who have patiently and courteously let me take advantage of their expertise. To name a few out of many: Benoît Bertrand, Lindsey Brown, Martin Cornish, Dr Elizabeth Cumming, the late Dr Theodore Decker, Laurence Fligny, Professor Pamela Robertson, Marijke Varrall-Jones, the late Michael Vermeer, Professor Oliver Watson, Ben Williams, and not forgetting all the Poppies.

Thanks also to my latest set of unsung heroes: the collectors and experts of the online interest groups who are always willing to help to identify the odd bits and pieces whose photos I post in the hope that they might turn out to be random treasure. One of my regular groups is the *ID My Pottery* group on 20th Century Forum at http://www.20thcenturyforum.com/. The others are on Facebook: *Collecting Chinese Ceramics & Art, British Studio Pottery Mystery Pots, Collecting Japanese Ceramics and Arts, What is my Rug?, Studio Pottery Identification and Appreciation, British Country Pottery Collectors, British Studio*

Pottery Collectors, and *Collecting Islamic and Gandhara Ceramics and Works of Art.* You can probably find an interest group specialising in just about any type of antique object that you can think of – but I haven't yet found one that does Burgundian sculpture.

Finally, thanks to my family for putting up with all the nonsense: to my lovely daughters Sarah and Hannah and their excellent husbands Iain and Niall, to my delightful grandchildren Samuel, Amy, Eliza, Celia and Oscar, and most of all to my beautiful, brilliant and ever-supportive wife Frances.

PERMISSIONS

Except where shown below, all photographs in this book are either my own images or are freely available in the public domain for reproduction without acknowledgement.

Images reproduced in the text

Page 11   Virgin of Flavigny: Image used with permission of PIASA and Laurence Fligny

Page 90   Bear and Staff: Photograph by Robert Freidus reproduced from The Victorian Web at http://www.victorianweb.org/art/architecture/pubs/28.html

Page 120   Mourner from the Tomb of Duke John the Fearless: Image by Shonagon from https://commons.wikimedia.org/wiki/File:Pleurant,_tombeau_de_Jean_sans_Peur,_60.JPG reproduced under the Creative Commons CC0 1.0 Universal Public Domain Dedication

Page 142   Theuley apostle: Image used with permission of PIASA and Laurence Fligny

Page 154   Auction brochure for The Saint: Image used with permission of PIASA and Laurence Fligny

Page 217   Bay Psalm Book: Image in public domain sourced from https://commons.wikimedia.org/wiki/File:Bay_Psalm_Book_title_page.jpg. Note that this image is not from the copy sold at Sotheby's New York in November 2013.

Images reproduced in plates section

Picture 4   The Jug: Image used with permission of Bonham's

Picture 5   Golden Egg Restaurant: Image supplied by Evening Standard / Hulton Archive / Getty Images

Picture 8   The Saint rear view: Image used with permission of PIASA and Laurence Fligny

Picture 9   The Saint: Image used with permission of PIASA and Laurence Fligny

Picture 10   Galle vase: Image used courtesy of The State Hermitage Museum, St. Petersburg. Photograph © The State Hermitage Museum. Photo by Yuri Molodkovets

Picture 11   Riemenschneider Virgin: Photograph from https://commons.wikimedia.org/w/index.php?curid=30983838 by Rufus46 – Own work, used under the Creative Commons Attribution-ShareAlike License

Picture 12   Saint and Virgin: Image used with permission of Laurence Fligny

Picture 13   Collyer Mansion: Image supplied by New York Daily News / New York Daily News Collection / Getty Images

Picture 15   Daumier Cartoon: le Crieur Public: Open access image reproduced from http://www.nga.gov/content/ngaweb/Collection/art-object-page.56774.html

Picture 16   Daumier Cartoon: la Salle des Ventes. Source: http://www.zeno.org – Contumax GmbH & Co. KG. Image reproduced from http://www.zeno.org/nid/20003968812

Picture 20   Wally Bird: Photograph used with permission © Victoria and Albert Museum, London

Picture 22   Doucai Chicken Cup: Photograph used with permission of Sotheby's

Picture 23   Kutchinsky Argyle Library Egg: Copyright © 2016 Rio Tinto

Picture 26   Peony Bowl: Photograph used with permission of Sotheby's

NOTES

1   *Art from the Court of Burgundy*, Musée de Beaux-Arts de Dijon and the Cleveland Museum of Art, 2004

2   Forsyth, William H, Curator Emeritus, Medieval Art, The Metropolitan Museum of Art, *A Fifteenth-Century Virgin and Child Attributed to Claux de Werve*, New York, Metropolitan Museum Journal 21, 1986

3   Sotheby's Auctioneers, Conditions of Sale, published at http://www.sothebys.com/content/dam/sothebys/PDFs/cob/N08823-COS.pdf

4   http://www.artloss.com/services/searching

5   Kreder, Jennifer Anglim, *Wrestling the Dead Hand of History: Perspectives on a Proposed State Department Commission on Nazi Looted Art*, in Cultural Heritage & Arts Review, American Society of International Law, Volume 1 Issue 1, Spring 2010, pp6-7

6   http://www.lootedart.com and http://www.lostart.de

7   Judge Tugendhat in Rachmaninoff v. Sotheby's and Eva Teranyi

8   https://en.wikipedia.org/wiki/Studio_pottery

9   de Waal, Edmund, *Bernard Leach*, London, Tate Gallery Publishing, nd, p26

10 Quotation from the Pottery Studio website, http://www.studiopottery.com

11 Jones, Jeffrey, *Studio Pottery in Britain 1900 – 2005*, London, A&C Black, 2007, p84. Quotations from Davis, Harry, *Harry Davis, Potter*, unpublished autobiography, typescript, p28 (held at Ceramic Archive, University of Wales, Aberystwyth)

12 Cooper, Emmanuel, *Leach and Cardew – The Early Years*, paper given at The Michael Cardew Centenary Symposium, University of Wales, Aberystwyth, UK, 27 – 28 June 2001

13 Ibid.

14 Harrod, Tanya, *The Last Sane Man: Michael Cardew, Modern Pots, Colonialism and the Counterculture*, New Haven, Yale University Press, 2012

15 Campbell, Sophie *Fired Up by St Ives Pottery*, article in Daily Telegraph, 10 September 2008, quoting John Bedding.

16 Cooper, Emmanuel, *op. cit.*

17 Harrod, Tanya, *op. cit.*, p57.

18 *International Contemporary Ceramics, Tuesday 20 March 2007*, Auction Catalogue, Bonhams 1793 Limited, London, 2007, pp12-13

19 *Cabinets of curiosities: the bookshops of Charing Cross Road*, in New Statesman, 11th October 2012.

20 Vessel, Edward A., Starr, G. Gabrielle and Rubin, Nava, *The brain on art: intense aesthetic experience activates the default mode network*, Frontiers in Human Neuroscience, 20th April 2012

21 Birmingham, Dr. Lesley, DVM, quoted at http://www.vetstreet.com/our-pet-experts/why-does-my-dog-point

22 Johnson, Chuck, *Training the Versatile Hunting Dog*, 2nd Edition, Wilderness Adventures Press, Belgrade MT, 2009, p102

23 Entry by A J Mann on *Hart, Andro (b. in or before 1566, d. 1621)* in Oxford Dictionary of National Biography

24 Oxford English Dictionary, Online version, "Eye, n.", 7th definition, see http://www.oed.com/view/Entry/67296?rskey=EvjNQ4&result=1&isAdvanced=false#eid4897966

25 Newell, Malcolm, *Mood and atmosphere in restaurants*, Barrie and Rockliff, 1965, p.22., quoted on Designing Britain website at http://www.vads.ac.uk/learning/designingbritain/html/goldenegg.html.

26 Perrone, Jane, *A swine of a vine: why you should plant Russian vine at your peril*, The Guardian, 24th September 2009, at http://www.theguardian.com/lifeandstyle/gardening-blog/2009/sep/24/gardens1

27 http://www.halslamppost.com/Safety%20Lamps/slides/American%20Safety%20Lamp%20A-H-G.html

28 Pasteur, Louis, *Discours d'Introduction de Doyen de la Nouvelle Faculté des Sciences à Lille*, 1854

29 From description of Lot 70,catalogue of *Haute Époque et Curiosités*, Piasa Auction, Paris, 7th June 2013

30 Kahsnitz, Rainer, *Carved splendor: late Gothic Altarpieces in Southern Germany, Austria and South Tirol:* Los Angeles, Calif, J. Paul Getty Museum, 2006

31 Baxandall, Michael, *The Limewood Sculptors of Renaissance Germany*, New Haven and London, Yale University Press, 1980

32 http://www.dr-decker-kunsthandel.de/

33 Laurence Fligny's website is at http://www.fligny-haute-epoque.com/

34 Subkowski, P. (2006). *On the psychodynamics of collecting.* The International Journal of Psychoanalysis, 87, 383–401.

35 *Obsessive Compulsive Disorders Factsheet,* © 2013 American Psychiatric Association

36 Nordsletten, Ashley E. and Mataix-Cols, David, *Hoarding versus collecting: Where does pathology diverge from play?* Clinical Psychology Review 32 (2012) 165–176

37 Freedberg, D., *Why Connoisseurship Matters,* in: Katlijne van Stighelen, ed., *Munuscula Discipulorum: Essays in Honour of Hans Vlieghe,* Turnhout: Brepols, 2006.

38 Quoted in Gibson-Wood, Carol, *Jonathan Richardson and the Rationalization of Connoisseurship,* Art History, Volume 7, Issue 1, pp. 38–56, March 1984

39 *ibid.*

40 Rosemary Hill, *Gentlemen Did Not Dig,* review of *The Society of Dilettanti: Archaeology and Identity in the British Enlightenment* by Jason Kelly, Yale, 2010, in London Review of Books, Vol. 32 No. 12 · 24th June 2010, pp 25–27

41 *ibid.*

42 See HMRC website at http://www.hmrc.gov.uk/manuals/bimmanual/BIM20205.htm

43 See http://www.artscouncil.org.uk/media/uploads/Guidance_for_Exporters_Issue_4_2014.pdf

44 Perris-Delmas, Stephanie, *A Saint John from Burgundy,* Article in La Gazette Drouot International, No 25, p.33, May 2013

45 Profit or Pleasure? Exploring the Motivations Behind Treasure Trends, Barclays Wealth Insights, Volume 15, 2012, published online at https://wealth.barclays.com/en_gb/home/research/research-centre/wealth-insights/volume-15.html

46 Quoted from the Art Investing page of the website of Beautiful Assets Advisors LLC, at www.artasanasset.com. At the date of final revision of this book, this website was no longer online. The Mei Moses Index was taken over by Sotheby's in October 2016, but the new web pages for Sotheby's Mei Moses had not yet been launched.

47 Hill, Sir R. and Hill, G. B., *The Life of Sir Rowland Hill and the History of Penny Postage,* London, Thos de la Rue & Co, 1880, Vol 1, Page 408

48 http://pennystampsgb.wordpress.com/about/the-penny-red/

49 http://www.stanleygibbons.com/stanleygibbons/view/content/plate77_pr

50 Champfleury, *L'hôtel des commissaires-priseurs,* E. Dentu, Paris, 1867.

51 Leach, Bernard, *A Potter's Book,* Faber and Faber, London, 2nd Edition 1945, p. xxv

52 Perry, Grayson, *Taste is woven into our class system,* in The Telegraph, 15th June 2013

53 *International Personality Item Pool Representation of the NEO PI-R™,* available at http://www.personal.psu.edu/j5j/IPIP/

54 Source: This is Money Historic Inflation Calculator, at http://www.thisismoney.co.uk/money/bills/article-1633409/Historic-inflation-calculator-value-money-changed-1900.html

55   See http://www.forbes.com/billionaires/

56   See   http://www.nytimes.com/video/nyregion/100000002574237/bay-psalm-book-sets-an-auction-record.html

57   Sender, Henny, *Lunch with the FT: David Rubenstein*, in Financial Times, 22nd March 2013

58   Transcribed from BBC Radio 4 programme *Four Thought*, 2nd July 2014, available at http://www.bbc.co.uk/programmes/b047zrl9 .

59   See http://gotheborg.com/marks/satsuma.shtml

60   *A National Treasure: 30 Years of Antiques Roadshow*, in The Independent, 31st August 2007

61   Quoted from National Trust for Scotland website at http://www.nts.org.uk/Charity/Our-work/History/